Born to Love Called to

Serve

RANDALL J. BREWER

BORN TO LOVE CALLED TO SERVE

CONTENTS

INTRODUCTION

There are many frontiers a man may cross in his lifetime. Some are physical - mountains climbed, battles fought, lands explored. Others are internal - fear confronted, pride broken, faith tested. Yet beyond all others stands one final frontier, greater and more demanding than any before it: love.

Love is not sentimental weakness, nor is it merely emotional warmth. It is the largest spiritual and emotional challenge known to man. It is the highest calling of the Christian life and the ultimate expression of who God is. Scripture does not say that God has love - it declares that God is love. To understand love, then, is to begin to understand God Himself. To live in love is to walk in the very nature and character of the Creator.

This is why love remains the last frontier. Many will conquer habits but never surrender their hearts. Many will learn doctrine but never practice devotion. Many will fight for truth yet fail to walk in grace. Love demands more than belief - it requires transformation. It calls for nothing less than the death of self and the resurrection of Christ within us.

In "Born To Love Called To Serve," you are invited to step beyond the shallow definitions of love and into its divine reality. This book is not a call to passive affection, but to active obedience. Love, as revealed in Scripture, is not a feeling to be managed - it is a life to be lived. It is costly, sacrificial, and courageous. It is the path Jesus walked, the cross He bore, and the command He gave to all who would follow Him.

Jesus summarized the entire law and the prophets with one declaration, "You shall love the Lord your God with all your heart, soul, mind, and strength - and love your neighbor as yourself." These words are simple, yet their implications are staggering. To love God fully requires total surrender. To love others rightly requires healed identity. And to love yourself properly requires understanding how deeply God loves you first.

This is where many struggle. We cannot give what we do not possess. A man who does not know he is loved will find it nearly impossible to love others well. Insecurity breeds control. Wounds breed walls. Fear breeds self-preservation. But when the love of God is fully received—when it is understood not merely as theology but as personal truth - it becomes a transforming force that reshapes how we see ourselves, how we treat others, and how we serve the world around us.

This book will take you on a journey into that understanding. "Born To Love Called To Serve" is an in-depth study of the true Christian life - one that moves beyond religious activity and into Christlike living. It will challenge you to examine not only what you believe, but how you live. It will show you that love is not optional for the believer; it is the defining evidence of authentic faith. Jesus Himself declared that the world would know His disciples not by their strength, success, or sacrifice - but by their love.

Throughout these pages, you will discover how love is both your origin and your destiny. You were born from love, redeemed by love, and called to live a life shaped by love. You will learn how God's love heals broken identity, restores purpose, and empowers obedience. You will see how love expresses itself through service - not as obligation, but as privilege. For when love is genuine, service is not burdensome; it is joyful.

This book will also confront the cost of love. Love requires a cross. It demands that we lay down pride, comfort, offense, and self-interest. To love as Christ loved is to take up His cross daily and follow Him - choosing humility over recognition, obedience over convenience, and service over status. Yet paradoxically, it is in this surrender that true freedom is found.

The journey ahead is both insightful and practical. You will not only explore what love means, but how to live it at home, in the church, in relationships, and in a world desperate for authentic Christianity. You will be guided to see people not as interruptions, but as assignments. You will learn to serve not to be seen, but because love compels you.

Ultimately, this book is an invitation to know God more deeply and to align your life with His destiny of love for you. It is a call to step beyond surface faith and into a life that reflects the heart of Christ. Love is the final frontier because it is where faith becomes flesh, belief becomes behavior, and discipleship becomes visible.

May these pages lead you to discover that you were born to love, and that in loving, you are called to serve—for this is the life Jesus lived, the path He modeled, and the legacy He left for all who would follow Him.

| 1 |

"BORN TO LOVE"

Nothing in this universe happens by accident. For everything there is a reason and a purpose. There is a reason for the sun, the moon, and the stars. There is a reason for summer and winter, spring and fall. There is a reason for rivers and oceans, trees and grass, rain and sunshine. For all things there is a reason and a purpose. There is also a reason and a purpose for you. God measures life not in terms of years or time but in terms of purpose. Purpose is the original intent or reason for a thing to exist. We are all created with a destiny and purpose, so the question needs to be asked, "Why were you born? For what purpose did God place you on this planet?" In both the Old and New Testaments people are commanded to "love the Lord your God with all your heart, with all your soul and with all your mind" (Deut. 6:5; Matt. 22:37). Jesus said in John 13:34, "A new commandment I give to you, that you also love one another."

Jesus also said to "love your enemies" (Matt. 6:44) and we are told to "love your neighbor as yourself" (Lev. 19:18). Husbands are to love their wives (Eph. 5:25) and wives their husbands

(Titus 2:4). The list is endless for love is the theme of the entire Bible. In fact, God "is" love (1 John 4:8). So why were you born? The answer is obvious. Clearly, you were born to love. Paul wrote in Eph. 5:12, "Therefore be followers of God as dear children. And walk in love, as Christ also has loved us and given Himself for us, an offering and a sacrifice to God for a sweet-smelling aroma." As born-again believers we are to be imitators of God as dear children imitate their parents. Jesus came to lay down His life for us and we ought to do the same for others. The Message Bible says, "Observe how Christ loved us. His love was not cautious but extravagant. He didn't love in order to get something from us but to give everything of Himself to us. Love like that."

We are commanded to love one another to the same measure as Jesus loved us. It is so important that you let God love you because your giving of love is limited to your receiving of love. When you let God love you, when you receive His love, you will learn to love yourself because you'll see who you are through His eyes. As a result of doing this you'll also be able to see others through the eyes of God and what follows will be a continual outpouring of love into their lives. By doing this you become a witness to the entire world. Jesus said, "By this all will know that you are My disciples, if you have love for one another" (John 13:35). The sinners of the world are not drawn into the Christian faith by us loving them but rather when they observe the demonstrated love that we have for one another. Whether we realize it or not people are watching how we live. Our actions speak louder than our words and this is why there must be zero tolerance for strife between fellow believers.

Strife is the manifested presence of the devil whereas love, joy, and peace is the manifested presence of God. Heb. 13:1 says, "Let brotherly love continue." The Message Bible tells us, "Stay on good terms with each other, held together by love." Our God is a covenant God and we need to begin to love one another with a covenant love that comes as a result of knowing Him. Jesus said in John 15:9,10 (MSG), "I've loved you the way my Father has loved me. Make your-selves at home in my love. If you keep my commands, you'll remain intimately at home in my love. That's what I've done - kept my Fathers' commands and made myself at home in his love." Jesus told us to abide in His love and this is what it means to live and make yourself at home in His love. You live inside yourself and not some geographical location. Living in a certain city won't make you happy even though many people think it will. You live from the inside out and if your heart is right, you can be happy anywhere.

If your heart is not right, you can live in a mansion and have all the money you need and still not be happy. The key to everlasting joy is to make yourself at home in His love. "These things I have spoken to you, that My joy may remain in you, and that your joy may be full" (John 15:11). Paul wrote in Rom. 13:8, "Owe no one anything except to love one another, for he who loves another has fulfilled the law." Love is a debt you owe to everybody even if you feel like they don't deserve it. It should be on the forefront of our minds that God loved each of us when we were yet sinners and also didn't deserve it. Love is not a feeling but rather is a spiritual force radiating out of your innermost being. God is love and His love is revealed and manifested by you being nice to someone. This love can produce good feelings but you can love without feelings or even with bad feelings. Love is a decision and when the right decision is made you can love somebody even when you want to tell them off or punch their lights out.

The nature of the flesh is to respond to hurt feelings. If someone slaps you, you want to slap them back harder. The key is to be led by the Spirit and not by fickle feelings that are forever changing from one moment to the next. Gal. 5:15,16 tells us, "But if you bite and devour one another, beware lest you be consumed by one another! I say then: Walk in the Spirit, and you shall not fulfill the lust of the flesh." Love does no harm to a neighbor (Rom. 13:10) and the Message Bible records these instructions from Romans 12, "Love from the center of who you are; don't fake it. Run for dear life from evil; hold on for dear life to good. Be good friends who love deeply; practice playing second fiddle" (vs. 9,10). "Bless your enemies; no cursing under your breath" (vs. 14). "Don't hit back; discover beauty in everyone. If you've got it in you, get along with everybody" (vs. 17,18). "Don't let evil get the best of you; get the best of evil by doing good" (vs. 21).

Love thinks no evil (1 Cor. 13:50) and takes no thought about how to hurt somebody. Neither should one rejoice if and when your enemy falls and gets hurt. God loves through you and you should help that fallen person get back on his feet and point him in the right direction. In the Spirit we are to "be strong in the Lord and in the power of His might" (Eph. 6:10) but in our relationships with other people we are to be harmless as a dove. Titus 3:1,2 tells us "to be ready for every good work, to be peaceable, gentle, showing all humility to all men." Love cares when something good happens to somebody else. Love is not jealous or envious but instead rejoices when somebody else gets blessed. John, the disciple of love who laid his head on the bosom of Jesus, gave what is probably the most prominent instruction about love when he wrote in 1 John 3:18, "My little children, let us not love in word or in tongue, but in deed and in truth."

The Message Bible says, "let's not just talk about love; let's practice real love. This is the only way we'll know we're living truly, living in God's reality." John knew that God will move when love is demonstrated. The entire Bible is a book of love and throughout its' pages are recorded several principles of covenant love that should govern the thoughts, words, and actions of every born-again child of God. John 15:12,13 tells us, "This is My commandment, that you love one another as I have loved you. Greater love has no one than this, than to lay down ones' life for his friends." One of the first things we learn about the love of God is that it always gives. John 3:16, probably the most famous verse in all of scripture, begins by saying, "For God so loved the world that He gave..." Just as faith without works is dead (James 2:26), so also love without works is dead. Love is an action and giving is the greatest expression of love. If we love, we give. We are the love child of a love God and love always gives.

Paul wrote in Gal. 2:20, "I live by faith in the Son of God, who loved me and gave Himself for me." Don't just give of your resources, give of yourself. Instead of paying to have your church painted, get up off that comfortable chair and go down to the church and help do the work. Don't love from a distance but personally get involved. 1 Tim. 6:18 says, "Let them do good that they may be rich in good works, ready to give, willing to share." Giving should be the lifestyle of every born-again believer and this includes a whole lot more than money. Finances is only a small part of giving and before money can be given we need to first be willing to cheerfully give of ourselves. We need to get involved in the lives of other people and when we do we'll quickly realize that there is always something we can give that will promote the lives of those we come in contact with. We can give people our love, time, loyalty, fellowship, counsel, prayers, our words and any natural resource we have at our disposal.

Love gives whatever is needed and we also need to be consistent in our giving. Daily look for ways to give and enrich those around you. Buy a co-worker a cup of coffee or bake a dozen cookies and give them to a neighbor. Give somebody you know a phone call and tell them how blessed you are to have them as a friend. Offer to baby-sit at no charge for a single mother with four children who never gets a chance to be by herself and do the things she truly enjoys. Take an elderly person to the shopping mall with you or a fatherless child to a ballgame. And, if nothing else, you can always give somebody a smile and a friendly "hello." Let people see the joy that is within you. And who knows? These acts of kindness may birth in them the desire to know the same God you know. What more can a person offer another than the opportunity to receive eternal life? John 4:23 says, "But the hour is coming, and now is, when the true worshipers will worship the Father in spirit and truth; for the Father is seeking such to worship Him."

Everybody likes praise. God likes praise. People like praise. Even cats and dogs like praise. Praise is a sign of acceptance and is this not the primary need of all people? Throughout history people have gone to great lengths to accomplish great deeds all for the purpose of being noticed and accepted by others. People have a craving to be received willingly and favorably. They want to be approved of and believed in. We need to learn to accept people not based on our preference or their performance but because God has accepted them. Paul says in Rom. 15:7, "Therefore receive one another just as Christ also received us, to the glory of God." The Message Bible states, "So reach out and welcome one another to Gods' glory. Jesus did it, now you do it!" Just as we praise and worship God for His worthiness, so must we compliment and lift up other people for theirs. Words are the most important thing in the universe. They can build up or tear down, and they reveal what is in a person's heart.

When you submit your life to God submit your words to Him as well. "Watch the way you talk. Let nothing foul or dirty come out of your mouth. Say only what helps, each word a gift" (Eph. 4:29 MSG). The NKJV Bible instructs us to "Let no corrupt communication proceed out of your mouth, but what is good for necessary edification, that it may impart grace to the hearers." Paul is telling us to take our words, wrap them with truth, love, and sincerity, and as a gift present them to whoever is close by. The NIV states, "Do not let any unwholesome talk come out of your mouths, but only what is helpful for building others up according to their needs, that it may benefit those who listen." Words that do not benefit another person must be left unspoken. Compliments spoken from the heart make people feel good about themselves and births in them the desire to respond back in a favorable manner to the person giving the compliment. This leads to unity among the brethren and this should be the ultimate goal of every believer.

A compliment spoken from the heart can "break the ice" between strangers and will open the door that leads to a life of love, fellowship, and faithful service to our Heavenly Father. If you will take the time and make the effort you will always find something good in the lives of people to compliment them about. And, by all means, be sincere in your praise giving. Nobody likes false praise. Covenant love means you will be real and honest in your relationships. Let your compliments come from a conviction in your heart that you really believe what you're saying. If you will remain sincere, in turn, you also will be blessed as you heap praises upon those around you. Prov. 15:23 says, "A man has joy by the answer of his mouth, and a word spoken in due season, how good it is." Our God is a giving God and there is no better indicator of His presence in our hearts than in the attitude we develop about giving. How you give determines and reveals what's inside of you.

Jesus said in Matt. 10:8, "Freely you have received, freely give." You received because God freely gave. It pleased the Father to have Jesus pay the price for our sins (Is. 53:10) and it pleased Jesus to do so (Heb. 12:2). You can't doubt Gods' love for us because He gave us the most precious thing He had - His Son! Jesus submitted His will to that of the Heavenly Father and went to the cross for us proving that suffering that doesn't benefit others is vain. Jesus shed His blood and freely gave up His life for us and because He lives in our hearts we can freely give to others. Godly love gives with no strings attached and with no thought of being repaid. If you're selfish and stingy or if you expect something in return from your giving then you're either not born-again or you're not letting the love of God lead you and guide you. If people owe you something because you gave to them then God is not your source - people are - and this is unbelief. If you want something in return, then you're not giving.

Love is not a loan, it's a gift that must be given quickly, willingly, and gladly. One must forever be on guard because the devil is a thief who will continually attempt to steal from you the proper motive you should have for your giving. Luke 4:5-7 reveals to us the selfishness of devilish giving, "Then the devil, taking Him up on a high mountain, showed Him all the kingdoms of the world in a moment of time. And the devil said to Him, 'All this authority I will give You, and their glory; for this has been delivered to me, and I give it to whomever I wish. Therefore, if You will worship before me, all will be Yours.'" Devilish giving is when you give expecting something in return from the person you gave it to. It's when you say, "I'll scratch your back if you'll scratch mine" (see Luke 6:30-36). The devil was bribing Jesus and by manipulation was trying to get something back from Him. Those who give this way have minds that have been blinded by the god of this age and will live a life of deception and destruction.

2 Cor. 4:4 (MSG) gives a description of those who submit to devilish giving, "All they have eyes for is the fashionable god of darkness. They think he can give them what they want, and that they won't have to bother believing a Truth they can't see. They're stone-blind to the day-spring brightness of the Message that shines with Christ, who gives us the best picture of God we'll ever get." The picture Jesus painted was of a loving and freely giving Father and when His example is followed, we'll overcome every attempt of the devil to get us to do otherwise. 1 John 3:14 says, "We know that we have passed from death to life, because we love the brethren. He who does not love his brother abides in death." When you lay down your life for the brethren sacrifices are made. You must give up something in order to walk in love. We live in a selfish world and the needs of other people aren't even noticed anymore. People are too busy thinking only of themselves and spend too much time on their jobs, hobbies, and the pursuit of worldly pleasures.

The devil is a master of preoccupation and if you'll let him, he'll consume all your time thus preventing you from having the time and resources to bless others. Selfishness is a work of the flesh and Paul writes in Gal. 5:19-21 (MSG), "It is obvious what kind of life develops out of trying to get your own way all the time: repetitive, loveless, cheap sex; a stinking accumulation of mental and emotional garbage; frenzied and joyless grabs for happiness; trinket gods; magic-show religion; paranoid loneliness; cut-throat competition; all-consuming-yet-never-satisfied wants; a brutal temper; an impotence to love or be loved; divided homes and divided lives; small-minded and lopsided pursuits; the vicious habit of depersonalizing everyone into a rival; uncontrolled and uncontrollable addictions; ugly parodies of community. I could go on." Love, on the other hand, freely gives and this is what separates devilish giving from Godly giving. The word "give' is in the Bible some 2000 times and giving is the greatest expression of love there is.

Giving is not what you do, it's what you are! God is love, and love gives. Paul wrote, "I have been crucified with Christ; it is no longer I who live, but Christ lives in me" (Gal. 2:20a). Jesus freely gave Himself to you and now you must give yourself to somebody else. Don't do this mournfully and act like it's a burden to you. Giving brings joy so put a smile on your face and help somebody cheerfully and willingly. Jesus said in John 13:17, "If you know these things, happy are you if you do them." The joy of the Lord is your strength (Neh. 8:10) and sadness makes you weak. If all you do is think of yourself you'll be sad and weak all the time and it's a bad witness to the world for a believer to be depressed. Remember, the world is watching you. If you help others you'll be stronger, happier, and more blessed than if you did something for yourself. We all have limits on our time, money, and resources and what you spend on yourself you can't spend on somebody else. It's a choice you'll have to make.

| 2 |

"LOVED BY LOVE"

Jesus was a master storyteller. The method of teaching adopted by Jesus was that of painting a parabolic picture for the people allowing it to tell its' own story. He was never without a parable when He spoke and like a skilled potter would mold and shape His messages to fit the experience and maturity of His listeners. These parables bore the stamp of originality and were given to influence the thoughts, words, actions, and purposes of all who listened. Later, when He was alone with His disciples, He would go over everything and give them a full explanation of the truth He was attempting to convey. Since many in His audience were farmers Jesus would often speak in their language for many could grasp the concept of seedtime and harvest. One such story is "The Parable of the Growing Seed" and is found in Mark 4:26-29. Of the four gospels this story is given by Mark alone and is one of the three parables which reveal the mysteries of the kingdom of God in terms of a sower's work.

Jesus said, "The kingdom of God is as if a man should scatter seed on the ground, and should sleep by night and rise by day, and the seed should sprout and grow, he himself does not know how. For the earth yields crops by itself: first the blade, then the head, after that the full grain in the head. But when the grain ripens, immediately he puts in the sickle, because the harvest has come." Much can be learned by a careful study of this parable and one of the foremost truths revealed is that our God is a God of order. One only has to look at a farmers' field to catch a glimpse of how God does things. First comes the blade, then the head, and after that the full grain in the head. God is sequence-minded and He never puts the cart before the horse. In the book of Genesis we read that the heavens and the earth were created in an orderly fashion. God had a plan for the first day of creation, then the second day, the third, and so forth.

Consider everything the high priests in the Old Testament had to do before they entered the Holy of Holies. They couldn't just waltz into the presence of God unannounced. No, cleansings had to be performed, and offerings had to be made (see Lev. 16). With much fear and trembling this was done in an orderly fashion and in a God-ordained sequence. If the proper order was not followed to the letter, it would mean the end of their life. A rope was tied to the ankle of the High Priest so he could be pulled out from behind the veil in case he didn't follow the prescribed sequence and dropped over dead. God is not the author of confusion (1 Cor. 14:33) and to Him sequence is a serious matter and so should it be for us. Paul writes, "Let all things be done decently and in order" (1 Cor. 14:40). People who wake up, get dressed, and go to work do so in an orderly manner. But the person who wakes up, goes to work, and then gets dressed is on their way to having a very bad day.

Without a doubt, a proper sequence is most important in everything we do. For example, sex before marriage is an action taken out of a proper, God-ordained sequence and many lives have been destroyed as a result thereof. To get your needs met there is a sequence to be followed. Matt. 6:33 tells us, "But seek first the kingdom of God and His righteousness, and all these things will be added to you." There is a sequence to be followed when it comes to our relationship with God and our war against the devil. James 4:7 says, "Therefore submit to God. resist the devil and he will flee from you." It is foolish to try to resist the devil without first submitting yourself to God. The seven sons of Sceva tried to do this and Acts 19:15,16 tells us what happened to them, "And the evil spirit answered and said, 'Jesus I know, and Paul I know; but who are you?' Then the man in whom the evil spirit was leaped on them, overpowered them, and prevailed against them, so that they fled out of that house naked and wounded."

James goes on to say in vs. 8, "Draw near to God and He will draw near to you. Cleanse your hands, you sinners; and purify your hearts, you double-minded." God's foremost command is for each of us to love and serve one another. You were born to love and called to serve and in our relationships with other people there is a proper order to do things. Paul also used the language of a farmer when he wrote in 1 Cor. 3:6, "I planted, Apollos watered, but God gave the increase." The Message Bible says, "We each carried out our servant assignment. I planted the seed, Apollos watered the plants, but God made you grow." Again, a prescribed sequence was followed thus allowing God to give life to the seed that was sown. In Lev. 19 God gave Moses the laws of social order and said in vs. 18, "You shall not take vengeance, nor bear any grudge against the children of your people, but you shall love your neighbor as yourself: I am the Lord." Jesus quoted this command to love your neighbor as you love yourself in Mark 12:31 as did Paul in Rom. 13:9.

The proper sequence here is that you must first love yourself before you can love your neighbor. You must become your own best friend and rejoice in the person God made you to be. You are a one of a kind original and there is nobody on this planet quite like you. Because of the cross you have been made the righteousness of God in Christ (2 Cor. 5:21) and Paul says in Rom. 8:16,17, "The Spirit Himself bears witness with our spirit that we are children of God, and if children, then heirs - heirs of God and joint heirs with Christ." The Message Bible says, "This resurrection life you received from God is not a timid, grave-tending life. It's adventurously expectant, greeting God with a childlike 'What's next, Papa?' Gods' Spirit touches our spirits and confirms who we are: Father and children. And we know we are going to get what's coming to us - an unbelievable inheritance."

Jesus said a great deal about love, but none was more important as what He said in John 13:34, "A new commandment I give you, that you love one another; as I have loved you, that you also love one another." Before you can love yourself or your neighbor you must have a divine revelation that God loves you. Then and only then can the love command be fulfilled in your life. Jesus prayed in John 17:23 "that the world may know that You have sent Me, and have loved them as You have loved Me." It takes faith to believe that the Heavenly Father loves you as much as He loves Jesus. Your mind cannot comprehend this much love. Your mind will tell you this is not so because Jesus never sinned, never rebelled, was never disobedient, and never displeased the Father. When Jesus was baptized "suddenly a voice came from heaven, saying, 'This is My beloved Son, in whom I am well pleased'" (Matt. 3:17).

Your mind will try to convince you that there is no way the Father can love you as much as He loves Jesus. But He does. In fact, He loves you so much that He sent Jesus to die for you (John 3:16). Your mind is limited in its capacity to believe such profound truths such as this so don't try to reason it all out. Just believe it by faith. Faith is a choice and does not require understanding. You can believe anything the Bible tells you if you would only choose to do so. It's not enough to just believe in God and that He exists. You have to believe that He loves you. James 2:19 says, "You believe that there is one God. You do well. Even the demons believe - and tremble." The Message Bible puts it this way, "Do I hear you professing to believe in the one and only God, but then observe you complacently sitting back as if you had done something wonderful? That's just great. Demons do that, but what good does it do them? Use your heads!"

Faith comes by hearing (Rom. 10:17) so you need to hear your-self say every day, "God loves me!!" Say it again, "God loves me!!" Once more, "God loves me!!" You need to meditate on this day and night. You need to confess it, sing about it, read about it, and hear good preaching about it. There is no life as exciting as the victorious life that comes from knowing God loves you. His great love has delivered you from the guilt of sin and the shame of your failures and mistakes. "Therefore, if anyone is in Christ, he is a new creature; old things have passed away; behold, all things become new" (2 Cor. 5:17). God re-members your sin no more (Jer. 31:34) and if you confess your sins, He is faithful and just to forgive you and cleanse you from all unrighteousness (1 John 1:9). If you're forgiven, you're for-given. If you're cleansed, you're cleansed. There is no condem-nation in Christ (Rom.8:1) and we have no fear of judgment and punishment. Indeed, He is the glory and the lifter of your head (Ps. 3:3).

John writes, "Whoever confesses that Jesus is the Son of God, God abides in him, and he in God. And we have known and believed the love that God has for us. God is love, and he who abides in love abides in God, and God in him" (1 John 4:15,16). There is a difference between knowing God loves you and be-lieving that He does. Divine revelation is needed for you to be fully developed in knowing the love God has for you. John called himself "that disciple whom Jesus loved" (John 21:7) and this should be your confession as well. Who are you? You're the one God loves. God is love and He loves you. You can't be any more loved than when you are loved by Love. God said in Jer. 31:3, "Yes, I have loved you with an everlasting love; Therefore with lovingkindness I have drawn you." God is drawing you into a love relationship with Him. He enjoys loving you and he delights in blessing you and showing you mercy. He is thinking about you today and He's got a plan for your life (see Jer. 29:11).

He'll lead you and guide you in the way you should go, and He'll never leave you or forsake you. He cares so much about you that He keeps count of the number of hairs on your head. His eyes roam to and fro across the earth looking for someone to show Himself strong on their behalf. Jesus said, "No longer do I call you servants, for a servant does not know what his master is doing; but I have called you friends, for all things that I heard from My Father, I have made known to you. You did not choose Me, but I chose you" (John 15:15,16). Your claim to fame is that you are loved by God and it is an insult to Him when you don't know and believe that. One day Jesus and His disciples were in a boat crossing over to the other side of the sea. "And a great wind-storm arose, and the waves beat into the boat, so that it was already filling. But He was in the stern, asleep on a pillow. And they awoke Him and said to Him, 'Teacher, do You not care that we are perishing?'" (Mark 4:37,38).

These disciples questioned whether or not Jesus loved them and fear gripped their heart. After rebuking the storm and a great calm fell upon the water Jesus turned to His disciples and "said to them, 'Why are you so fearful? How is it that you have no faith?' And they feared exceedingly..." (vs. 40,41a). One way to know if you truly believe God loves you is whether or not there is fear in your life. If you fear you won't be able to pay your bills this month then you're not fully convinced in your heart that God loves you. If cancer runs in your family and you fear that one day you'll catch this dreaded disease, then you are not totally persuaded that God loves you as much as He loves Jesus. But if you're walking in love, you'll have no fear. 1 John 4:18 says, "There is no fear in love, but perfect love casts out fear, because fear involves torment. But he who fears has not been made perfect in love."

Faith works by knowing how much God loves you. Faith works through love (Gal. 5:6) and this is the key to your victory in life and for overcoming the trials that come your way. Heb. 11:6 tells us, "But without faith it is impossible to please God, for he who comes to God must believe that He is and that He is a rewarder of those who diligently seek Him." The Message Bible says, "It's impossible to please God apart from faith. And why? Because anyone who wants to approach God must believe both that He exists and that He cares enough to respond to those who seek Him." Faith is a choice. You chose to believe in the goodness of God, that He is, and that He will reward you if you seek Him diligently. David wrote in Ps. 27:13, "I would have lost heart, unless I had believed that I would see the goodness of the Lord in the land of the living." Faith is activated and works by love and it's this perfect love that will cast fear out of your life. The word "cast" means 'to throw out not caring where it lands.'

Without fear in your life, you won't be afraid of the devil, people, death, car crashes, cancer, or of losing your job. Paul wrote in 2 Tim. 1:7, "For God has not given us a spirit of fear, but of power and of love and of a sound mind." When you're fear-less, you're a problem to the devil because he can't scare you. Rom. 8:37 says you "are more than conquerors through Him who loved us." Gods' love gives you the victory every time. Paul writes, "Now thanks be to God who always leads us in tri-umph in Christ" (2 Cor. 2:14). The closer you walk with God the more He'll manifest His love in your life. Just walk outside and look around and you'll see the goodness of God fully dis-played. All that you see He made for you. He made the sun and the moon and all the planets so that the earth could be here and He made the earth so that you could be here. He made it all for you. That magnificent mountain range is for you as is that beautiful rainbow and the green grass that grows near your home.

The reason the sun shines by day and the moon by night is for you. The reason the ocean rolls onto the sand is for you. The stars twinkle at night, and the wind blows and the trees sprout their leaves all for you. The flowers bloom across the fields and the birds sing their beautiful harmonies for you. All these things say with a loud voice, "God loves you!!" Every meal you eat God is saying "I love you!" Every breath you take and every time your heart beats God is saying "I love you!" Rom. 8:31,32 says, "What then shall we say to these things? If God is for us, who can be against us? He who did not spare His own Son, but delivered Him up for us all, how shall He not with Him also freely give us all things?" The birth of Jesus said to the world, "God loves you!!" and if He gave you Jesus He'll heal your body and give you a sound mind. He'll give you a nice house to live in and a car, a job, and a family. He'll help you comb your hair in the morning, and He'll help you drive to work each day.

He is the living God "who gives us richly all things to enjoy" (1 Tim. 6:17). All things are yours because of the great love He has for you. It is because of His unfailing and never-ending love that you have been crowned with glory and honor (Ps. 8:5). Never doubt the love of God. When you do, you doubt God for He is love. Every day you're alive He demonstrates His love for you beyond question. John writes, "In this the love of God was manifested toward us, that God sent His only begotten Son into the world, that we might live through Him" (1 John 4:19). He could give no greater gift. He loved us while we were His enemies and not for what we were doing for Him. He does not have to do one more thing to prove that He loves you. He's already done it. Paul asks, "Who shall separate us from the love of God? Shall tribulation, or distress, or persecution, or famine, or nakedness, or peril, or sword?" (Rom. 8:35).

He answers his own question in vs. 38,39, "For I am persuaded that neither death nor life, nor angels nor principalities nor powers, nor things present nor things to come, nor height nor depth, nor any other created thing, shall be able to separate us from the love of God which is in Christ Jesus our Lord." The Message Bible says, "I'm absolutely convinced that nothing - nothing living or dead, angelic or demonic, today or tomorrow, high or low, thinkable or unthinkable - absolutely nothing can get between us and Gods' love because of the way Jesus our Master has embraced us." As Jesus hung and bled on the cross the Father was showing you how much He loves you.

The cross is a picture of love; it's what love looks like. Jesus paid the highest price that could ever be paid. And He did it all for you. 1 John 3:1 says, "Behold what manner of love the Father has bestowed on us, that we should be called children of God!" The word "behold" means 'look.' Look how much the Father loves you!

You are an amazing, one-of-a-kind, child of the living God! He bought you with a price and you are most valuable to Him. You are the apple of His eye (Zech. 2:8) and you can have boldness on the day of judgment because the One sitting on the throne loves you. You are loved by Love and God is not quiet about how much He loves you. He wants the whole world to know it. Jesus said in John 17:22,23, "And the glory which You gave Me I have given them, that they may be one just as We are one: I in them, and You in Me; that they may be made perfect in one, and that the world may know that You have sent Me, and have loved them as You have loved Me." In the book of Revelation Jesus told John to write these profound words to the church in Philadelphia, "Indeed, I will make these of the synagogue of Satan, who say they are Jews and are not, but lie - indeed I will make them come and worship before your feet, and to know that I have loved you' (Rev. 3:9).

Imagine that. The enemy will be brought to your feet and shown that God loves you. The Message Bible states it like this, "And watch as I take those who call themselves true believers but are nothing of the kind, pretenders whose true membership is in the club of Satan - watch as I strip off their pretensions and they're forced to acknowledge it's you I've loved." God wants the whole world to know that he is a God of love and that He loves you. Go public and tell people all that God has done for you. Love your neighbor and tell them if you draw near to God, he'll draw near to you. If you seek Him with your whole heart He'll be found by you. If you'll ask, you'll receive. If you knock, it will be opened unto you. He is a good God and when you reach out to Him, He will respond back to you. If you believe in the love and mercy of God you can enjoy your life even knowing you've sinned and come short of the glory of God.

Mercy means you don't get the punishment you deserve but rather get the blessings you don't deserve. All this and more because God loves you so much that He gave you Jesus. You are loved by Love and Gods' grace will pardon and cleanse you and make you whole. 1 John 4:10,11 tells us, "In this is love, not that we loved God, but that He loved us and sent His Son to be the propitiation for our sins. Beloved, if God so loved us, we also ought to love one another." Herein is the threefold sequence of fulfilling Gods' command to walk in love. God loves you, you love yourself and then you love your neighbor. Loving other people is the stamp of approval that you have been born again and believe that you are loved by Love. John writes, "We know that we have passed from death to life because we love the brethren. He who does not love his brother abides in death" (1 John 4:14).

John, the apostle of love, the one who openly confessed that he was loved by Jesus, tells us in 1 John 3:11, "For this is the message that you heard from the beginning, that we should love one another." He went on to say in vs. 16-24 (MSG), "This is how we've come to understand and experience love: Christ sacrificed His life for us. This is why we ought to live sacrificially for our fellow believers, and not just be out for ourselves. If you see some brother or sister in need and have the means to do something about it but turn a cold shoulder and do nothing, what happens to Gods' love? it disappears. And you make it disappear. My dear children, let's not just talk about love; let's practice real love. This is the only way we'll know we're living truly, living in Gods' reality. It's also the way to shut down debilitating self-criticism, even when there is something to it. For God is greater than our worried hearts and knows more about us than we do ourselves.

And friends, once that's taken care of and we're no longer accusing or condemning ourselves, we're bold and free before God! We're able to stretch our hands out and receive what we asked for because we're doing what He said, doing what pleases Him. Again, this is Gods' command: to believe in His personally named Son, Jesus Christ. He told us to love each other, in line with the original command. As we keep His commands, we live deeply and surely in Him, and He lives in us. And this is how we experience His deep and abiding presence in us: by the Spirit He gave us." Without question, God loves you. You are loved by Love and by faith you believe that and love Him back. Now, when the shouting subsides, go out today with open eyes and a willing heart, and let God use your words, actions, and kindness to become a living blessing in someone else's life.

| 3 |

"YOUR OWN BEST FRIEND"

The time drew near for Jesus to fulfill His calling and purpose for coming to planet Earth. Within a few short
hours He would be beaten, ridiculed, spat upon, and shamefully
hung naked on a cross between two thieves. In the upper room
during the last supper Jesus prayed these words, "I do not pray
for these alone, but also for those who will believe in Me
through their word; that they all may be one as You, Father, are
in Me and I in You, that they also may be one in Us" (John
17:20,21). The Message Bible says, "So they might be one heart
and mind with Us." Jesus came to bridge the gap of sin that
separated people from the Father and to bring unity among
themselves. He came with the purpose of turning all people
everywhere into one, big, happy family. He said, "I am the vine,
you are the branches" (John 15:5). Together as joint heirs with
Christ people everywhere are to become "like-minded, having
the same love, being of one accord, of one mind" (Phil. 2:2).

The Message Bible says, "Agree with each other, love each
other, be deep-spirited friends." This is called the law of unity

and without it a plundering will take place within the body of Christ causing much division and pain. Jesus Himself said, "Every kingdom divided against itself is brought to desolation, and every city or house divided against itself will not stand" (Matt. 12:25). Clearly, unity should be the goal of every born-again believer for your very existence depends on it. David wrote in Ps. 133:1, "Behold, how good and how pleasant it is for brethren to dwell together in unity." What this means is that you are to have a continual courtship with other believers. When you are courting somebody in the natural you are always on your best behavior and will do anything to win their affection and approval. You need to delight to be in the presence of others and strive to promote and further their welfare and calling in life. Phil. 2:4 says, "Let each of you look out not only for his own interests, but also for the interests of others."

Believers worldwide are joined together in a covenant relationship because of the shed blood of Jesus. The bonding element that holds them together is love, the "bond of perfection" (Col. 3:14). Heb. 13:1-3 states, "Let brotherly love continue. Do not forget to entertain strangers, for by so doing some have unwittingly entertained angels. Remember the prisoners as if chained with them, and those who are mistreated, since you yourselves are in the body also." The love of God is no ordinary love. It is a love that continues to love no matter what. The love of God will always focus on the one loved with thoughts of self secondary. Jude 21 says to "keep yourselves in the love of God." If you will do this the body of Christ will be undivided because the love of God always seeks and desires unity. It is God's desire that His children dwell together as a family having one heart, one soul, and one interest. Ps. 133:2 says dwelling together in unity "is like the precious oil upon the head, running down on the edge of his garments."

This ointment was holy and was not made for common use. So must brotherly love be. To dwell together in unity, all believers must love with a pure heart that is solely devoted to God and the fulfillment of His will. As with the oil, holy love is also of great price and is precious indeed. It is like ointment and perfume that will rejoice the heart. It is the "oil of gladness" that brings exaltation, celebration, and exceeding joy. If people will take the time to develop a love relationship with one another then dwelling together in unity will be "like the dew of Hermon, descending upon the mountains of Zion" (Ps. 133:3). The morning dew represents fertility and growth. Love will grow when hospitality and brotherly kindness is practiced on one another. Pleasant in its manifestation, love can span all gulfs and distances and can bind together all things that seem to be apart. For sure, love is the solution to every problem and it is through love that unity comes to the body of Christ.

Without a doubt, walking in love should be the ultimate goal of every born-again believer. Before that can happen, however, the Bible says the prerequisite to loving others is to first love yourself. Loving yourself is not vanity or pride, it's God's plan and purpose for your life. Jesus considers this to be of the utmost importance, so much so that He commands you to do it. Matt. 22:35-39 says, "Then one of them, a lawyer, asked Him a question, testing Him, and saying, 'Teacher, which is the great commandment in the law?' Jesus said to him, 'You shall love the Lord your God with all your heart, with all your soul, and with all your mind. This is the first and great commandment. And the second is like it. You shall love your neighbor as yourself.'" Jesus put loving yourself into the same category as loving God because, if you don't love yourself and have a healthy respect for who you are in Christ, you will never be able to properly love other people.

Many people struggle with this and have a civil war raging on the inside of their inner man because they don't understand you can't give away what you don't have. If you don't love yourself, you're not going to be able to love other people. Too many people in the world don't like themselves and are not at peace with who they are. They feel like they don't measure up to the standards set up by the world around them and their self-esteem is based on the bad things other people have said to them. Somebody said this and then somebody else said that. Continually they hear words that tear down instead of building up. Their lives are being controlled by what somebody said and most of the time they just barely know who that somebody is. The Bible refers to the enemy as "the accuser of the brethren" (Rev. 12:10) and he'll use other people to point out all your faults and shortcomings. Nobody is perfect, especially those who continually point their finger at you and tell you how bad you are.

Yes, all people have sinned, failed, and fallen short of the glory of God (Rom. 3:23). The apostle Paul wrote, "For the good that I will to do, I do not do; but the evil I will not to do, that I practice" (Rom. 7:19). The Message Bible says, "I can will it, but I can't do it." He says in vs. 24, "O wretched man that I am! Who will deliver me from this body of death?" Too often a person's self-worth is determined by how other people feel about them. They fall into the abyss of despair and condemnation if others have negative things to say about them. They become addicted to the approval of others and fall prey to their opinions, words, and actions. This has caused lives and relationships to be destroyed and have led many to commit the selfish, diabolical act of suicide. These people refuse to love themselves unless others love them first. They forget that God loved the world while they were yet sinners, so much so that He sent His only Son to die for them. How much more love and approval do you need?

Eph. 6:14 (GWT) tells you to "put on God's approval as your breastplate." This piece of armor covers your heart, the center of your being, the way you feel about yourself deep inside. It is in your heart that you receive God's forgiveness and His mercy that endures forever and His love that never fails. The truth is, people who speak negatively of you only do so because they don't love themselves. They reason in their subconscious that if you're such a flawed individual then they're not so bad after all. By making you look bad, they in turn feel good about who they are. And yes, their words may sting like piercing arrows because much of what they say may be true. The good news is that your value is not based on what other people say about you but is based solely on the fact that you are a child of the Most High God. Paul said in Eph. 2:10, "For we are His workmanship, created in Christ Jesus." The NLT says, "For we are God's masterpiece. He has created us anew in Christ Jesus."

Understand that you are not yet a finished product. You are a work in process and throughout your life God is continually molding and shaping you into the person He wants you to be. He is the potter and you are the clay. You're on the potter's wheel of grace, mercy, and love. Paul says in Phil. 1:6 that you can be "confident of this very thing, that He who has begun a good work in you will complete it until the day of Jesus Christ." You may not be where you should be but thank God you're not where you used to be. You go from glory to glory as you are daily being transformed into the very image of God (2 Cor. 3:18). The Message Bible says, "And so we are transfigured much like the Messiah, our lives gradually becoming brighter and brighter and more beautiful as God enters our lives and we become like Him." Your self image is a picture of yourself that you carry in your heart. You need to love yourself in a healthy way and see yourself the way God sees you.

The Bible says you are a new creation in Christ and all your sins have been washed away. You are the righteousness of God in Christ Jesus (2 Cor. 5:21) and you've been set apart and chosen to be an ambassador for Christ (vs. 20). You are fearfully and wonderfully made (Ps. 139:13,14) and God put you together precisely as He wanted. For sure, there is no one quite like you in all the earth. He perfectly, genetically, and distinctly formed you in your mother's womb and caused you to become the person you are today. You are so special that God counts the hairs on your head. You are distinguished, marked, and unique. It was God's purpose and plan for you to have your personality, gender, and nationality. He chose the color of your hair and the color of your eyes and He chose how tall you would be. He caused you to be born at this particular time in history. He created everything about you and, like He did in the beginning when He created the heavens and the earth, God looks at you and says, "It is good!"

God also created you to feel good about yourself. He created you to feel complete, to feel whole, to feel confident and secure. Look inside your heart and see your true value and worth. Love your life and don't ever minimize who God made you to be. You're someone special and you need to daily celebrate yourself and who you are in Christ. Love your life and be filled with passion and zeal. Do something special for yourself today. Throw a party for yourself and have a big celebration. Don't expect life to be exciting, you be exciting. Life is what you make it and if you have holy fervor and zeal then your life will be exciting. It starts from the inside out so love yourself and love your life. Become your own best friend. By far, one of the most important and beneficial things you can ever do for yourself is to learn how to love yourself in a proper way. You have probably said "I love you" countless times to your loved ones but how many times have you said this to yourself?

The first step to loving yourself is to stand in front of the mirror, look yourself in the eye, and say loud and clear, "I love you!" Jesus said to love God with all our heart, soul, and mind. Your emotions are a part of your soul so get emotional in your love for God. Clap your hands, stomp your feet, jump in the air, and shout praises to your King. At the same time, get emotional and express yourself in your love for your neighbor and, most importantly, in your love for yourself. Be happy for who you are and for the person God made you to be. Don't desire to be somebody else but joyfully be content and satisfied with how the Lord put you together. After all, God doesn't make junk. How many times have you looked at your friends and relatives and loved them exactly as they are? You then turn and look at yourself in the mirror and hate what you see. This is not how God wants you to be. You are not supposed to have negative feelings about yourself. It's true, people who don't love themselves are emotionally handicapped.

If you don't get along with yourself, you're not going to get along with anybody else. The greatest gift you can give the world is a healthy you. You need to be spiritually healthy, physically healthy, and emotionally healthy. Many churches tell their congregations what wretched sinners they are. Religious spirits will always make you feel guilty and bad about yourself. When the people leave the church service they feel worse than before they went in. People shouldn't leave the church feeling like a rat and a bum who won't ever amount to anything. No, God's perfect will is for people to know that their value and worth is rooted in Christ and Him alone. It is not based on your achievements or where you live or how much money you have. Neither is it based on what you know, who you know, or how many college degrees you have. It's all based on who you are in Christ. Col. 2:9,10 says, "For in Him dwells all the fullness of the Godhead bodily, and you are complete in Him Who is the head of all principality and power."

The word "complete" means 'to be satisfied, finished, perfected, filled up, assured (confident, secure, knowing who you are).' The Amplified Bible says, "You are made full in Him." Too many people are still seeking to be loved by others. If you know God loves you, and you love yourself, then being loved by others won't be on the forefront of your mind. Instead, you'll have the freedom to step out of yourself and seek to love others and be a blessing to them. A good, healthy self-esteem will make you amazingly happy, well adjusted, and will give you the determination to go further in life than what others think possible. People who love themselves in the right way are in touch with their God-given dreams and aspirations. They believe they have something to offer the world and are more likely to make a positive difference in the lives of other people. If you love the person God made you to be, then you can value and respect those people you come in contact with.

It's sad but true that some religious authors condemn the whole concept of loving yourself. They think it's being self-centered and arrogant. They don't realize there is a way to love yourself without worshiping yourself. When you love yourself the right way, you're recognizing and rejoicing in God's view of your worth. Look into the mirror of God's love and see your reflection in Calvary's price tag. Let's be honest here. Self-love is a horse that you can fall off on either side. You can love yourself too much to the point of arrogance or you love yourself not enough to the point where you hate yourself. There is such a twisted perception in the world regarding one's self-worth that most Christians don't even know how to love themselves or that they're supposed to. This is why they fall into the trap of always seeking to win the approval of other people. Loving yourself is very, very important, so much so that Jesus included it in the two greatest commandments.

It's easy to see by the Lord's command to "love your neighbor as you love yourself" that you must make loving yourself a top priority in your life. As you do that on a daily basis, always stay connected to God because loving yourself is one area where, if you're not careful, you can really get out of balance on. Many people go to one extreme or the other. In today's self-centered society, many have gone to the extreme by being concerned about their own personal well-being and their own agendas to the exclusion of everyone else. All some people think about is "me, myself, and I." The world totally revolves around them and their own personal goals and desires. These people will do anything and everything to constantly get their own way, even if it means hurting other people. These types of people are incapable of bonding with or loving anyone but themselves. Love that is selfish and self-centered is totally opposite from the sacrificial, self-giving love God wants all people to have.

On the other hand, when you comprehend God's love, when you become His friend and deeply know that He loves you, you won't need to focus all your attention on loving yourself. The more you experience God's unfailing love and His graciousness that He pours out on you, the more you'll think of Him and your neighbor and the less you'll think of yourself. You can be sure you're loving yourself in the right way when you start to love others more as a result of how you feel about yourself. When you make loving others your goal, everything else will automatically fall into place. Life and everything in it just makes sense. Confusion is thrown out the door. You can have the confidence that God will always be there to help keep you in balance with the way you are loving yourself. You will, however, have to stay on top of your game, always making sure you don't get too full of yourself and start sliding down to the extreme of becoming too self-centered. Don't ever let your guard down.

The command to love your neighbor as you love yourself is essentially saying to treat other people as well as you treat yourself. The Bible presumes that people already love themselves too much and that is the problem. Jesus gave the love command so that people take their eyes off of themselves and start to care for others. Someone wrote, "Loving yourself makes you a vessel for the aroma of God's grace. The fragrance of your self-worth perfumes many lives, including your own." Most relationship problems come as a result of not loving yourself. Remember, if you don't love yourself, you won't be able to love other people in a proper way. You are commanded to love and have relationships with God and people but at the same time you need to also have a positive relationship with yourself. Let's face it, you can never get away from yourself. Wherever you go, there you are. So if you don't love yourself, you are going to have one miserable, wretched life.

Your attitude about yourself determines whether or not you will live and enjoy a good life. It's easy in a success driven world to come to a point where you believe you just don't measure up. Don't ever compare yourself to other people and stop trying to be like them. There will always be somebody whose grass is greener than your own. Instead, be who you are and the person God made you to be. You're talented, you're creative, you're strong in the Lord and in the power of His might" (Eph. 6:10). Be positive and rise higher to a new level of confidence, a new level of boldness. Your future is bright and the best is yet to come. God sees you as a champion. He sees you as His very own masterpiece. He regards you as a strong, courageous, successful, and overcoming person. An angel appeared to Gideon and said, "The Lord is with you, you mighty man of valor" (Judges 6:12). The Amplified Bible calls him, "You mighty man of fearless courage." Always see yourself as a priceless treasure in the eyes of God.

God believes in you even more than you believe in yourself. Develop a healthy self-image based on what God's Word says about you and not on where you live, what style of car you drive, or what other people say about you. Remember, you will never rise above the image you have of yourself in your own mind. As God helps you grow you will change but you will always be you. Your uniqueness is God-designed, and He did not create you to be somebody else. Every day strive to become God's best version of who you are. How does a person love themselves in a good, healthy way? First, stop criticizing yourself. "Death and life are in the power of the tongue" (Prov. 18:21). If you always belittle yourself then little is all you'll ever be. People believe what they hear themselves say so put a guard over your mouth. To love yourself like God loves you, you must see yourself as Jesus sees you. Everybody has strengths and weaknesses and when you fall, forgive yourself and go on. It's that simple.

God loves you so much that He extends mercy and casts away all your transgressions (Ps. 103:11,12). If you would embrace His mercy and take your eyes off of your transgressions as He has, you would love yourself far more than you ever thought possible. And don't ever forget Rom. 8:1, "There is therefore now no condemnation to those who are in Christ Jesus, who do not walk according to the flesh, but according to the Spirit." The Parable of the Prodigal Son is the only place in scripture where the Bible pictures God running (Luke 15:20). To whom was He running? To a person who made grievous mistakes and failed miserably. Nothing you've done is too much for the mercy of God and, the moment you take one step toward God, your loving Father will come running to you. You are His prized possession, and He'll welcome you with arms wide open. Nothing you've ever done, or ever will do, can separate you from the love of God and His desire to be a blessing to you.

Become your own best friend. Love, trust, and respect yourself. See yourself through the same eyes of compassion the way you would look at a friend. Accept yourself for who you are and don't judge yourself so harshly. Understand that self-love must come from you. Others cannot affirm or love you the way you can so stop looking to other people to do what only you can do yourself. Treat yourself well and find ways to prosper yourself and replenish your soul. Start with your physical appearance. If you look good, you'll feel good. Wear what you like and what you are comfortable in. It's not necessary to blindly follow the latest trend even if it doesn't suit your tastes and desires. Don't wear what you don't like just to keep yourself in tract with what others are wearing. No, wear what pleases you.

Give attention to yourself and never neglect what matters most to you. Take time to look after yourself, to groom yourself and to take care of your well-being. Love always starts within.

You are a child of the King of kings and Lord of lords so start treating yourself like royalty. Get rid of those used dishes you use all the time and start using the best china that's collecting dust in the cabinet. Buy yourself that new fishing pole or that fancy pair of shoes you've been looking at the past few months. Pamper yourself and bless yourself on purpose. God commands you to love yourself so start doing it. It's okay to love yourself while God is in the process of changing you into His image. Nobody is perfect and God has already approved of and accepted you just as you are. Get in agreement with God and start feeling good about the way He made you. You are God's own special child so start confessing positive things about yourself. Say out loud, "Greater is He who is in me than he who is in the world. I'm the head and not the tail. I'm above and not beneath. I can do all things through Christ which strengthens me. I will come behind in no good thing because God loves me and I love myself."

If you will focus on how much God loves you and the price He paid to redeem you, you'll come to see yourself as God sees you. God thinks you're worth dying for and that should make you feel very special indeed. Knowing that will help you understand just how much you're really worth as a child of the Most High God. Too often self-worth is based on what other people tell you about yourself. However, the one, true authority on your self-worth is Jesus and, since He gave His own life up for you by dying on a cross, then that should tell you how valuable you really are. Start today. Make a quality decision to do yourself a favor and love yourself. God loves you so you can love yourself. God accepts you so you can accept yourself. God cherishes you so you can cherish yourself. Seeing yourself as God sees you is what it means to have a good self-image. It also means that you will live a long, good, happy, and prosperous life. So love yourself and become your own best friend. Do it today.

| 4 |

"YOUR BROTHER'S KEEPER"

The world as we know it today exists because people sought for answers to questions brave enough to be asked. "What lies beyond the horizon? What's it like on the ocean floor? Can a man fly? Is there a cure for polio? How can we land a man on the moon and return him safely back to the earth? Can we predict the weather? Is it possible for a man to travel faster than the speed of sound? Is there life on other planets? Can a computer be made to fit in the palm of your hand?" If a question could be asked, then an answer had to be found. That's just how human nature is and it was the pursuit of all these answers that caused man to seek God and reach down deep inside himself in order to create a world that nobody in times past ever dreamed could ever exist. The Bible says knowledge will increase in the last days (Dan. 12:4) and indeed it has, all because of questions asked and people with enough faith, courage, and perseverance to seek for the answers.

For those who have been born-again and gained the privi-lege of being called the children of God the Bible is a book of questions and answers. It is interesting to note that the first question ever asked by a man was made by one who had just murdered his own brother. Gen. 4:8,9 says, "Now Cain talked with Abel his brother; and it came to pass, when they were in the field, that Cain rose up and killed him. Then the Lord said to Cain, 'Where is Abel your brother?' And he said, 'I do not know. Am I my brother's keeper?'" Along with "What must I do to get saved?" (Acts 16:30) this inquiry by Cain ranks as one of the most important questions asked in all of scripture. The reason this question is so profound is because your answer to it will determine what happens to your life in the here and now as well as your eternal destiny in the age to come. Cain did not realize the significance of what he asked. He was being rude, obnoxious, and tried to avoid the admittance of guilt that he had just killed his brother.

His words have come to symbolize people's unwillingness to accept responsibility for their own actions and for the welfare of their fellow man. Still, this question imposes a relevance for all born-again believers and must be answered by all. "Am I my brothers' keeper?" Your quest to find the answer to this question should not be a long one because the entire Bible is a book about love and clearly teaches us that we indeed do have a responsibility to care and watch out for one another. Paul wrote in 1 Thess. 4:9,10, "But concerning brotherly love you have no need that I should write to you, for you yourselves are taught by God to love one another; and indeed you do so to-ward all the brethren who are in all Macedonia. But we urge you, brethren, that you increase more and more." The Message Bible tells us, "You're God-taught in these matters. Just love one another! You're already good at it; your friends all over the province of Macedonia are the evidence. Keep it up; get better and better at it."

John, the apostle of love, tells us in 1 John 1:3, "that which we have seen and heard we declare to you, that you also may have fellowship with us; and truly our fellowship is with the Father and with His Son Jesus Christ." In Greek the word for "fellowship" is 'koinonia' and it is the highest degree of love two people can generate toward one another. The word means "fellowship, partnership, social intercourse, companion, communion, partaker." John later goes on to say, "Beloved, let us love one another, for love is of God; and everyone who loves is born of God and knows God. He who does not love does not know God, for God is love" (1 John 4:7,8). You can be born-again and know very little about God. When you get saved you meet God and get acquainted with Him, but that doesn't mean you know Him. If you don't know love, you don't know God. Love is not something God has, it's what He is. God is love! If you don't see things through the love perspective, you don't see it as God sees it.

God sees everything through the eyes of love. The agape love of God is a fruit of the spirit and is the most powerful, the most dynamic, and the most dominate force in the world. Knowing God and His love will put you on a higher plane of living, higher than the plane you attained when you got born-again. This love is not selfish but carries with it the overwhelming desire to be a blessing to somebody else. God's love will always manifest itself with actions that line up with His Word and gives for the purpose of blessing the recipient. Paul writes these encouraging words in 1 Cor. 16:14, "Let all that you do be done with love." The world today is craving for love like never before. We all have within us the need to love and be loved. Inwardly our hearts are yearning for the acceptance that only a covenant relationship can bring. The story of David and Jonathan is but one example in the Bible of what the love of God is all about.

1 Sam. 18:1,3,4 says, "And it was so, when he had finished speaking to Saul that the soul of Jonathan was knit to the soul of David, and Jonathan and David cut a covenant because he loved him as his own soul. And Jonathan took off the robe that was on him and gave it to David, with his armor, even to his sword and his bow and his belt." Nobody had more reason to dislike David than Jonathan. Because he was Sails' son Jonathan was next in line to be king. David, however, was anointed by God through Samuel to be the next heir to the throne but still Jonathan cut a covenant with him. Jonathans' rival to the throne now became his closest friend. Their mutual love and affection was sincere and in 1 Sam. 20:4 Jonathan told his close friend with whom he was now bonded, "Whatever you yourself desire, I will do it for you." By giving David his robe and weapons Jonathan proclaimed that all he had now belonged to the future king of Israel.

David's enemies were now Jonathan's enemies, and both vowed to fight their covenant partner's battles as if they were their own. Each had become their brothers' keeper. A covenant is the most sacred thing that can exist between two people. It is an irrevocable, solemn and binding agreement between two or more parties in which each promises to perform certain deeds for the other. A blood covenant was often made between tribes, families, or individuals based on their needs, strengths, and weaknesses. One tribe, for example, may be good at farming while another was skilled in the art of warfare. An agreement would be reached where the farmers would provide food for the warriors while the warriors would provide protection for the farmers. By making a covenant together they each filled in the gaps caused by the other's weaknesses. A blood covenant is a union in which all assets, talents, debts, and liabilities are held mutually.

A blood covenant meant you were totally and forever giving yourself away to somebody else. Nothing could ever be yours alone again. All that you were, all that you had or ever would have, became the equal property of your covenant partner. The body of Christ desperately needs to become more covenant minded. The central theme of this God-given bond is love and that we need one another. Solomon wrote in Eccl. 4:9-12, "Two are better than one, because they have a good reward for their labor. For if they fall, one will lift up his companion. But woe to him who is alone when he falls, for he has no one to help him up. Again, if two lie down together, they will keep warm; but how can one be warm alone? Though one be overpowered by another, two can withstand him. And a threefold cord is not quickly broken." The blood covenant was originated by God and not man. It started in the Garden of Eden when God slew the animals to clothe Adam and Eve after they sinned.

In the Hebrew language the word for "covenant" means 'to cut flesh' or 'to make an incision.' When a covenant is 'cut' there is always a shedding of blood as a sign of the pledge between the two parties. Lev. 17:11 says, "For the life of the flesh is in the blood." No blood, no life. In the Old Testament some covenants were made by cutting their thumbs, wrists, or palms and mixing their blood together. In fact, this is where the handshake came from. Today we are "made nigh by the blood of Christ" (Eph. 2:13). Jesus shed His blood so we wouldn't have to shed ours and we come into a covenant relationship with God through faith in that blood. We need to realize that the blood covenant is a very sacred thing even today for it forms a bond between two people that creates a relationship that is stronger than normal family ties. When the world observes this union that is centered around the love of God they'll be drawn into a covenant relationship with Christ and other believers.

Through the action of believers fulfilling their part of the covenant we have in the blood of Jesus, when you become your brother's keeper, they'll see for themselves that the Lord came to give us life and give it more abundantly (John 10:10). The body of Christ would be a haven of rest and protection for all the world if more of its' members had a David or a Jonathan in their lives. And where does one find such a friend? The first place to look is in the mirror. Don't waste your time waiting for somebody to come up and knock on your front door because chances are it will never happen. Instead, make a commitment to become a friend. Friendships don't just happen on their own. They are planned and cultivated, and it starts with you. It is common knowledge that good things don't just happen to people. Life is what you make it and more times than not we are the ones who have to make good things happen. The same can be said about covenant relationships.

Prov. 18:24 says, "A man who has friends must himself be friendly, but there is a friend who sticks closer than a brother." With Christ as your Lord and example prepare your heart to become a lifelong friend to another, to become part of a three-fold cord that is not easily broken. Love is what the world is looking for, and love is what God and the Christian experience is all about. Take the first step and be willing to reach out and get involved with other people. Don't sit around and wait for someone to come and offer you their hand in friendship. You make the first move and begin by asking the Lord to place in your heart the name of a person who desperately needs a true friend in their life. For sure there is someone who is desperately waiting to hear your voice, read your message, or feel the reassurance of your presence. What you choose to say or do today may be the very lifeline God uses to bring them hope, strength, and encouragement right when they need it most.

In Paul's last letter before his death, he wrote about a true friend who was in his life. 2 Tim. 1:16-18 states, "The Lord grant mercy to the household of Onesiphorus, for he often refreshed me, and was not ashamed of my chains; but when he arrived in Rome, he sought me out very diligently and found me. The Lord grant to him that he may find mercy from the Lord in that Day - and you know very well how many ways he ministered to me at Ephesus." Onesiphorus had ridden his donkey a long distance to get to Rome and in spite of being tired and weary he searched hard for Paul until he found him. Love seeks to bless other people and this same love will energize you and give you strength and endurance because you're in the flow of what God desires. God can use you on a regular basis and if He puts somebody on your heart don't make a feeble attempt to help them, do it diligently. Don't sit around all day thinking only about yourself and about what you want and what you don't have.

Don't murmur and complain about how other people don't love you and never come to visit you. This will steal your peace and joy and make you old before your time. Paul said "for all seek their own" (Phil. 2:21) but the love of God will move you to seek another's benefit and well-being (1 Cor. 10:24). The Message Bible says, "We want to live well, but our foremost efforts should be to help others live well." Paul wrote in Phil. 2:19, "But I trust in the Lord Jesus to send Timothy to you shortly, that I also may be encouraged when I know your state." Paul was in a cold, damp prison cell when he penned these words and his foremost thought was the well-being of the brethren in the Philippian church. When you become your brothers' keeper you need to show interest in others no matter what's going on in your own life. Too many people talk about their problems all the time. Everybody has problems! Love is not selfish and love does not talk about problems.

Love asks people how they're doing without telling them what's wrong in your life. In Phil. 2:3,4 we read, "Let nothing be done through selfish ambition or conceit, but in lowliness of mind let each esteem others better than himself. Let each of you look out not only for his own interests but also for the interests of others." This is the highest form of love there is, and this is what it means to be your brother' keeper. The Message Bible says, "Don't push your way to the front; don't sweet-talk your way to the top. Put yourself aside and help others get ahead. Don't be obsessed with getting your own advantage. Forget yourselves long enough to lend a helping hand." Paul encouraged the church at Rome to "Be kindly affectionate to one another with brotherly love, in honor giving preference to one another" (Rom. 12:10). The NIV Bible states, "Be devoted to one another in love. Honor one another above yourselves." Love will esteem others better than yourself and will show preference to their wants, needs, and desires.

This doesn't mean other people are better than you, but you act like they are. If you esteem them, you will give them preference. You will serve them and give of yourselves to them. This is the heart of the Master. This is Christianity! Jesus said, "For even the Son of Man did not come to be served, but to serve, and to give His life as a ramson to many" (Mark 10:45). 2 Cor. 5:15 tells us, "And He died for all, that those who live should live no longer for themselves, but for Him who died for them and rose again." Jesus also said in Matt. 10:38, "And he who does not take his cross and follow after Me is not worthy of Me." Those who become their brothers' keeper will lay down their lives for other people and do this on a daily basis. You must make a sacrifice so others can benefit. This is the key to fullness of joy. You satisfying yourself all the time will not satisfy your soul. Selfish people are the most unhappy people in the world. Billionaires are miserable and often commit suicide. You simply can not satisfy a selfish person.

To be a Christian means to be like Christ for He is our example. Love serves and is glad to do it even when it's not convenient. You must be flexible to be your brothers' keeper for you may be needed in the middle of the night or be asked for money you needed for something else. People need you when they need you so you must be willing to rearrange your priorities so that you'll be available during their time of need. Examine your life and get rid of worthless things that take away your time from serving God and others. Things you do that God doesn't tell you to do will drain you and wear you out. The grace isn't there and this is why people are so tired all the time. They're doing things they shouldn't be doing and wasting time on things God didn't tell them to do. Learn to say "no" to things that would preoccupy you. Don't go shopping or fishing when you're supposed to stay home and pray and be still before the Lord.

God speaks in a still, small voice and it's during these quiet times when divine direction will come. The covenant bonding of a God-centered friendship involves a willing-ness to conform and become what the other person in the relationship needs. Love is not selfish and sooner or later it will become necessary for you to put the needs of your friend above your own. Prov. 17:17 says "a friend loves at all times" and true friendships bring with it endurance and stability. You can always depend upon your friend, and your friend can always depend on you. The best friends are the ones who stick by your side no matter what happens and is a person you can talk to about anything. A true friend is one who walks in when the rest of the world walks out. Prov. 27:9 says, "Ointment and perfume delight the heart, and the sweetness of a man's friend does so by hearty counsel." One of the many reasons a person should daily study the Bible is so he will be able to give Godly advice to a friend in need.

"The heart of the righteous studies how to answer" (Prov, 15:28) and Prov. 15:13 says, "And a word spoken in due season, how sweet it is." Words of advice and counsel from a true friend are pleasant because they are used to lift up and not tear down. A friend should always strive to promote and advance the life of the person he is in fellowship with. At the same time, love is also honest. When a friend sees something that needs to be corrected, he will reach out in love and give Godly counsel to his friend and encourage him as the correction is made. The Bible says, "Faithful are the wounds of a friend but the kisses of an enemy are deceitful" (Prov. 27:6). The Word also says in Prov. 28:23, "He who rebukes a man will find more favor afterward than he who flatters with the tongue." Words spoken in love will never be mistaken for criticism. A friend who speaks words of wisdom should also strive to perfect the art of listening.

God created us with one mouth and two ears and oftentimes all a person needs is a friend who will listen to them express the needs and concerns of their heart. Psychiatrists earn hundreds of dollars an hour because years of college has taught them that more can be accomplished by listening than through talking. How better off we'd be if each of us had a Godly friend who would be there for us during out time of need. It would be a lot cheaper, too. We are commanded by God to love because people everywhere have a need to be loved and accepted. No amount of achievement can fulfill the need for acceptance. It is a void that only love can fill. Insecurity comes from a lack of one-on-one relationships and can cause people to do great accomplishments for the sole purpose of getting accepted by others. As Christians we are "rooted and grounded in love" (Eph. 3:17) and because we have been "accepted in the Beloved" (Eph. 1:6) it has become our responsibility to share with others that God has accepted them as well.

This will cause hearts to be filled with joy, and it is only joyful believers who are able to reach out and lead others to Christ. We cannot demonstrate to the world the love of God without a loving relationship with one another. The best friends are the ones who love Jesus together and a church is only as strong as the relationships among its' members. Covenant relationships are continuous and should last a lifetime. Many people give roses when they want to make a friend but give thorns and briars afterward. They then wonder why the friendship failed. You get out of a friendship what you put into it and we must continue to treat people the way we treated them when we were first trying to gain their trust and confidence. True friendships are very rare indeed. Some people will go an entire life and never find a true friend. But don't give up. A true friend is worth a lifetime of work. Friendships have to be born and nurtured. They require time, effort, and a lot of sacrifice. And it all begins with you.

Become a friend to somebody in need, and watch what happens when compassion takes the place of indifference. A simple act of friendship can restore dignity, awaken hope, and remind a weary soul that they are not alone. In giving your time, attention, and kindness, you often discover that your own heart is strengthened in the process. True friendship has a quiet power - it changes lives, starting with yours. It has been said that there are two types of people in the world: those who make deposits into your life and those who make withdrawals. Depositors bring encouragement, truth, strength, and accountability, leaving you richer in faith, character, and purpose. Withdrawers drain joy, peace, and focus, often without any intention of building what truly matters. The real question is not only what type of person you want in your life, but what type of person you choose to be every single day.

| 5 |

"THE LOVE COMMAND"

The world would be a better place and life wouldn't be so complicated if people would just learn to follow the instructions that govern whatever it is they are trying to do. Car accidents happen when people drive on the wrong side of the road or forty miles over the speed limit. People risk an overdose on medicine when they don't follow the doctors' instructions that are printed on the bottle label. Divorces take place and lives are shattered when the vow to stay committed to one another "till death do us part" is broken. Instructions are everywhere, from the model airplane you bought your son to the cookbook that lays on the kitchen counter. The new lamp stand you just brought home from the store has instructions in it as does the power tools that hang in your garage. These instructions are not given to make you feel restricted in what you can or cannot do. They are given to help you live a better life.

Problems arise when people think they know more than the creator of the product and give no regard to the instructions given. This is what happened in the Garden of Eden when

Adam and Eve did not follow God's instructions to not eat the fruit from the tree of the knowledge of good and evil. They cast aside what God said, they did things their own way, and this is why the world is in the condition it is today. God's will for people is that they be willing and obedient (Is. 1:19) to follow all the instructions He gives us. Because of sin and rebellion people have not done so and now Gods' instructions come in the form of commands. Moses did not come down from Mt. Sinai with the Ten Suggestions, he came down with the Ten Commandments. Just like in the military, a command is an order that must be obeyed whether you like it or not. You have no say-so in the matter. It's not a suggestion, it's not an option, it's not a high ideal. It's an order and you must do it!

The Old Testament law was a set of commands that had to be obeyed in order to restore what was lost in the Garden of Eden. When Jesus came He fulfilled the law totally and gave us the one command that takes precedence over all the others. He said in John 13:34, "A new commandment I give to you, that you love one another; as I have loved you, that you also love one another." The love command is an order from the King of kings and Lord of lords, the everlasting Head of the church. Jesus is the Captain of our salvation and when He gives an order, He expects it to be carried out. It's not a choice! You are ordered by God to love one another just like Jesus loves you. Get this settled in your heart, the New Testament commandment is love. It's not a suggestion or an option. It's a command that must be kept whether you feel like it or not. You don't have to feel love toward someone to keep the order. It's an act of your will, an act of obedience.

The Old Testament teaches people to love. Lev. 19:18 says, "you shall love your neighbor as yourself: I am the Lord." Love was taught from the beginning so why does Jesus say this is a "new" commandment? In the Old Testament you loved your neighbor as you loved yourself but in the New Testament you love as Jesus has loved you. Jesus taught a brotherly love as opposed to a neighborly love. 1 John 2:10 tells us, "He who loves his brother abides in the light, and there is no cause for stumbling in him." Jesus came to show us a higher level of love, a love that will bring you to the point of being willing to sacrifice yourself for the sake of another. This is New Testament love. This is Christianity. A Christian will take on a burden that is not their own and use their faith, energy, and resources to meet the need and get the burden removed. The love of God has been shed abroad in your heart and to love as Jesus loved you takes a willingness to get your hands dirty with somebody else's problems.

Gal. 6:2 says, "Bear one another's burdens, and so fulfill the law of Christ." The Message Bible says, "Stoop down and reach out to those who are oppressed. Share their burdens, and so complete Christ's law." The law of Christ is the law of love. God will lead you and guide you in the way you should go but direction won't come until you first take your eyes off of yourself and consider the needs of other people. 1 Thess. 4:9,10 says, "But concerning brotherly love you have no need that I should write to you, for you yourselves are taught by God to love one another; and indeed you do so toward all the brethren who are in all Macedonia. But we urge you, brethren, that you increase more and more." God will personally teach you how to love one another and we are to increase in this love more and more.

The Message Bible says, "Keep it up, get better and better at it."

The Wuest translation says, "You yourselves are those taught by God with a view to loving one another with a love that impels you to deny yourselves for the benefit of the one whom you love." To be taught is the responsibility of every believer (Col. 3:10) and only those taught by God and led by His Spirit can keep the love command. Ps. 25:4,5 says, "Show me Your ways, O Lord; Teach me Your paths. Lead me in Your truth and teach me, for You are the God of my salvation; On You I wait all the day." Ps. 71:17 states, "O God, You have taught me from my youth; and to this day I declare Your wondrous works." Consider Ps. 143:10, "Teach me to do Your will, for You are my God; Your Spirit is good. Lead me in the land of uprightness." Isaiah writes, "Come, and let us go up to the mountain of the Lord, to the house of the God of Jacob; He will teach us His ways, and we will walk in His paths" (Is. 2:3).

God's call to His own has always emphasized unselfish love. His teaching is not that which provides information alone but that which creates disciples who will live in responsive obedience to Gods' will. People think the bulk of Christian love is talk, that if they tell somebody they love them then they have obeyed the love command. That is not so. Love is an action. 1 John 3:18 says, "My little children, let us not love in word or in tongue, but in deed and in truth." Keeping the love command means you do something and until you do your love is empty. Love always shows itself in action. James 2:15,16 tells us, "If a brother or sister is naked and destitute of daily food, and one of you says to them, 'Depart in peace, be warmed and filled,' but you do not give them the things which are needed for the body, what does it profit?" Keeping the love command will cost you something but you must take up your cross and endure hardness as a good soldier (2 Tim. 2:3).

You can keep the love command with God's grace and help, and He is personally going to teach you how. You must receive His help by faith, and you've got to be willing to learn it, do it, and grow in it. If you've already been loving one another then you must increase and do it more and more. Jesus said in John 15:10-12, "If you keep My commandments, you will abide in My love, just as I have kept My Father's commandments and abide in His love. These things I have spoken to you, that My joy may remain in you, and that your joy may be full. This is My commandment, that you love one another as I have loved you." Walking in love is fun! His joy will abide in you and will give you the strength to walk in love every day. Your joy will be full and you'll be the happiest you've ever been. The more you walk in love, the more happy you'll be. As a disciple of Christ you live to give, you live to bless people and to help remove their burdens. You're so busy doing things for other people that you forget about yourself.

You're already happy and fulfilled, satisfied and blessed. Your joy is full and your needs are met because what you make happen for others God will make happen for you. Eph. 6:8 says, "Knowing that whatever good anyone does, he will receive the same from the Lord whether he is a slave or free." The Message Bible says in vs. 6-8, "Don't just do what you have to do to get by, but work heartily, as Christ's servants doing what God wants you to do. And work with a smile on your face, always keeping in mind that no matter who happens to be giving the orders, you're really serving God. Good work will get you good pay from the Master, regardless of whether you are slave or free." You've got every reason to obey the love command and no good reason not to. It's not always easy, but it is always fun. Love is given as a command because your flesh may tell you some people aren't worth loving. This is precisely why we are to love them because those who need love the most deserve it the least.

We must never forget that at one time we were all in the same dead spiritual condition. Thankfully we read in Rom. 5:8, "But God demonstrates His own love toward us, in that while we were still sinners, Christ died for us." 1 John 4:10,11 tells us, "In this is love, not that we loved God, but that He loved us and sent His Son to be the propitiation for our sins. Beloved, if God so loved us, we also ought to love one another." There are a lot of Christians who Jesus is not their Lord. He's their Savior but not their Lord. The word "Lord" means He's in charge and you're not. He gives the orders. Sad to say, this is not the case with millions of believers. They want to be in charge of their own lives, and this is precisely why it's in the mess it's in today. But if Jesus is your Lord, then you will do what He says and do it cheerfully. And it was Jesus Who said in John 15:12, "This is My commandment, that you love one another as I have loved you."

Walking in love is the evidence that you are a real Christian. It's not about going to church or carrying your Bible or quoting scriptures or having your name on some membership roster. It's about whether or not you obey the order. Do you keep the love command? Do you love one another as God loves you? Jesus said "By this all will know that you are My disciples, if you have love for one another" (John 13:35). Jesus is talking about how we love each other as Christians. Divided churches and divorces among Christian couples destroy our witness to the world. If Jesus is your Lord then you will obey the order to love one another as He has loved you, and you will be excited doing it. Remember, it's the doers that get blessed. You can go to church all your life and watch other people praise God and love others but until you do it yourself you are just taking up space and are of little or no value to the kingdom of God.

Love is not something you talk about from time to time, it's what you live in and do every day, every night. It's a full-time job so get excited about obeying the love command. Th good news is that you can obey this order even when you don't feel like it. Feelings have nothing to do with it. In fact, love is strongest when you have no feelings. Real love shows up when you bless somebody when you'd rather slap them and walk away vindicated. The greatest gift you can give to another person is to believe in them and to love them, to treat them like they're important and valuable. Thankfully, God won't leave you hanging. You won't be left wondering what it is you're supposed to do. He tells you to love one another and then He teaches you how to do it. He takes you by the hand and leads you in the way you should go. Rom. 12:9,10 says, "Let love be without hypocrisy. Abhor what is evil. Cling to what is good. Be kindly affectionate to one another with brotherly love, in honor giving preference to one another."

All pain and tragedy and suffering is caused by the selfishness of man, but the Godkind of love prefers his brothers. When you prefer somebody, you yield to their wants and needs and let them get what they want first. In Greek the word "prefer" means 'to go before and lead; taking the lead to show deference.' God is teaching you to take the lead in preferring one another. Don't wait for somebody to treat you good, take the lead and treat them good first. Carnal Christians walk by feelings but mature Christians who take the lead walk by faith, hope, and love. No matter how they feel, no matter what they think, no matter what other people have done to them, they always walk in love and do it with a smile on their face. If the whole church took genuine delight in honoring one another and excelled in showing mutual respect, the atmosphere would be transformed by love, unity, and humility.

If the whole church would take delight in honoring one another, and excel in showing respect for each other, you would have heaven on earth. If every member would take the lead in seeking to outdo the other in showing compassion and helping to meet one another's needs, then the world would be turned upside down. If every member chose to take the lead in compassion - eagerly looking for ways to serve, help, and uplift others - the culture around us would be radically transformed. When meeting one another's needs becomes a joyful competition rather than a reluctant duty, love moves from words into powerful action. A community marked by selfless care would radically disrupt the world's patterns of selfishness, power, and indifference, revealing a way of life that cannot be explained apart from God. When love is lived sacrificially and consistently, the reality of God's kingdom becomes unmistakably visible - no longer a theory to be debated, but a force to be encountered and experienced.

The early church did this and we read in Acts 2:44,45, "Now all who believed were together, and had all things in common, and sold their possessions and goods, and divided them among all, as anyone had need." The Lord spoke about this to the prophet Isaiah when He said in Is. 58:1, "Cry aloud, spare not." Do not hold back in showing preference to one another. Spare not! He continues in vs. 6,7, "Is this not the fast that I have chosen: to loose the bonds of wickedness, to undo the heavy burdens, to let the oppressed go free, and that you break every yoke? Is it not to share your bread with the hungry, and that you bring to your house the poor who are cast out; When you see the naked, that you cover him, and not hide yourself from your own flesh?" He then said in vs. 10,11, "If you extend your soul to the hungry and satisfy the afflicted soul, then your light shall dawn in the darkness, and your darkness shall be as the noonday. The Lord will guide you continually."

You can't steer a parked car but if you will step out and take the lead in obeying the love command God will lead you and guide you continually. Paul continues this train of thought in Phil. 2:3,4, "Let nothing be done through selfish ambition or conceit, but in lowliness of mind let each esteem others better than himself. Let each of you look out not only for his own interests, but also for the interests of others." The Message Bible says, "Don't push your way to the front; don't sweet-talk your way to the top. Put yourself aside and help others get ahead. Don't be obsessed with getting your own advantage. Forget yourselves long enough to lend a helping hand." Esteeming others as better than yourself is the highest form of love there is. When you treat people like they're better than you, when you regard them as being more important than you are, your life will be better than it's ever been before. Giving more honor to others does not mean they are better than you, but you do treat them that way.

Jesus preferred us when He hung on the cross. People mocked Him and blasphemed Him when they said, "He saved others; Himself He cannot save" (Matt. 27:42). He put our needs above His own and by doing so He showed us how to keep the love command. Two thousand years ago Jesus left the splendor and majesty of heaven and came to earth to live as a man. He came to be a servant of all people everywhere and shortly before His death He set the example by kneeling down in front of His disciples and washed their feet. He laid aside His garments and put on a slaves' towel and in love even washed the feet of the one He knew would betray Him. Jesus was not elevating the disciples because they had earned His level, but because He believed in who they could become through His grace and calling. He treated them with the dignity of sons and leaders, inviting them to rise into the fullness of what God was shaping them to be.

At that moment Jesus took the role of a slave, and the disciples had the role of a master. Afterward He sat back down and explained the meaning of what had just taken place. "Do you know what I have done to you? You call Me Teacher and Lord, and you say well, for so I am. If I then, your Lord and Teacher, have washed your feet, you also ought to wash one another's' feet. For I have given you an example, that you should do as I have done to you. Most assuredly, I say to you, a servant is not greater than his master, nor is he who is sent greater than he who sent him. If you know these things, happy are you if you do them" (John 13:12-17). The Message Bible closes out this passage with these promising words, "If you understand what I'm telling you, act like it - and live a blessed life." The happiest people in the world are those who take the lead and serve. The willingness to serve, the willingness to put others above yourself, is the mark of spiritual greatness.

Like Jesus you can wash peoples' feet every day and treat them like they're better than you. You can defer to what they want because you've been told to do so, you've been ordered to keep the love command. The standard or the measure of how you love other people is how Jesus loves you. He said in Matt. 20:28, "Just as the Son of Man did not come to be served, but to serve, and to give His life s a ransom for many." Paul said the same thing in 1 Cor. 10:24, "Let no one seek his own, but each one the others' well-being." Living a selfish life is worse than dying. A self-centered life is a hellish life, a life of hurt, misery, and pain. The more you try to get what you want and the more you step on other people to get there, the more miserable you'll be. You can have three mansions, two airplanes, one yacht, and twelve sports cars and still not enjoy them if all you do is think about yourself. God planned it that way. He put something in you that demands more than self-gratification.

He placed in you a void that only He can fill. He placed in you the need to walk in love and if you don't take heed to the call to love others as Jesus loves you then all these luxuries will be like gravel in your mouth. But when you walk in love you will be on the threshold of some glorious things. God will come into your midst and manifest Himself. His glory will increase more and more until you know that you know that you know He is here. And where God is, there is love. This is how you are able to keep the love command. Like the Master you'll suffer before you'll let somebody else suffer. You'll sacrifice what you want and need in order to ease the pain of other people and help remove their burdens. Your highest desire is to help their dreams come true so that they'll reach their full potential in Christ. Jesus came to make you feel wanted and when you care for other people you make them feel wanted also. Every day you have choices to make. Will you prefer others or not?

Are your thoughts and actions centered on yourself or on other people? Are you going to do all the talking or remain silent and let other people talk? Are you going to focus on getting your own needs met or are you going to take the lead and help meet the needs of other people? It is profanity to only think of yourself and is a violation of the love command. Preferring others is going to cost you something every day but when you esteem others as being better than yourself God will see to it that you get what you need and want. You'll cast your cares on Jesus and

trust Him to supply what you need and want instead of you trying to do it yourself. You're too busy preferring other people
to think about yourself but you can have the confidence that
God is thinking about you every minute of every day. Take the
lead and prefer other people. Count those around you as being
more excellent than yourself. Jesus came to serve and you do
the same. This is the law of Christ. This is true Christianity.
This is love.

| 6 |

"A DEBT OF LOVE"

L ove is a costly thing. Jesus said, "If anyone desires to come after Me, let Him deny himself, and take up his cross daily, and follow Me" (Luke 9:23). The Message Bible says, "Don't run from suffering, embrace it. Self-sacrifice is the way, My way, to finding yourself, your true self." The story is told of a lieutenant addressing his platoon, "I'm looking for volunteers. Chances are, this mission won't succeed and many of you won't come back alive. If you're interested, step forward," Everybody looks around and then takes a collective step backward, leaving an unsuspecting volunteer standing alone. This is not how it is in the army of the Lord. God is looking for men and women who are willing to step beyond comfort, security, and convenience in order to obey His call. He honors those who quietly sacrifice everything to serve others, even when their obedience is never seen, recognized, or repaid by people because heaven always takes notice.

Oswald Chambers once said, "If we are devoted to the cause of humanity we will be crushed and broken-hearted, for we shall often meet with ingratitude. But if our motive is love for God, no ingratitude will hinder us from serving our fellow man." God is looking for a few good men, followers who will do something different by making a positive difference in the lives of other people. To obey this command to love you must give up those expectations that life be lived on your terms and be willing to pay the price so that God's purposes can be fulfilled on planet earth. What's more, He expects you to do it daily. Minute by minute, hour after hour. God is not asking you to do something He hasn't already done Himself. 1 John 3:16 tells us, "By this we know love, because He laid down His life for us. And we also ought to lay down our lives for the brethren." The Message Bible says, "Christ sacrificed His life for us. This is why we ought to live sacrificially for our fellow believers and not just be out for ourselves."

Are you willing to die daily (1 Cor. 15:31)? This is harder than physical death because it means to deny yourself and obey God even when it goes against the grain. Still, that's what you've been called to do when you step forward with a willingness to obey the love command. Paul writes, "But indeed I also count all things loss for the excellence of the knowledge of Christ Jesus my Lord, for Whom I have suffered the loss of all things, and count them as rubbish." (Phil. 3:8). To many people sacrifices are associated with regret and sadness but to God it's an act of love that brings joy and gladness. Paul wrote in 2 Cor. 12:15, "And I will very gladly spend and be spent for your souls." It is a great privilege to be given the opportunity to make a sacrifice for other people. There is, however, no reward unless your sacrifices are done very gladly. You're not just glad to make the sacrifice, you're very glad. God loves a cheerful giver (2 Cor. 9:7) and if your sacrifice isn't given very gladly then it's not very godly.

Gladness is the qualifier as to whether or not you are sincere in what you're doing. Give with a smile on your face as you consider that the sufferings of this present time are not worthy to be compared with the glory which shall be revealed in you (Rom. 8:18). Christianity is about finding out what God wants you to do and then doing it. It's about being a doer of the Word and not a hearer only (James 1:22). 1 John 4:7,8 reveals specifically what God wants you to do with your life, "Beloved, let us love one another, for love is of God; and everyone who loves is born of God and knows God. He who does not love does not know God, for God is love." Love is the indicator that one has been born again and knows God. It doesn't matter how religious you are, or how many scriptures you can quote. What matters is whether or not you obey the command to love others as Jesus loves you. Paul writes in Rom. 13:8, "Owe no one anything except to love one another, for he who loves another has fulfilled the law."

The Message Bible says, "Don't run up debts, except for the huge debt of love you owe each other. When you love others, you complete what the law has been after all along." John writes, "Beloved, if God so loved us, we also ought to love one another" (1 John 4:11). The word "ought" is derived from the root word "owe." Love is a debt owed to people and God is telling you to pay your debts. The reason this is so important is because people see God by seeing you. God is love and, when you love others, people come in contact with Him. Deep calls unto deep (Ps. 42:7) and the creation calls unto the Creator. The Creator is love and He lives inside of you. No other religion has this, and no false god can make that claim. Love is not a thing you achieve; it's a force you become. God is love, He is all powerful, and you are made in His image. Jesus became the love of God everywhere He went and you are to do the same. Let the love of God consume you!

Love people so much that you'll diligently look for and find ways to bless them. Jesus did things other people wouldn't do because of the love He operated in. Mark 1:40 tells how a leper came to Jesus asking to be made clean. "And Jesus, moved with compassion, put out His hand and touched him, and said to him, 'I am willing; be cleansed'" (vs. 41). Jesus touched the leper! You don't do that! But love does. Compassion is God's love in action and Jesus made it personal when He touched the leper. Love is the power with which God accomplishes His will on planet earth. There is nothing more powerful than love. God is love and His love makes you strong. It makes a difference when you do things motivated by love. It increases the value of whatever you do so take the love of God and minister it to people one person at a time. Keep yourself in the love of God (Jude 21) and work on a level where He operates.

Love takes the limits off God and when you walk in love God is unlimited in what He can do in and through you. Everything God does benefits other people. Ps. 19:8 says, "The statutes of the Lord are right, rejoicing the heart; The commandment of the Lord is pure, enlightening the eyes." God can use you to change somebody's world and to bring rejoicing to their heart. There is no greater blessing than that. Love is the bedrock to your success at being a child of God. There is such a distorted concept of love in the world that people rarely walk in the true light of Godly love. They ignore love to their own peril and need major mind renewal when it comes to the subject of love. Jesus said in John 15:13, "Greater love has no one than this, than to lay down one's life for his friends." How many people actually do this? Love never thinks of itself. It always thinks about the other person. As Jesus hung on the cross He was concerned about the relationship His tormentors had with the Father.

This is why he said, "Father, forgive them, for they do not know what they do" (Luke 23:34). In John 10:14,15 (MSG) Jesus said, "I am the Good Shepherd. I know My own sheep and My sheep know Me. In the same way, the Father knows Me and I know the Father. I put the sheep before Myself, sacrificing Myself if necessary." He continues in vs. 17,18, "This is why the Father loves Me: because I freely lay down My life. And so I am free to take it up again. No one takes it from Me. I lay it down of My own free will." Jesus was not a victim. He was not helpless in the hands of those who crucified Him. In the Garden of Gethsemane He willingly let the people take Him. This is love in action and is the same love you are commanded to walk in. Laying down your life is not merely an act of obedience; it must be a willing surrender marked by joy and gladness of heart. True sacrifice is proven not by what you give up, but by the spirit in which you give it freely, gladly, and without regret.

The value of something is established by what somebody is willing to pay for it. "Where your treasure is, there your heart will be also" (Matt. 6:21). Abel brought the best he had, Cain did not. If you're not willing to gladly sacrifice all you have then you cannot be the Lord's disciple (see Luke 14:27). Nothing can be more valuable than God and you've got to be willing to pay any price to follow Him. The rich young ruler walked away sad when Jesus told him to sell all he had, give to the poor, and come follow Him. The price was not too high for the young ruler to pay. Instead, his love for Jesus was too small. When there is true, genuine love, when you love God with all your heart, soul, and strength, there is no price too high to pay. When love for God is genuine - rooted in the whole heart, soul, and strength - obedience stops being a burden and becomes a willing offering. True love counts no cost as too great, because devotion to Him is valued above comfort, convenience, or self-preservation.

The disciples got beat for preaching the gospel and Acts 5:41,42 tells us, "So they departed from the presence of the council, rejoicing that they were counted worthy to suffer shame for His name. And daily in the temple, and in every house, they did not cease teaching and preaching Jesus as the Christ." Don't tell Jesus you love Him, show Him! Love God with all you've got. Hold nothing back! God smells the fragrance of a Godly sacrifice. Paul wrote how he received "the things which were sent from you, a sweet-smelling aroma, an acceptable sacrifice, well pleasing to God" (Phil. 4:18). If it's a godly sacrifice, somebody else is benefiting from what you've done. Excel in hospitality and seek for opportunities and the resources to build up and increase your brethren in Christ. People are most valuable to God and a person after God's own heart will value what He values. In the Parable of the Feast (Luke 14:15-24) those first invited did not go because other things were of greater value to them.

The things of God are supposed to be a big deal and those who walk in love see value where others do not. Shortly before Jesus went to the cross "a woman came to Him having an alabaster flask of very costly fragrant oil, and she poured it on His head as He sat at the table" (Matt. 26:7). Spices and ointments were like gold and very expensive. This particular flask of oil was worth a year's wages, but the woman valued Jesus more than the money. Judas Iscariot rebuked the woman for doing this and when Jesus told him to leave her alone, he immediately left to go to the high priests and asked, "What are you willing to give me if I deliver Him to you?" (vs. 15). Like the rich young ruler he valued money more than he valued Jesus. Some people say it's too hard and it cost too much to obey God and keep the love command. These same people have time and money for everything else, but when it comes to God, they say the price is too high. Is that the case or do they not value the things of God enough?

Those who truly love God and value what He values are the ones who will gladly sacrifice for Him. They'll endure hardness like a good soldier and do whatever it takes to complete the mission. You must make up your mind as to what matters most to you. Paul said he would very gladly spend and be spent for those he ministered to. When you're spent you've got no more to give. You've given it all. Abraham was a man who was willing to give God anything and everything. He left his people to go to an unknown destination and in Gen. 22:2 God asked him to offer his son Isaac as a burnt offering. Surely this was too high a price to pay. Abraham didn't think so for the next day he rose up early and set out on a journey to obey the Lord's command. He took God at His word that through Isaac his descendants would outnumber the stars in the sky and if need be God could raise his son from the dead. This is why he was called the friend of God and his faith will always be honored.

Jesus taught in Matt. 13:45,46, "Again, the kingdom of heaven is like a merchant seeking beautiful pearls, who, when he had found one pearl of great price, went and sold all he had and bought it." This man was seriously and deliberately searching for goodly pearls for he treasured what God treasures. In order to secure the costliest gems, he would travel far and was prepared to secure them no matter what the cost. This is what happens when you love God on purpose and value what He values. You'll go out of your way to search for ways to honor Him and be a blessing to other people. You will gladly spend yourself and be spent because in your heart there is no price too high to pay, no cost too great. In the Parable of the Hidden Treasure we read, "Again, the kingdom of heaven is like treasure hidden in a field, which a man found and hid; and for joy over it he goes and sells all that he has and buys that field" (Matt. 13:44).

The joy factor is a key element in the sacrifices you make to keep the love command. Jesus said in John 15:11,12, "These things I have spoken to you, that My joy may remain in you, and that your joy may be full. This is My commandment, that you love one another as I have loved you." The Message Bible says, "That My joy might be your joy, and your joy fully mature." Jesus is telling you to have a self-sacrificial love so that your joy will be full. Neh. 8:10 says the joy of the Lord is your strength and when you walk in love, you'll be a strong Christian. You'll be bold and strong; you'll walk in your authority as a child of God. You'll have confidence toward Him (1 John 3:21) and your faith will work when you walk in love. People think if you walk in love you'll be unhappy all the time and never get what you want. True happiness is found in selfless love, because those who live only for themselves and refuse to walk in love for God and others will always come up empty inside.

Those who obey the command to love are living in overflowing joy and it's the cheerful, sacrificial giving that allows God to open up the windows of heaven and pour you out a blessing there is not room enough to contain. The Lord said in Ezek. 34:26, "I will make them and the places all around My hill a blessing; and I will cause showers to come down in their seasons; there shall be showers of blessing." God will cause you to be a blessing to somebody else so always care about people and cheer them on. Encourage them to press on and keep going no matter what obstacle they may face. And if need be, reach inside your wallet and give them all that you have. Be willing to spend and be spent for others. Examine yourself. How happy have you been lately? How joyful? Christians are supposed to be the most joyful people on the planet. Joy is the environment of heaven and when you walk into a room the sun shines and the birds sing.

God's love is the light that shines and this same love should be seen on your face. Love does not frown and pout when it doesn't get its own way. Love rejoices in the truth (1 Cor. 13:6) and when truth wins out somebody gets set free. Love is genuinely glad when other people get blessed. Love is not jealous or envious and rejoices more over another person's victory than it does its own. Jesus said, "What man of you, having a hundred sheep, if he loses one of them, does not leave the ninety-nine in the wilderness, and go after the one which is lost until he finds it? And when he has found it, he lays it on his shoulders, rejoicing. And when he comes home, he calls together his friends and neighbors, saying to them, 'Rejoice with me, for I have found my sheep which was lost!'" (Luke 15:4-6). Love makes the effort and takes the time to notice another person's blessing. If a friend gets a new car, rejoice with them and offer to buy the first tank of gas and pay for their first oil change.

Have a celebration party! Invite people over and celebrate their victory and the good that has happened to them. Those in heaven rejoice when spiritual progress is made on earth (Luke 15:7) and we should do the same. Real love rejoices and is accompanied by real joy and real strength. Shortly before His betrayal Jesus told His disciples, "You have heard Me say to you, 'I am going away and coming back to you.' If you loved Me, you would rejoice because I said, 'I am going to the Father,' for My Father is greater than I" (John 14:28). Jesus is leaving and the disciples are not happy. Something good is about to happen. The price of sin is about to be paid and fellowship with the Father will soon be restored. This is good news and worthy of celebration, but the disciples could only think of how the Lord's departure would affect them. People who are miserable and unfulfilled are those who only think about themselves, what they want, what they need, and what somebody didn't do for them.

They live to satisfy themselves and this is why most of the world is unhappy. All of mankind is about to benefit from the Lord's departure and Jesus told the disciples to rejoice if they truly loved Him. People in the world today are not celebrating enough. Love builds up, it edifies, and it rejoices in another person's victory. Paul wrote in 1 Cor. 10:33, "just as I also please all men in all things, not seeking my own profit, but the profit of many, that they may be saved." Care so much for other people that you celebrate and rejoice when they get born-again or when their house gets paid off or they get a promotion at work. Love seeks not its own and will diligently search for ways to be a blessing to other people. This is the key to finding true joy. God is love and when you obey Him completely you will find all the satisfaction you'll ever need. Love means nothing unless you do it, unless you put actions to your words.

Paul writes in Rom. 16:26 (MSG), "All the nations of the world can now know the truth and be brought into obedient belief, carrying out the orders of God, who got all this started, down to the very last letter. "If you believe God, you'll obey Him. Jesus said, "If you love Me, keep My commandments" (John

14:15). The key to success in anything is commitment. A missionary society wrote to David Livingstone and asked, "Have you found a good road to where you are? If so, we want to know how to send other men to join you." Livingstone wrote back, "If you have men who will come only if they know there is a good road, I don't want them. I want men who will come if there is no road at all." There is a price to pay to fulfill the call to keep the love command and the down payment is commitment. Commitment demands that you apply yourself by giving the very best you have and to give priority to that which you are committed to.

The level of your commitment reveals the level of your love for God and other people. This is why there is no such thing as love at first sight. There is no commitment there. People who live together without being married lack commitment. They want to keep one foot out the door in case they want to quit the relationship and leave. It's like a biker who backs his motorcycle into the parking space. He wants to be able to leave quickly in case things get rough and out of hand inside the bar. Commitment will cost you! People need you when they need you, not when it's convenient. Commitment will hold a marriage together when the fun is gone. Commitment will rise up in the middle of the night and will go to great lengths to express itself. Prov. 17:17 says, "A friend loves at all times, and a brother is born for adversity." Love that is not seen is not love. Paul wrote Timothy, "Be diligent to come to me quickly; for Demas has forsaken me, having loved this present world, and has departed for Thessalonica" (2 Tim. 4:9,10).

Demas had no commitment. He forsook Paul just as Judas forsook Jesus and sold Him out. A lack of commitment is when people say, "What's in it for me?" You're not loving people if you're always complaining about what they're not doing for you. Don't judge people for not loving you. God told you to love them. Do it because He told you to. Do it for Him. Love people who don't deserve it. Forgive them and bless them because you love God. When you do God will manifest Himself and become more real to you than any living person. Jesus said, "He who has My commandments and keeps them, it is he who loves Me. And he who loves Me will be loved by My Father, and I will love him and manifest Myself to him" (John 14:21). God will fill up your life and your house and your car with His presence and you'll be filled with His thoughts and His Spirit. Yes, love is a costly thing, but it is a price well worth paying. As Dwight L. Moody once said, "Faith makes all things possible...love makes all things easy."

| 7 |

"THE LOVE TEST"

The debt of love is one debt you will always owe and never be able to pay off fully. You'll never reach the place where you can say you've loved others as much as you ought. No matter how long you've been a Christian and how much you have grown and matured, you still have room to grow in love. Since you can never exhaust the debt of love, you must keep working to pay it off. Paying off debts is hard because it requires denying yourself in order to reach your goal. You have to take your focus off yourself and put it on others and their needs in order to work at this debt of love that you owe. Since self-denial runs contrary to your flesh, love will require constant effort and thought. Do you love difficult family members? Do you love your angry boss at work who yells at you all the time and treats your coworkers better than you? Do you love those in the church who rub you the wrong way? If so, how did you show it in your words and behavior?

If they irritated you, did you respond with patience and kindness or did you get angry and retaliate with harsh words? John

Calvin wisely observed that "nothing flows away so easily as love" and that is why there are 55 New Testament commands to walk in love. Sometimes we think that love should be spontaneous and effortless but Biblical love is not automatic. It's a lifelong process and you've got to work at walking in love on a daily basis for the rest of your life. If you don't focus on it and work hard at it, it easily flows away. Love is an effort and you will be tested. God will tell you to do something for a person who won't appreciate it and won't say "thank you." He'll then tell you to do something extra nice for them the next time you see them. Hearing people say "thank you" feeds the flesh and that's why you want to hear it all the time. Just remember that you're not doing it for them, you're doing it for God, and your reward comes from Him. Love is a sacrifice and every sacrifice has its reward.

First comes the cross, then comes the glory. Rom. 8:17 says we are "joint heirs with Christ, if indeed we suffer with Him, that we may also be glorified together." The flesh is lazy and it always wants what's easy and free. Love will always cost you something and you can't wait for a feeling to motivate you. It is an effort and you must do it on purpose. You must give attention to your love walk. You must study the subject of love in the Word day in and day out, day after day. God is calling you to excellence. He is a God of excellence, a God of integrity, and He says love is the more excellent way (1 Cor. 12:31). You must take the conditions off your love for others. You can't love them only if they treat you right and if they say "thank you" all the time. Love people unconditionally. Love them on purpose because God told you to and not because you got some mushy feeling when somebody said, "Thank you." You are God's representative so get yourself off your mind and treat people with love and respect.

There is a simple test to see if you are of God and striving daily to walk in love. 1 John 3:10,11 says, "In this the children of God and the children of the devil are manifest: Whoever does not practice righteousness is not of God, nor is he who does not love his brother. For this is the message that you heard from the beginning, that we should love one another." The Message Bible says, "Here's how you tell the difference between God's children and the Devil's children: The one who won't practice righteous ways isn't from God, nor is the one who won't love brother or sister. A simple test." Are you striving daily to walk in love and do what's right or are you only concerned about how people treat you? Vs. 14 states, "We know that we have passed from death to life, because we love the brethren. He who does not love his brother abides in death." The Message Bible says, "Anyone who doesn't love is as good as dead."

Death is when you say, "What about me?" and refuse to obey God's command to love others as He has loved you. A command is an order, and you are ordered by God to walk in love. You experience God when you abide in His manifested love and the only thing that can truly satisfy you down on the inside and make you happy is when God uses you to be a blessing to somebody else. You can be a multi-billionaire and still be the most miserable person on the planet. It satisfies you deep inside when God uses you to help somebody get their needs met. This is the love of God being manifested through you and is the only thing that will give you fullness of joy. We live in a love starved society, and one only has to go to the shopping mall to see bizarre and weird behavior. Security cameras have filmed women fighting over who gets to buy the last purse sitting on the shelf. Prisons are filled with people who during an act of road rage committed deplorable crimes against another person.

The list is endless because people are selfish and only think of themselves. Even in evangelical churches there are many who claim to be born again but do not love others and don't even make an effort to do so. They are angry, unkind, impatient, abusive in their speech, self-centered in their daily lives, and judgmental of others. They spread malicious gossip with great delight and are defensive if you try to point out any of their sins to them. In Rom. 12:9 Paul said, "Let love be without hypocrisy. Abhor what is evil. Cling to what is good." There is a strong tendency among believers to put on a mask of love to cover hearts that are full of selfishness, jealousy, manipulation, and even hatred. The epitome of love with hypocrisy was when Judas betrayed Jesus with a kiss (Luke 22:48). Outwardly it looked as if he really cared for Jesus but in reality he was giving Jesus over to bloodthirsty men who would torture and kill Him. The Message Bible says, "Love from the center of who you are; don't fake it."

Paul is calling you to pass the test and have a sincere love that flows from your heart. Paul knew more than anybody that the enemy of your faith walks around like a roaring lion seeking whom he may devour (1 Peter 5:8). He is a thief who comes to kill, steal, and destroy (John 10:10). In his early travels Paul founded a series of churches in the Roman province of Galatia and a few years later he wrote them these special words, "For all the law is fulfilled in one word, even in this: 'You shall love your neighbor as yourself.' But if you bite and devour one another, beware lest you be consumed by one another!" (Gal. 5:14,15). The Message Bible says, "If you bite and ravage each other, watch out - in no time at all you will be annihilating each other, and where will your precious freedom be then?" Satan steals the Word from people and hinders their effort to fulfill the love command by getting them angry and offended.

Anger is the cruelest of all emotions and is a manifestation of selfishness, pride, and hatred. People who get angry think they're superior and always look down at other people. They are unable to walk in love because they're too busy being upset about what they don't like or about what somebody did or didn't do to them. Solomon wrote in Eccl. 7:9, "Do not hasten in your spirit to be angry, for anger rests in the bosom of fools." Anger will make a fool of you because "a fool vents all his feelings, but a wise man holds them back" (Prov. 29:11). It is far better to exercise self-control and obey the words of James 1:19,20, "Therefore, my beloved brethren, let every man be swift to hear, slow to speak, slow to wrath; for the wrath of man does not produce the righteousness of God." One thing interesting about people is they're everywhere you go. You can't get away from them and no matter where you go there will always be people who will rub you the wrong way.

Without even knowing why they'll dislike you and begin to say things in an effort to destroy your character and rob you of the peace that is in your heart. These people are nothing more than puppets on a string controlled by the devil as he attempts to destroy your life and the mission for God that you are on. The spirit of offense is like a cancer that if not dealt with will destroy your home, your health, your ministry, your relationships, and everything else that pertains to your life. The word "offense" means 'that which causes one to trip or stumble' and is one of the most harmful and dangerous things that could ever happen to you. The devil is out to separate you from the Lord and His people and he uses offense to cause you to feel displeasure, to get angry and hurt, and to disconnect from those you should be loving. Many people no longer go to church because they got their feelings hurt and got offended. Somebody sat in their favorite chair or else the pastor didn't shake their hand after the service.

The devil wants you to lose your faith and stop walking in love and he uses offense to do it. If not dealt with offense will make you grow bitter inside and soon you'll stay home from church and do nothing for the kingdom of God. Instead of getting offended be like a nail - the harder you get hit, the deeper you go in God. Two thousand years ago when Jesus walked the earth He made it clear to His listeners that He would one day return again to the earth. This sparked the interest of all those who heard Him say this and one day He was asked, "Tell us, when will these things be? And what will be the sign of Your coming, and of the end of the age?" (Matt. 24:3). He was unable to answer the first question because only the Heavenly Father knows when the end will be (vs. 36) but He was able to make known to them the signs that would precede His glorious return. He then spent nearly two chapters expounding on the answer to their second question.

Natural calamities will occur and the actions of the godly and ungodly alike are recorded in great detail. Any person who is even remotely aware of the conditions of the world around them will quickly come to the correct conclusion that all the predictions have been fulfilled and we are indeed living in the last days. Jesus can and will return any day now. As a believer you must pay particularly close attention to what Jesus said in vs. 10-13 because it contains a warning to all those who claim to be children of God. What He says may shock you for His words reveal the stark reality of what will happen to many believers in the last days. Pray you are not one of them. "And then many will be offended, will betray one another, and will hate one another. Then many false prophets will rise up and deceive many. And because lawlessness will abound, the love of many will grow cold. But he who endures to the end shall be saved."

The Message Bible says, "Going from bad to worse, it will be dog-eat-dog, everyone at each other's throat, everyone hating each other. In the confusion, lying preachers will come forward and deceive a lot of people. For many others, the overwhelming spread of evil will do them in - nothing left of their love but a mound of ashes." It is a stab in the heart to realize that these verses describe the actions of born again believers and not the wicked sinners of the world. The office of prophet is a ministry given to the church and false prophets and lying preachers will not deceive non-saved sinners because they won't be preaching to them. Those who will be deceived are cold-hearted believers who are unable to tell the difference between right and wrong. Their sin will dull their spiritual senses and will take away their ability to hear from God. Truly there is a price to pay for sin and dullness of hearing and a lack of discernment are two of them.

Notice also in vs. 12 where it says "the love of many will grow cold." The word "love" in this verse is the Greek word 'agape' which is the God-kind of love. Only believers can have this kind of love and Jesus is saying that many people who are saved and born again will have this God-given love turn cold within their hearts and as a result will begin to betray and hate one another. Christians hating Christians! What causes this love to grow cold? lawlessness! Sin! Offense! The absence of holiness in the lives of wayward believers! It is a shame to know that Christian divorces now outnumber the divorces of the community of non-believers. Churches everywhere are grasping the idea that homosexuality is an acceptable behavior and some are electing openly gay clergymen to the highest offices in the organization. What must the Lord be thinking? Churches are split nearly every day and each night many believers go to bed bitter and angry at their fellow brothers and sisters in the Lord.

What caused these evil feelings to take root in these people? To answer that you must go back to the beginning of our scriptural context and see what Jesus said. Matt. 24:10 begins by saying, "And many will be offended..." Notice it doesn't say a few will be offended but many! Believers being offended at one another are those who have failed the love test and is a sign that the end of the age is fast approaching. The Amplified Bible gives an even more clear picture of the repulsive condition many members of the body of Christ are now in. It says they "will begin to distrust and desert Him (Whom they ought to trust and obey) and will stumble and fall away and betray one another and pursue one another with hatred." It is a sad commentary that sin in the church is even listed in this category of end-time events. For sure, the root of bitterness runs deep. The word "offense" also means 'to create resentment, injustice, insult, to hurt the feelings of.'

Unaddressed hurt never remains small; it quietly takes root in the heart. When wounds are ignored, they harden into bitterness, reshaping how a person thinks, feels, and responds. Over time, that bitterness can mature into anger and even hatred, poisoning relationships and distorting judgment. Healing begins when hurt is confronted honestly, forgiven intentionally, and released before it gains power. In Greek the word means 'to bait a trap, to ensnare.' It's the part of the trap where the bait is laid. It pleases the flesh to lash out at others when one's appetite for self-centeredness is not filled to full capacity by those around them. Getting offended is a bitter reaction to not getting one's own way and only selfish and self-centered people get offended. Sadly, these same people often turn to uncontrolled anger that causes them to do harm to the one whom they are offended at. The Bible is filled from cover to cover with stories of people who got caught in the deadly trap of offense.

In Genesis 4 Cain got offended when God rejected his offering and as a result rose up and murdered his brother Abel. The sons of Jacob got offended when their younger brother Joseph told them about his God-given dream that foretold a day when they would all bow down before him. King Saul was jealous when more attention and praise was given to David and once offended tried on several occasions to murder the anointed heir to the throne. In the New Testament Martha got offended because her younger sister Mary sat at the feet of Jesus instead of helping with the serving of the guests. Let us not forget what offended hearts did to the Lord Jesus Christ after He spent His entire life doing nothing but good to those around Him. He healed the sick, lifted the broken, spoke truth in love, and extended mercy yet He was rejected, mocked, and crucified. This sober truth reminds us that faithfulness to God does not guarantee applause from people, but it does guarantee eternal significance.

| 8 |

"NEVER FAILING LOVE"

Several hundred miles off the coast of Guam is the Mariana Trench, the deepest place in the ocean. The depth of the ocean is mind-boggling and the Mariana Trench is nearly seven miles down. The water pressure at the bottom of the trench is 15,931 pounds per square inch yet there is life there surviving despite the pressure and the darkness. It is hard to fathom just how deep the Mariana Trench is but it's much more difficult to comprehend the infinite depth of God's love for you. The apostle Paul was hard pressed to describe this love but he prayed that his readers would be able to somehow grasp the love of Christ which surpasses all knowledge. To the saints in Ephesus he prayed "that Christ may dwell in your hearts through faith; that you, being rooted and grounded in love, may be able to comprehend with all the saints what is the width and length and depth and height - to know the love of Christ which passes knowledge; that you may be filled with all the fullness of God" (Eph. 3:17-19).

The word "comprehend" means 'to take eagerly or to seize and thus to make something one's own or to hold as one's own; to gain control of through pursuit; to grasp mentally; to apprehend with the mind; to perceive.' The word carries the idea of mentally grasping something while "apprehend" suggests laying hold of it for yourself. It is possible to understand something but not really make it your own. The Message Bible translates Paul's prayer this way, "And I ask Him that with both feet planted firmly on love, you'll be able to take in with all Christians the extravagant dimensions of Christ's love. Reach out and experience the breadth! Test it's length! Plumb the depths! Rise to the heights! Live full lives, full in the fullness of God." God wants you to live in four dimensions: the breadth, length, depth, and height of His love - a love that is immeasurable and never failing. These were terms used to express the totality of the universe and astrologers utilized them in their calculations.

The universe is infinite and so also is God's love for you. "Yes, I have loved you with an everlasting love; Therefore with lovingkindness I have drawn you" (Jer. 31:3). God loves you with infinite dimensions and to an endless degree. The love of God extends from eternity past to eternity future. Christ's love is like His Name, and that is Wonderful (Is. 9:6). So wonderful is His love that it is above all creatures, beyond measure, contrary to all nature. Time did not begin His love and time shall never end it. Paul prayed that you would comprehend the love of God in its total fullness, that you would know fully and completely the totality of God's love for you. He wanted every aspect of your being - spirit, soul, and body - to know and experience and come into a relationship with the love of God. The good news is that you can attain what Paul is saying in this prayer. Paul was anointed when he wrote these words and the Spirit would not give the church a prayer that can't be answered.

The love of God is as high as the heavens above the earth and as wide as the east is from the west. The only way to know and comprehend this love is to love others as He has loved you. When you demonstrate your love for Jesus by following His command to walk in love, He will manifest Himself to you in a loving, special way. John 14:21 (AMP) says, "The person who has My commands and keeps them is the one who really loves Me and I too love him. I will let Myself be clearly seen by him and make Myself real to him." Those controlled by their emotions don't know the love of God but the person that endeavors to show it will come to comprehend it in a rich, full way. You may not always be able to feel love for the unlovable at the outset but you can be willing to be the channel through which love flows. As Christ's love through you broadens, lengthens, deepens, and heightens, you will come to know and experience the vastness of His great love.

Everything that pertains to your life gets its strength and nourishment from the love of God. You must be established in that love because love never fails, never becomes obsolete, never comes to an end. Love abides forever and, when you are rooted and grounded in love, you also are firm, solid, and you'll never come to an end either. You'll never fail because you're standing on the firm foundation of God's holy love. Paul was praying that the foundation of your life would be anchored in the love of God. In order to fully comprehend the magnitude of God's love, you must first be rooted and grounded in that same love. Being "rooted" means 'to become stable, to render firm, to be firmly established, to be strengthened with spiritual roots, to be firmly fixed with the focus upon the source of such strength.' The children of God are established and settled securely in the love of Christ. They are rooted deeply in the soil of love and are able to grow strong and massive.

In Christ, believers find life-giving soil "that they may be called trees of righteousness, the planting of the Lord, that He may be glorified" (Is. 61:3). Never forget that everything you do is for the purpose of giving glory to God. The Message Bible says, "Rename them 'Oaks of Righteousness' planted by God to display His glory." A tree must sink its roots deep into the soil if it is to have nourishment and stability. As a believer you have been permanently and completely rooted deep into the love of God. Paul writes in Col. 2:6,7, "As you have therefore received Christ Jesus the Lord, so walk in Him, rooted and built up in Him and established in the faith, as you have been taught, abounding in it with thanksgiving." Psalm 1:2,3 says blessed is the man whose "delight is in the law of the Lord, and in His law he meditates day and night. He shall be like a tree planted by the rivers of water that brings forth its fruit in its season, whose leaf also shall not wither; and whatever he does shall prosper."

Jer. 17:8 says, "For he shall be like a tree planted by the waters, which spreads out its roots by the river and will not fear when heat comes; but her leaf will be green, and will not be anxious in the year of drought, nor will cease from yielding fruit." The born-again believer must be rooted and grounded in love as a way of life, a life of kindness, selflessness, brokenness, and meekness. It is the life of Christ finding expression in and through the life of the believer. Love is the soil in which your life must have its roots, and it is the rock upon which your faith must ever rest. The word "grounded" describes the foundation which lies beneath, with reference always to something secure and permanent in itself. It means to ground securely, deeply, and firmly founded, like a building rising higher and larger. The picture conveyed is that of a house which is so firmly fixed on a foundation that it is not moved by winds and floods or by the stormy waves of suffering or the loud howling roar of your adversary the devil.

Love is the key to the fullness of God. If you want to get filled up with God, then you must walk in love. You are to be rooted and grounded in that love which is unconditional, sacrificial, and always giving. When you're walking in love, you're walking in God for God is love (1 John 4:8). Nothing in your life will fail if love is your motivation. You can't be defeated, you won't be destroyed, you can't be undone. Jesus looked like He was defeated when He hung on the cross but He wasn't. The love of God is a force that has all the appearance of weakness and yet is the strongest force that exists. To His tormentors and mockers Jesus appeared weak as He hung on the cross. To the world He looked defeated but on that cross was pure love and it couldn't be defeated. Jesus spread His arms out on the cross and said, "This is how much I love you." That's the breadth of

God's love and it has the ability to encompass the entire world and to reach every person.

The length of God's love is how far love will go and extend itself to help or reach another person. Jesus said, "Greater love has no one than this, than to lay down one's life for his friends" (John 15:13). The depth of the love of God causes you to not be changed or be altered by bad circumstances and the pain of rejection. You may feel hurt and pain but love will overcome all the hardships you go through. It's too deep to be dominated by it. The height of God's love is the magnitude of good it can achieve in the heart of someone who gives it and receives it. Love never fails and it was the fullness of God's love that raised Jesus up three days later. Because of that love, death and the grave was forever defeated, as was sin, sickness, and poverty. Your relationships at home, church, school, and work will remain and endure forever if you are rooted and grounded in love. If the motivation factor behind all you do is love, even if you do or say something at the wrong place and time, God will turn it around in your favor.

You can mess things up but if you are rooted and grounded in love, even if what you did was wrong, when it crumbles it will crumble back into love. Love will pick you up, set you on your feet, and send you on your way. You can not be defeated if you are walking in love even though many times you may look defeated and weak. If you are responding to life in the love of God you are going to come out on top every time. The blocks you build your life upon may crumble but they'll crumble back into love. Pick up the pieces and keep walking in love. If someone strikes you and you turn the other cheek, the love of God will stop them from hitting you on the other side. There is no way to be defeated or undone when you walk in the love of God. It is impossible to fail. Real love has staying power. The world is changing around you day by day but the love of God never changes, never ends, and never fails (1 Cor. 13:8). Love is eternal. It never dies. It will last forever and it never, not at any time, never at all, fails!

Jude 21 tells you to "keep yourselves in the love of God, looking for the mercy of our Lord Jesus Christ unto eternal life." 1 Cor. 13:13 says, "And now abide faith, hope, love, these three; but the greatest of these is love." Not only are these spiritual forces but are also the three basic needs that every person has. A person has to have these three things if their life is to be fulfilled and complete. There will never be a day throughout all eternity when you won't need faith, hope, and love. These three things remain and endure forever. You were created to believe and in order to walk in faith you must have hope, a confident expectation, a dream, an aspiration. Without faith and hope people despair and give up on life. Both are needed in abundance but the greatest need a person has is love. Not only does a person need to receive love, they even more so need to give love. Yes, the need to give is the greatest need you'll ever have. You were created in the image of God. God is love and love always gives (John 3:16).

Prosperity hasn't manifested in the church like God desires it to because the only reason most people want money is so they can buy themselves a new car or anything else that will satisfy their sensual cravings. God wants you to have nice things but He's not going to give them to you if you're not walking in love. He knows that without the motivation of love you won't enjoy these material things anyway. The proper motive for prosperity should be so you can be a blessing to someone else. Love always gives. When you do that God will add all these material benefits into your life. Jesus said in Matt. 6:33, "But seek first the kingdom of God and His righteousness, and all these things shall be added to you." Prosperity must be rooted and grounded in love, as does healing. Don't desire healing so you can watch TV without pain. Get healed so you glorify God and use your physical strength to do more for Him and other people. Get rooted and grounded in love first, then believe God for healing and prosperity.

Many people refuse to love because they've been deeply hurt in the past. They come into the faith from backgrounds where love was not experienced. Maybe your parents abused you verbally or physically and perhaps you were in a series of abusive relationships that left you hurt, battered, and bruised. You had no role models to show you how to love other people and today you ridicule Jesus and take His Name in vain. It is urgent, once you trust in Christ as your Savior, to learn from God's Word and from more mature believers how to love others in a practical, daily manner. You will need to unlearn many bad ways of relating to others that you brought with you from the past. You will need to relearn how to think and speak and act in loving ways, especially toward those who have wronged you. If you do not learn to love others as Christ loves you, know with certainty that you will fester with bitterness and anger, causing your relationship with Christ to suffer.

Rather than thinking angry thoughts about how somebody wronged you, begin to pray for that person that he or she would come to know Jesus. Forgive them and look for opportunities to return good for evil. Then let love extend to your speech. Put off abusive speech that tears down the other person and cease from gossip and slander. Put on speech that builds up and edifies and begin to practice loving deeds, looking to serve others and becoming a blessing to them. Become zealous for good works (Titus. 2:14). If you really want to walk in love then you better be ready to work at it. Loving people who are unlovable is the hardest thing you will ever have to do and as soon as you try the devil will rise up and attack you. Love is spiritual warfare and you can never love without being vulnerable and opening yourself up to hurt. It can't be done. Not loving, however, will hurt you more than anything another person can do to you. It is better to have a soft heart that can be hurt than a cold heart that can't.

Love is deep and can overcome hurt feelings and the pain that rejection and bad circumstances bring. Love never fails and, if you're white hot on fire with love, the devil can't touch you. Ps. 84:11 says, "For the Lord God is a sun and shield; The Lord will give grace and glory: No good thing will He withhold from those who walk uprightly." Choose love and don't draw back if you've been hurt. God will shield you and protect you. Open yourself up and love again because love will pick you up and give you the victory that you long for. The greatest need you have is to love and be loved, and if nobody else will love you, God will. Bask in that love. If people love you, great! If they don't, so what? God loves you and this gives you the motivation and power to love people no matter how they feel about you. Jesus came to meet your need to be loved. Always and forever you are loved! People have to love and be loved and this is why Jesus gave the command to love one another. It's man's greatest need.

Love is how unity comes to the body of Christ. The church will never come into unity based on what people believe. Believers loving one another is the key to unity, prosperity, healing, and faith. It's the key to the power of God, the key to everything God has and is. The love of God needs to be your chief objective, the foremost thought in your thinking. You have to constantly be thinking about and dwelling on the question, "What would love do?" What would love say and how would love respond in the situation you find yourself in? If people call you names and say bad things about you, keep yourself in the love of God at all costs. If you're not in the love of God you're in Satan's territory which is ruled by hatred and deceit. The majority of Christians and sinners alike have not seen God as He truly is. Rom. 2:4 says God is rich in goodness, rich in forbearance, and rich in longsuffering. Love puts up with a lot of things and it's the goodness of God that leads people to repentance.

The love of God seeks unity and desires reconciliation and, the more you love other people, the more you'll know God and comprehend the depth of His love. Remember, God loves the people you don't like and He wants you to love them as He has loved you. Love is the nature of God. His character, essence, and temperment is love. He can't do anything outside of love. He acts in love, He talks in love, He responds in love. A person's nature is revealed by close observation and, the more you dwell in the presence of God, the more you'll learn that His nature is love. Since God is love, you can be love also. You can be patient and kind, not rude, jealous, or envious. Learning the concepts of walking in love will change your life because it teaches you to take your eyes off yourself and put them on other people. Nobody is going to be happy as long as they are selfish and think about themselves all the time. Jesus died for all mankind and it's this same nature of love that you must adopt as your own.

Your life may be a mess but walking in love opens the door for God to change you. If you don't like who you are, then go out and do something nice for somebody else. God will change you if you do. You'll be changed into the image of God which is the image of love. You'll be changed from glory to glory, from love to greater love. As you get rooted and grounded in love, you'll be able to comprehend with all the saints the four dimensions of God's eternal and glorious love. This same love will radiate out of you and will become your very own. For love to grow, it has to flow. It has to get out of your heart and into your words and deeds. It has to govern your actions and your bank account. Listen to what people say, be attentive to what they need and want, and then reach out and be a blessing to them. Also, everybody you give to doesn't need to be poverty stricken. Give to somebody who has more than you. They may not need what you give them but do need the love or the example of what walking in love is really like.

Love is not measured by verbal expression; it's measured by actions. Your love for God is measured by your obedience to His commands. 2 John 5 says, "And now I plead with you, lady, not as though I wrote a new commandment to you, but that which we have had from the beginning: that we love one another." The Wuest translation calls it "that commandment which we have been having continually from the beginning." The disciples were continually going back to love, drawing the church's attention back to this truth. John exhorts his readers no less than ten times in his writings to love one another. He places great emphasis on this subject because of its importance to the integrity of Christianity. True love is bound by the truth of God's will. Love finds the manifestation in responding to the will of God as revealed in His Word. Truth and love are the riverbanks between which God flows. In essence, love is applying God's Word to life's experiences. When you obey the Word, you are walking in love.

God is love and since God and His Word are the same, then the Word is love. 2 Cor. 11:3 talks about "the simplicity that is in Christ." The Message Bible calls it "the simple purity of your love for Christ." The simplicity of Christ is love. In the Garden of Eden life was pretty simple. They only had one command - don't eat the fruit of the tree of the knowledge of good and evil. You also have one command to obey, the command to walk in love. Love should be a habit you perform daily, a divine love that is sacrificial in its essence. It's not concerned how its been hurt but only how it can help. Nothing will mature you faster as a Christian. John continues in 2 John 6, "This is love, that we walk according to His commandments, that as you have heard from the beginning, you should walk in it." God's command is a statement of His will and the content of this love comes by revelation. Love is more than sentiment for it also involves content.

Shakespeare said, "Love reasons without reason." This is the opposite of what God says. God says that love always contains content, a divine revelation of what the true love of God is all about. Man cannot artificially produce divine love on his own. Love manifests itself by responding to the content of God's will. Keeping God's will out of a sense of duty and with little love for God is not true love. Sentimental love without God in it is as dry as last year's bird's nest. It has no depth and is as dry as the dust. True love is hard to counterfeit. You can tell whether your belief and trust in God is genuine by the nature of your love. It's a response to the grace of God in Christ and love that is real does not lie beyond the sphere of action. Love must be seen and not only heard. Love as an emotion or sentiment has no accountability but love in action reveals what you truly believe. Faith applies truth to experience and love presents the patent test of the genuineness of belief.

God will personally instruct you how to love unlovely people. He'll show you how He loves them so you can love them the same way. Let love urge you and prompt you to do the right thing. Don't grow weary and give up for the love of God is too deep to quit. Loving one another reveals how much you love

God so keep pressing forward with a never failing love no matter how people may respond back to you. Natural people get their natural nature from their parents but spiritual people get their spiritual nature from God. When you became a new creature in Christ you got yourself a new nature. Rom. 5:5 says that the love of God has been shed abroad in your heart. God's love nature is in you! God is love and so are you! Say out loud, "I am love!" Love is the greatest need of man and God wants to use you to help meet that need. As you do, then and only then, will you be filled with the fullness of God and be able to comprehend the riches of the love of God that He has for you.

| 9 |

"RADICAL LOVE"

Walking in love is the Mount Everest of all Christian behavior. Jesus sets the standard of love that we are to follow as high as it can possibly be set. He said in John 13:34, "A new commandment I give to you, that you love one another; as I have loved you, that you also love one another." Jesus said that our love for others must match the love He has for us. This radical love is not just a special requirement for the super-committed. It is clearly God's standard for all His children. He continues in vs. 35, "By this all will know that you are My disciples, if you have love for one another." The love you have for your Christian brothers and sisters must be marked by a devotion that is characteristic of a loving, close-knit, and mutually supportive family. Radical love must be developed and as you grow to be more like Jesus you'll soon develop a genuine interest in others where you'll seek to serve and not be served.

Daily you must fight against the common hindrances to love such as selfishness, pride, impatience, the love of the world and the things in the world that will pull you down. In other words, you must die to yourself. Even Paul said, "I die daily" (1 Cor. 15:31). Love is a sacrifice, but it is a joyful sacrifice. Jesus said in John 15:11, "These things I have spoken to you, that My joy may remain in you, and that your joy may be full." What separates the false from the true is joy. Radical love gives you radical joy which in turn gives you radical strength (Neh. 8:10). People who walk in radical love are never weak and depressed because they're full of strength and the joy of the Lord. Peter spoke of radical love when he wrote, "Since you have purified your souls in obeying the truth through the Spirit in sincere love of the brethren, love one another fervently with a pure heart" (1 Peter 1:22).

The sincere agape love of God describes the quality of love bestowed by God and does not refer to an easy, sentimental reaction to our personal likes and desires. Instead, radical love is a fruit of the Spirit in a yielded believer who is then enabled to do the supernatural and not just the natural. The believer is able to love the unkind and the unlovable, can love in spite of insult and injury and love when love is not returned. Peter goes on to say, "And above all these things have fervent love for one another" (1 Peter 4:8). The phrase "above all" reminds the saints that love is the prerequisite to all proper exercises of Christian behavior. Courtesy without love is a cold thing and generosity without love is a harsh thing. Love makes all other virtues what they should be. Love is the badge of honor that a believer displays openly, especially in times of testing and persecution. It is with radical love that you'll be able to give your life away and obey the Lord's rules for kingdom living.

Jesus said in Luke 6:27-30 (MSG), "To you who are ready for the truth, I say this: Love your enemies. Let them bring out the best in you, not the worst. When someone gives you a hard time, respond with the energies of prayer for that person. If someone slaps you in the face, stand there and take it. If someone grabs your shirt, gift wrap your best coat and make a present of it. If someone takes unfair advantage of you, use the occasion to practice the servant life. No more tit-for-tat stuff. Live generously." Peter is saying that a radical love is a fervent love that flows from a heart that is pure. The word "fervent" is literally the picture of one who is stretched out. It pictures an intense strain and unceasing activity which normally involves a degree of intensity and perseverance. The Greek word "ektenes" was used to describe a horse whose legs are fully extended while galloping.

It was also used as a medical term describing the stretching of a muscle to its limit and in Grecian athletes described a runner with the taut muscles moving at maximum output, straining and stretching to the limit in order to win the race. Peter is calling us to a love which is "fully stretched out" and manifested in an all-out manner with an intense strain. This presents the clear picture that love is not something that will just happen but is something you will have to work at like an Olympic athlete who strives to master his area of expertise with all his energy. An aggressive love that is "stretched out" allows you to reach out and touch someone with strenuous and sustained effort. Christian love is not an easy, sentimental reaction but is energetic and demands all your mental and spiritual energy. Radical love is the love that never fails and into which every atom of one's strength is directed. Love never disappoints and never lets anyone down. It can always be depended upon and is always reliable.

Walking in radical love will always be a benefit to other people and it will take you out of the prison of selfishness you've been living in most of your life. Love never quits and walks away. It cares more for others than it does for itself and it patiently and passionately bears with others for as long as patience is needed. Love doesn't demand others to be like itself but rather is so focused on the needs of others that it bends over backwards to become what others need it to be. Love suffers long (1 Cor. 13:4) and is like a candle that has a long wick and is prepared to burn a very long time. A person with radical love is ready to forebear, to patiently wait when a person doesn't quickly respond back to them in a proper way. To be patient means to be long spirited, to be long tempered. Heb. 10:36 says, "For you have need of endurance, so that after you have done the will of God you may receive the promise."

Life is a marathon and when you realize we're in this for the long haul the sooner you'll see the need for love, faith, and patience. The level of patience in your life is the same level of faith that you have. If you lose your patience, you lose your faith. They go hand-in-hand. When you have no faith you stop believing God and you no longer please Him. Patience motivated by radical love is developed through exercise. Most people want things quickly and pass up opportunities to develop patience and walk in love. They get upset driving behind a slow car and lose their temper when they have to stand in line at the check-out counter at the store. Love is generous and the more you exercise patience by displaying acts of aggressive kindness the stronger it will become, the more it will develop. Faith works by love and if you don't stop loving you won't stop believing and lose your faith. To be patient and kind means to be adaptable to the needs of others and to love people so much that you become all things to all men (1 Cor. 9:22).

Love is a Person. God is love (1 John4:8) and radical love is a force, a nature, a commandment, an action. There is no defense against love and the devil has nothing in his arsenal that can stop it or slow it down. Love is tolerant and patient but is also kind while it is patient. Being patient reveals how deep your love and strength goes. The more impatient you are, the more weak in faith you are. It is not okay to be impatient and demanding with one another. Never have the attitude that says, "I want it and I want it now!" Don't be so ambitious and self-centered and so consumed with yourself that you never think of the needs or desires that others have. Love is humble and never seeks its own way. Love is not rude or discourteous. It's not careless or thoughtless, nor does it carry on in a fashion that would be considered insensitive to others. Radical love has an attitude that is submissive and will always adapt itself to the needs and desires of other people.

Real love will step out of line and let others go first even if it means they'll get the best and you'll have to settle for second best. That's okay. Do it for God. It won't matter a century from now anyway. Make it your business every day to glorify God by walking in love and preferring other people above yourself. People are supposed to see your love for love hidden is not real love. The Message Bible says, "Live a lover's life, circumspect and exemplary, a life Jesus will be proud of: bountiful in fruits from the soul, making Jesus Christ attractive to all, getting everyone involved in the glory and praise of God" (Phil. 1:11). Too many people live in their own world where everything is about them. The flesh is selfish and everything is always about me, me, me! It is time for the church to rise up and adopt a new way to live. It's time to change the way you look at the world. It's time to turn your eyes away from yourself and onto the lives of others.

Forgetting about yourself is very liberating and will give you a freedom you've never experienced before. Let the biggest joy you have come from seeing the smile you put on someone else's face. God can use you for miracles where you become a dream come true for those you meet. Ask Him to show you people with needs without getting anything in return. Radical love is not based on what you get back. Consider what Paul said in 2 Cor. 12:15, "And I will very gladly spend and be spent for your souls; though the more abundantly I love you, the less I am loved." The Message Bible says, "I'd be most happy to empty my pockets, even mortgage my life, for your good. So how does it happen that the more I love you, the less I'm loved?" Paul was saying he wasn't getting anything in return from these people, but he was going to keep on loving them anyway. That's the radical love of God! Love is a decision. It's a choice you make to value people and do good things for them no matter if they respond back to you or if they don't.

You won't find this love in the selfish world we live in because the radical love of God is good to people all the time. It steps in when the rest of the world steps out. To be totally and completely developed in love is Christlike perfection. To be just like Jesus is to be love, a radical love that abounds to every good work (2 Cor. 9:8). The love of God is the manifestation of all the excellencies of God. He is love and you must daily pursue your calling to also be love. The true love of God is when you love and do nice things for the person who does nothing for you. You can't love people if you fear being taken advantage of all the time. Fear comes in when you're concerned that something bad will happen to you instead of being concerned about what you can do for somebody else. People spend more time trying not to be hurt than they do reaching out to others with a sincere heart and pure motive.

People who walk in fear are self-centered and are forever focused on the bad things they thought somebody did to them. "You ignored me at church last week. You didn't talk to me. You didn't call me on the phone. You didn't give me what I thought I needed." People put up walls so they won't get hurt but those same walls also prevent the love of God from flowing out as it should. It takes great determination to walk in love. The radical love of God is strong and fearless and is never concerned about itself at all. 1 John 4:18 says, "There is no fear in love; but perfect love casts out fear, because fear involves torment. But he who fears has not been made perfect in love." Love throws fear out thus enabling you to yield to the love that has been shed abroad in your heart (Rom. 5:5). Love is a choice and is independent of how you feel and how other people treat you.

You can love somebody and there is nothing they can do about it.

Love is a command. If God said you can do it, you can do it. Love others as God loves you. Be radical. Become love to somebody else. The number one call in a person's life, the top priority, is to walk in radical love. Paul said, "So, no matter what I say, what I believe, and what I do, I'm bankrupt without love" (1 Cor. 13:3 MSG). Prosperity and success in the business world should not be your top priority but developing a strong, successful love walk. Jesus said in Matt. 6:33 to seek first the expansion and the full development of God's kingdom and this is done through walking in love. A walk is made up of several steps and is the slowest form of transportation known to man. Slow down and live life one step at a time. A decision is made to take each step and in the walk of love lots of decisions have to be made every day, all day long. Decisions determine direction and direction determines destiny.

You need a kingdom mentality and every morning when you wake up and every night when you lay down you need to make the decision to simplify your life and walk in love. Too many distractions and complications in life can hinder your love walk and cause people to put other things first, especially their own personal needs and desires. There's more to life than having money in the bank and a lifelong membership at the yacht club. Most of the world is either spiritually dead or spiritually asleep and this is why Paul says in Eph. 5:14, "Therefore He says: 'Awake, you who sleep, arise from the dead, and Christ will give you light.'" The Message Bible says, "Climb out of your coffins." The only thing you need to do to be carnal is nothing. Decide to be a doer of the Word and not a hearer only (James 1:22). Get focused on the right thing. Walking in love must be the first and foremost priority in your life and everything else a distant second.

The nicest and greatest place to live on planet earth is in the radical love of God. He who dwells in love, dwells in God and God dwells in him. God is love and so are you. There is nothing love won't fix. Enough love will heal your body and make those headaches go away and cause your liver to function properly. It will get your debts paid off and restore broken relationships and will make you the head and not the tail. 1 Cor. 13:13 says, "And now abide faith, hope, love, these three; but the greatest of these is love." The Message Bible says, "Trust steadily in God, hope unswervingly, love extravagantly. And the best of these is love." Love has to be the top priority of your life, the foundation of everything you believe, say, and do. When you believe in that love and act on it, there is nothing you can't receive from God. Your light will rise in obscurity, and the Lord will guide you continually and He'll satisfy your soul in a bad economy, during seasons of drought and lack.

He'll water your garden and make fat your bones when you walk in love and think about God and what He wants you to do. Hundreds of things are fighting for your mind time, those things you think about instead of God. If you are not careful you can get so caught up in these distractions that days turn into weeks and weeks turn into years and suddenly half your life is gone. Get sold out to Jesus and think about Him all the time and meditate in the Word day and night (Josh. 1:8). People will think you're strange but so what? Who cares what people think? If Jesus was their Lord, they'd be doing the same thing. The world is way too busy. People are running around like a chicken with its head cut off, going here and there and not really going anywhere. They're so busy they don't know if they're coming or going and their lives are spinning out of control. Now is the time to slow down and make a decision on what's important to you and act accordingly.

God is calling you to walk in love and you need to put everything on hold and answer the call. Jesus said, "Many are called, but few are chosen" (Matt. 20:16) because only a few people slow down enough to answer the call. Those who seek first the kingdom must also do so with their time. Time is a limited, precious commodity and if you're too busy to love your neighbor as you love yourself then you're too busy. There is only so much time in a day and what amount of time you spend on one thing you can't spend on another. You can't have it both ways. It's a choice you have to make. And once today is gone, it's gone forever. You can't get it back, you only have what's left. What will the Lord find you doing when He returns? You don't have enough days and years to waste doing those things not relevant to the kingdom of God. Prioritize your time! Unclutter your schedule and get rid of those things you do that have no eternal significance.

Lay aside those things that take up your time, thoughts, and energies. If you don't, life will pass you by and you'll miss out on the will of God. You can't serve two masters. You can't serve yourself and God. Kick yourself off the throne of your life and put God there. Say, "not my will but Your will be done." Pursue love (1 Cor. 14:1) and set your mind on things above, not on things on the earth. "Pursue the things over which Christ presides. Don't shuffle along, eyes to the ground, absorbed with the things right in front of you. Look up and be alert to what is going on around Christ - that's where the action is. See things from His perspective" (Col. 3:1,2 MSG). Love is costly. It cost Jesus His life and the Father His Son. Every time you walk in love it will cost you something. You will be asked to give away something you want to keep, say something you don't want to say, and behave in a way you don't want to behave.

This is why you must be reading about and studying love all the time because it's one of the hardest things to get and maintain. Most people struggle in life and are forever asking Jesus to hasten His return to planet earth to relieve them of all their suffering. Jesus does not want to come back just to bail you out of all your troubles. He wants to come back for a strong and victorious church, a church that is walking in love and obeying all His principles, a church that is radical and stirred up and on fire every day, day in and day out. You are His representatives on the earth and you are to be working the works He gave you to do and occupying until He comes. The truth of the matter is that you should desire Him to delay His return so you can do more for Him, not less. Love will protect you as you seek first His kingdom. Love "bears all things, believes all things, hopes all things, endures all things" (1 Cor. 13;7). The word "bear" means 'to cover as a roof covers a house.'

There are many seasons of life, and not all seasons are pleasurable. Some seasons are stormy and very difficult, but love will protect you exactly as a roof shields and guards the inhabitants of a house from snow, rain, heat, and cold. Love endures all things and it never quits, never surrenders, and never gives up. Real love never throws in the towel and never accepts defeat. It is always pressing on, reaching forward, and straining to fulfill that which it's been called to do. Love never fails! God is love. It's not what He does, it's Who He is. You too, are love. And since God and love are perfect, you also are called to radical perfection. Jesus said in Matt. 5:48, "Therefore you shall be perfect, just as Your Father in heaven is perfect." The Amplified Bible says, "You, therefore, must be perfect [growing into complete maturity of godliness in mind and character, having reached the proper height of virtue and integrity], as your heavenly Father is perfect."

The Message Bible puts it this way, "In a word, what I'm saying is 'Grow up.' You're kingdom subjects. Now live like it. Live out your God-created identity. Live generously and graciously toward others, the way God lives toward you." One can not sidestep the context of when Jesus commanded you to be perfect. He said these words right after He said to "love your enemies, bless those who curse you, do good to those who hate you, and pray for those who spitefully use you and persecute you" (Matt. 5:44). A carnal Christian is one who only obeys the Word when it's easy to do so. It's easy to love those who love you back, to love the rich church member but despise the poor. Character is forged in the dark places of life, where no applause is heard and obedience to God is chosen without recognition. Perfection is revealed when you learn to love those who do not love you back, reflecting the heart of Christ who loved us while we were yet undeserving.

Love is an act of your will and perfection comes when you talk to people when you feel like being quiet, when you smile when you feel like frowning, when you give away that what you want to keep, when you're nice when you're worn out and tired and don't feel like being nice, and when you put up with people whom you'd like to slap and put in the trash can. This is how you imitate God. This is how you become radical. This is how perfection comes. Love does the impossible and it all begins when you seek first God's kingdom. David said, "Trust in the Lord, and do good; Dwell in the land, and feed on His faithfulness. Delight yourself also in the Lord, and He shall give you the desires of your heart" (Ps. 37:3,4). You delight yourself in the Lord by doing what pleases Him and putting His holy law in your heart (see Ps. 40:8 and Rom. 7:22). God has not promised to gratify all your fleshly desires and the appetites of your body but to grant all the desires of the heart, the cravings of the renewed, sanctified soul.

The desire in the heart of a Godly person is to know God, to live for Him, to please Him and to be pleased in Him. Nothing pleases God more than when you become your brother's keeper and love your neighbor as you love yourself. God is not a genie in a bottle waiting for your command for Him to fulfill your wildest dreams. No, He is God and we are to fulfill His dreams. When your life is so in harmony with the Savior's that your only goal is to see Him face to face, then this oneness produces the likeness of Jesus in your earthen vessel. Your delight is in the Lord and Him alone. Out of this great union between you and God comes a change of heart. No longer are you driven to the material things of this world but are more hungry for the things of God's heart. His heart becomes your heart and His desires become your desires. He then gives you the desires of your heart that you were intended to have before they were muddied by the selfishness of sinful thinking.

When all is said and done, the measure of a life is not found in achievements, applause, or accumulation, but in obedience to God's will. Living His dreams means aligning your desires with His purpose and allowing His plans to shape your decisions each day. God's will anchors your life to something eternal, far greater than temporary success or personal ambition. When His purpose becomes your priority, your life gains clarity, direction, and lasting meaning. In the end, doing His will and living His dreams is the one true goal that gives your life eternal significance. Say out loud, "Lord, show me Your heart and let me dream Your dreams." When you surrender your own plans and begin living for His dreams, life becomes richer, deeper, and far more exciting than anything you could design on your own. The true adventure of life does not begin with human ambition, but in discovering and walking out the heart of God. Let the adventure begin.

| 10 |

"EXCEL IN LOVE"

When the apostle Paul first met the Lord on the road to Damascus his key question was, "Lord, what do you want me to do?" (Acts 9:6). From that day forward Paul devoted his life doing what the Lord told him to do and saying what the Lord told him to say. Our God is a God of love, and He used Paul in a great way to teach the church how to be transformed into His image and to love one another as He has loved us. During his second missionary journey Paul and Silas brought the message about Jesus the Messiah to the city of Thessalonica (Acts 17:1). Many people became believers but a riot soon arose and they had to flee, narrowly escaping with their lives. A short time later Paul became concerned that the believers in this infant church might fall away from the faith due to the opposition they were facing so he sent Timothy to encourage them. When Timothy returned with the good news that those in the church had remained faithful Paul wrote them a letter to express his joy.

Their faith, hope, love, and perseverance in the face of opposition was exemplary and Paul's affection for them is evident in every line he wrote. He encourages them to increase in their new-found faith, to excel in their love for one another, and to rejoice, pray, and give thanks always. So proud of them was he that he wrote in 1 Thess. 2:19,20 (MSG), "Who do you think we're going to be proud of when our Master Jesus appears if it's not you? You're our pride and joy!" As Paul penned these words to his dear brothers and sisters in the Lord his love was so strong that the desire rose up in him to one day return and visit them once again. This desire was expressed in 1 Thess. 3:11,12, "Now may our God and Father Himself, and our Lord Jesus Christ, direct our way to you. And may the Lord make you increase and abound in love to one another and to all, just as we do to you."

The Message Bible says, "May God our Father Himself and our Master Jesus clear the road to you! And may the Master pour on the love so it fills your lives and splashes over on everyone around you, just as it does from us to you." Paul continues to encourage his readers to excel in love a few verses later when he wrote, "But concerning brotherly love you have no need that I should write to you, for you yourselves are taught by God to love one another; and indeed you do so toward all the brethren who are in all Macedonia. But we urge you, brethren, that you increase more and more" (1 Thess. 4:9,10). The Message Bible says, "Just love one another! You're already good at it; your friends all over the province of Macedonia are the evidence. Keep it up; get better and better at it." Love is a behavior you choose to operate in because you represent God and He told you to do it. If you have received the gracious gift of eternal life, then you owe a debt of love to all people.

The good news is that you don't have to pay this debt with love that you generate on your own. Rather, you pay it out of the limitless overflow of God's love toward you. To excel in love the first and foremost thing you must do is realize that it's not about you. You must get yourself off your mind and reject all thoughts of selfishness. Love is a sacrifice and if you want to be free you must first forget about "me." Prov. 30:15,16 says, "The leech has two daughters, crying, 'Give! Give!' There are three things that are never satisfied, four things never say, 'It is enough'; The grave, the barren womb, the earth that is not satisfied with water, and the fire the never says, 'It is enough.'" The NL Bible says, "The leech has two suckers that cry out 'More! More!'" The EV says, "The leech has two daughters, and both have the same name, 'Give me!'" A big horse leech is a parasite, a creature that lives off the life of something else. It's like a mosquito that sucks the blood out of its host.

The life is in the blood, and a parasite takes the life out of something else in order to sustain their own self. In Hebrew the word "leech" literally means 'to suck' and it is sad but true that with some people in different situations there is no pleasing them. No matter what you do or how nice you are it is never enough. They don't realize it but they are a "sucker" much like a leech and they always cry out, "Give! Give! More! More!" They complain because you didn't do this and you should have done that. They are never satisfied and are forever trying to pull something out of someone else in order to sustain their greedy and selfish ways. The biggest root cause of problems in relationships is selfishness and a failure to walk in the commandment to love. Husbands tell their wives, "If you'll submit to me, I'll love you" and wives tell their husbands, "If you'll love me, I'll submit to you." Both are saying "Give me." Paul says in 1 Cor. 10:24, "Let no one seek his own, but each one the other's well-being."

Don't be a leech who pulls on people for something all the time. Love seeks not its own and it doesn't think about "me" and what "I" need. Don't have a selfish attitude. Remember, it's not about you. You must die to your self and learn to think of others and put their needs above your own. God cares about hurting people and He expects you to care about them as well. We read in Luke 10:25-28, "And behold, a certain lawyer stood up and tested Him, saying, 'Teacher, what shall I do to inherit eternal life?' He said to him, 'What is written in the law? What is your reading of it?' So he answered and said, '"You shall love the Lord your God with all your heart, with all your soul, with all your strength, and with all your mind," and "love your neighbor as yourself."' And He said to him, 'You have answered rightly; do this and you shall live.'" Jesus was saying, "You know the answer, now do it." The AMP Bible says in vs. 28, "If you do this you will enjoy an active, blessed, endless life in the kingdom of God."

People who are not happy rarely, if ever, do things for other people. They are "suckers" and all they ever think about is "Me! Me! Me!" Being saved is no guarantee of happiness. If you are selfish and full of yourself, you will never be happy. Our society drives people to selfishness and this same "Give me!" attitude has crept into the church. We want more and more and more yet we are never satisfied with what we have. We try to buy happiness yet are some of the most miserable people in all the world. You cannot be happy until you get yourself off your mind and reach out to somebody in need. God wants you to prosper and have nice things, but He doesn't want you to forget the poor, the lost, the needy, the naked, and the destitute. You can not outgive God. Take care of somebody else and God will take care of you. Find somebody who is hurting and try to make a difference in their life. Be passionate about the things God is passionate about. Be more caring when it comes to helping people in need.

The first century church did God's work with great power but the more selfish we become the less power there is available to us. It's time for a change! It's time to start doing what the Bible tells you to do! Jesus called us to love one another, and this means you have to do something. You can do anything but one thing you can't do is nothing. There is more to life than making money. When you're on your death bed it's not going to matter how much is in your bank account. Get out of your comfort zone and go be a blessing to someone else. Who cares if the pews at church have padding on them or not or if your air conditioner didn't work one day this week? Stop being the center of your life. Forget about yourself. Get yourself off your mind and excel in loving one another. God will lift you up from the deepest pit, but He won't lift you out of your easy chair. That you have to do yourself. God will open doors for you, but it is you who must get out of your comfort zone and walk through them.

Give God something to work with. Just as thrust is the power that pushes an airplane forward so it can gather speed and lift off the ground, use love to provide forward motion in your life and thrust you into a radical life of being a blessing to other people. You will never walk on water unless you're willing to get out of the boat. If you want to swim you are going to have to go ahead and take the plunge. Some people spend their whole lives waiting for the perfect time to do something. Little do they know that there is rarely a perfect time to do anything. What is important is to get started. As you walk in love put one foot in front of the other and that momentum and forward motion will provide you with the lift you need to soar like an eagle in your service to other people. An ancient Chinese proverb says, "The journey of a thousand miles begins with the first step." Even if there are a thousand things you cannot do, there is always something you can do.

It may seem small and insignificant, but the eyes of God are on you. He is watching to see what you do with the opportunities He has given you. Your response determines whether or not He entrusts you with more. Love doesn't just happen on its own. You have to pursue it. 1 Cor. 14:1 (AMP) says, "Eagerly pursue and seek to acquire this love." You can pray for God to help you walk in love but He's not going to do it for you. The Message Bible says, "Go after a life of love as if your life depended on it - because it does." Without love you are a useless nobody. Love is not a feeling, it's a "willing"! Get up each morning and will yourself to love somebody on purpose. God will show you what to do but He won't make you do it. Love is an action word. It's a verb, not a noun. Real love is seen and measured in how you treat people. If love is not demonstrated in visible actions and genuinely felt in human connection, it remains nothing more than empty words rather than a living truth.

A hypocrite is somebody who talks the talk but doesn't walk the walk. A hypocrite speaks loudly about principles but quietly ignores them in practice. They tell people what to do but don't do it themselves. They preach love but don't live it. They have a scripture for everybody and they're proud of how much more they know than you. They're judgmental and think they're better than everybody else. Hypocrites are "suckers" and the good news they preach to everybody else isn't working for them because they don't do the things to cause people to see their love. Don't judge people and look down your holy nose at them. Nobody is better than anybody else and you don't impress the world by being religious. Hypocrites are "traitors, headstrong, haughty, lovers of pleasure rather than lovers of God, having a form of godliness but denying it's power. And from such people turn away" (2 Tim. 3:4,5).

If you're not happy maybe it's because you're not excelling in love and not doing anything for somebody else. It's the goodness of God that leads people to repentance (Rom. 2:4) and God wants to be good to somebody through you. If you're good to people, they'll be more open to listen when you talk to them about Jesus. An anointing abides in you (1 John 2:20) so wherever you go do something good to somebody whether you feel like it or not. Get up every day and put yourself on deposit before God and say, "Use me, Lord. Here I am. Send me." Don't wait for somebody to say, "I'm hurting. Please help me." Go find somebody! David writes in Ps. 68:5,6a (NIV), "A father to the fatherless, a defender of widows, is God in His holy dwelling. God sets the lonely in families, He leads out the prisoners with singing." Go to your pastor and ask for a list of all the widows and single parents in the church and then go out and do something for them. Bless them, encourage them, visit them, take them shopping.

Forget the attitude that says, "What about me?" and go find a single mom and give her some money and take her and her children to lunch. Pay her rent this month and send her some gift certificates to stores without letting her know you did it. Adopt a widow and visit them and care about them. Being lonely is a terrible thing and days are long and painful when nobody calls or visits you. Remember those in prison. Write them often and encourage them to have faith in God and that all hope is not lost. Do something and stop passing by on the other side of the street (Luke 10:31,32). You can't love people from a distance. "If a brother or sister is naked and destitute of daily food, and one of you says to them, 'Depart in peace, be warmed and filled,' but you do not give them the things which are needed for the body, what does it profit?" (James 2:15,16). How often at church do people hug one another, say "I love you with the love of the Lord," and then part ways and don't see or hear from each other until the following Sunday?

Never tell a person you love them if you're not ready and prepared to get personally involved with their lives. If you're not ready to do this then your words are cheap and meaningless. People need to "see" Jesus. Being a Christian is not just about going to church on Sunday. It's about developing the character of God in our own lives so that people can actually see Jesus in what we do and say. We need to display the same love, attitude, and behavior that God has toward His Son and all the people in the world. Love wants to give and doesn't feel put out when asked to do so. It looks for reasons and opportunities to get involved. This should be your goal in life. It shouldn't be to have enough faith so that you can get everything you want, or to get to the point where nothing bothers you and the devil never comes against you. Your goal and purpose in life is to be living epistles read by all men, to represent God in this earth, to act like Him so that people who need Him can see Him through you.

True happiness is not found by chasing our own wants and needs, but by forgetting ourselves and pouring our lives into something greater than us. When self fades and purpose, service, and love take its place, joy follows as a natural result. Remember, it's not about you. Those who truly love Jesus are always alert for opportunities to be a blessing, because His love compels them to look beyond themselves. Their faith is not passive or private - it is expressed through intentional acts of kindness, service, and compassion toward others. Job writes, "When the ear heard, then it blessed me, and when the eye saw, then it approved me; Because I delivered the poor who cried out, and the fatherless and he who had no helper. The blessing of a perishing man came upon me, and I caused the widow's heart to sing for joy" (Job 29:11-13). He continues in vs. 15,16, "I was eyes to the blind, and I was feet to the lame. I was a father to the poor, and I searched out the case that I did not know."

Job took it upon himself to look for ways to bless other people. He was a man who excelled in love and further evidence of this is seen in Job 31:16-22, "If I have kept the poor from their desire, or caused the eyes of the widow to fail, or eaten my morsel by myself, so that the fatherless may not eat it (But from my youth I reared him as a father, and from my mother's womb I guided the widow); If I have seen anyone perish for lack of clothing, or any poor man without covering; If his heart has not blessed me, and if he was not warmed with the fleece of my sheep; If I have raised my hand against the fatherless, when I saw I had help in the gate; Then let my arm fall from my shoulder, let my arm be torn from the socket." Everything we've been given by God should be used to bless another person's life. Job said if he could not use his arm to bless somebody then yank it out because he had no use for it. Love is a sacrifice and you can't love people without giving something up that is valuable to you.

Give to the missionary who comes to your church the money you've been saving for your dream vacation so he can feed the poor in Calcutta. Let the single mother borrow your new car when hers has broken down. Stay home from that fishing trip with your buddies so you can help paint the walls of the Sunday school classroom. Help your neighbor move into their new home when you'd rather watch the championship ballgame on

TV. Make investments into the lives of other people and do it cheerfully without grumbling and complaining. Take the initiative and offer to do these things without being asked. Most people don't do this. Most people are "suckers" who make demands on other people and say "Give me! Give me!" Declare war on selfishness and be good to people on purpose. When you give with a right attitude, you're more like God than at any time in your life. Love is a beautiful thing, and the world is hungry to see what real love is really like.

It's your job to show them that the true love of God is not selfish, it seeks not its own, and is a higher, deeper love than what the world knows. Love is carried through vessels, and it is your responsibility to be good to people all the time and show them what God is really like. Get stirred up in love and be willing to be used by God to bless somebody else. Heb. 10:24 says, "And let us consider one another to stir up love and good works." Actively seek to make somebody's life better. The word "seek" means to get up and go after it. Turn off your television, pull yourself out of that easy chair, and go out and do something good to somebody. Show the world that you know God and through you let them see what He is like. 1 John 4:7,8 says, "Beloved, let us love one another, for love is of God, and everyone who loves is born of God and knows God. He who does not love does not know God, for God is love." You can't know God and go around being a 'sucker' all the time.

If you're continually using people for your own benefit, you don't know God. Gal. 6:2-5 states, "Bear one another's burdens and so fulfill the law of Christ. For if anyone thinks himself to be something, when he is nothing, he deceives himself. But let each one examine his own work, and then he will have rejoicing in himself alone, and not in another. For each one shall bear his own load." The Message Bible continues in vs. 7,8, "Don't be misled: No one makes a fool of God. What a person plants, he will harvest. The person who plants selfishness, ignoring the needs of others - ignoring God! - harvests a crop of weeds. All he'll have to show for his life is weeds! But the one who plants in response to God, letting God's Spirit do the growth work in him, harvests a crop of real life, eternal life." The love of God that comes "to" you doesn't benefit others until it flows "through" you. Ask yourself, what are you doing to help somebody? What are you doing to make somebody's life better?

Don't be super spiritual and go to Bible studies all the time. Go into the world and "be" a Bible study to those in need. Live what you've learned. Religion that never moves beyond words and rituals is empty if it does not express itself through love and service to others. True faith proves its value when it reaches beyond belief and actively does good for someone in need. This is what it means to be so heavenly minded that you're no earthly good. Start to creatively ask God, "What can I do?" You have compassion because God is in you and there is always something you can do. Don't ever assume you can't do anything. You can help relieve all the suffering in the world if you will let God baptize you with the fire of love (see Ps. 97:3). Jesus died so people can be set free and it's your God-given obligation to get yourself off your mind and go out and do something for someone else. There is more going on in the world than what's going on inside the four walls of your house.

People who are "suckers" don't walk in love because it's an effort and will cost them something, but Paul says in Eph. 5:1,2, "Therefore, be followers of God as dear children. And walk in love, as Christ also has loved us and given Himself for us, an offering and a sacrifice to God for a sweet-smelling aroma." It's time to take a stand against complacency where you no longer close your eyes to the needs of others. Love finds a way to help. It makes no excuses. You are already equipped with the love of God, and that love carries the power to bring real hope, healing, and positive change into the lives of others. Faith was never meant to stay comfortable or confined - it is meant to move, to serve, and to show up where it is needed most. So get off your couch and go do something good for someone else. Stop waiting for a better moment to arrive. Do it now, today, right this minute, because obedience delayed is opportunity lost and tomorrow is never guaranteed.

| 11 |

"LOVE IN ACTION"

Since the dawn of time love has been one of the most mis-understood and abused words known to man. We all know love is important and that we are told to love one another but most people would be hard pressed knowing how to do that. One mistake many Christians make is they think if they've heard a lot about love that they're good at it. This is deceptive thinking because it's not what you know that counts, it's what you do. The time is now for people to make up their minds and become a doer of the Word and not a hearer only (James 1:22). Do the Bible. Do what it says to do. If the Bible says pray, then pray. If the Bible says to sing praises and shout, then sing and shout. If the Bible says give, give. If the Bible says be a witness, then be the best witness you can possibly be. If the Bible says to have joy, then have joy to the fullest. And if the Bible says to love, then love "with all your heart, with all your soul, with all your mind, and with all your strength" (Mark 12:30).

You've got to do it and work at it day after day, year after year. Jesus said in John 15:10a, "If you keep My commandments, you will abide in My love." You need to live, stay, and continue in the love of God. You've got to grow in this love and learn more things and put it into practice. When the decision is made to do this, then God will personally step in and teach you how to love one another (see 1 Thess. 4:9). What was once a mental concept to you can become a reality in your life when you put into practice that which you've heard. Walking in love is just not an ideal, it's something you do. It's an action, a command that must be followed wholly. You can only learn so much from instruction, the rest you'll learn by doing it. It's the doing that causes growth to come and in time walking in love will become second nature to you. You can do it without even thinking about it. Yes, God will teach you how to love but divine revelation only comes when you put the Word into practice.

Wake up in the morning and lay down at night meditating on things you can do to keep the love command. Daily ask yourself, "Did I keep the command? Did I follow orders?" If not, it will open the door to the enemy in your life. Be aggressive in your love for God and other people and by all means do not be led and controlled by your feelings. You can feel different in ten minutes than how you feel now and fifteen minutes after that you'll feel different again. Feelings are fickle and are forever changing. If you live by how you feel, before long you'll be a basket case. Spiritual people are not controlled by their feelings, carnal people are. That's why they're carnal. They quit when things get hard or when they don't feel like doing something. When you walk by feelings you cut yourself off from the blessings of God. The true love of God is not a feeling, it's a command, an order, and you can love the strongest when your feelings are at their worst.

The command to love would be an easy order to follow if all we had to do was love our family, friends, and loved ones. Even the heathen do that and in truth this is a selfish love because more than likely these people will love you back (see Luke 6:32,33). The love of God, however, is different. It is not an ordinary love. It is a love that goes beyond our sensual feelings and reaches into the realm of the supernatural. So powerful and unique is the love of God that we are commanded to love the unlovable, to be kind to the unkind. Jesus said in Luke 6:35, "But love your enemies, do good, and lend, hoping for nothing in return; and your reward will be great, and you will be sons of the Highest. For He is kind to the unthankful and evil." The Message Bible continues this revelation of love in vs. 36-38, "Don't pick on people, jump on their failures, criticize their faults - unless, of course, you want the same treatment. Don't condemn those who are down; that hardness can boomerang.

Be easy on people; you'll find life a lot easier. Give away your life; you'll find life given back but not merely given back - given back with bonus and blessing. Giving, not getting, is the way. Generosity begets generosity." Those who need love the most deserve it the least but still the command goes out to love them the same way Jesus loves you. Luke 6:28,29 says to "bless those who curse you and pray for those who spitefully use you. To him who strikes you on the one cheek, offer the other also. And from him who takes away your cloak, do not withhold your tunic either." This is love in action. The walk of love is an exciting, adventurous journey and the Bible is our road map showing us the direction we should go. Ps. 103;7 says, "He made known His ways to Moses, His acts to the children of Israel." God will make known His ways to you and if you're willing and obedient He will personally teach you how to love one another.

Love is an action and the foundation this is built on is Rom. 13:10, "Love does no harm to a neighbor; therefore, love is the fulfillment of the law." Love is the only law you need! Love does no wrong to any one and that's why it satisfies all of God's requirements. It shouldn't cost people to be around you so become more aware of the affect your actions and words have on other people. Don't butt in line at the grocery store and don't cut people off on the highway. The flesh is self-centered and you can be so caught up with yourself that you walk over other people without ever knowing you're doing it. It should grieve you if through willingness or ignorance you have hurt somebody else. Be not hard-hearted but be sensitive to those around you. Have a tender heart and ask God to help you not hurt anybody. Be the type of person people can trust because they know you're not going to hurt them or take advantage of them.

People today don't trust those they should be able to trust. Husbands and wives don't trust one another because they know they're the ones who can hurt them the most. You can't hurt people when you're walking in love. Love prefers the other person and does no harm to a neighbor. A Secret Service agent will take a bullet before they'll let the president take one. Likewise, love will hurt itself before it hurts another person. You can be physically strong on the outside but be pitifully weak on the inside. Weak people hurt others trying to prove they're strong but this only shows how weak they really are. A strong person will absorb the punch and take the pain thus making life easier for the other person. Paul wrote in 2 Cor. 12:15, "And I will very gladly spend and be spent for your souls; though the more abundantly I love you, the less I am loved." Paul took the pain of not being loved in order that he could be a blessing to those he was ministering to. This is what happened when Jesus went to the cross.

He loved the Father and us so much that He said, "I'll go to the cross. I'll take the pain. I'll do it." He endured the cross with joy (Heb. 12:2). Likewise, the Father so loved the world that He took the pain of seeing His only begotten Son hanging on the cross for those who were yet alienated from Him. To be God-like is to be willing to take the place of someone who is hurting. Jesus was willing to take your place on the cross and He did. Even today He is taking your place at the right hand of God "since He ever lives to make intercession for you" (Heb. 7:25). The more we learn who God is and what He's like the more we'll desire to be like Him. He's big! He's strong! He's tough! He's love! He's got you covered. He takes the pain for you and smiles all the while He's doing it. If you love somebody you won't allow yourself to hurt them. Don't look at people when they're down. Don't exploit and reveal the faults of those around you but instead cover it with love.

1 Peter 4:8 says, "And above all have fervent love for one another, for 'love will cover a multitude of sins.'" This is not a
lying and deceiving cover-up but a willingness to not expose
and publish your brother's faults and past mistakes. We read
in Prov. 17:9, "He who covers a transgression seeks love, but he
who repeats a matter separates the best of friends." After the
great flood "Noah began to be a farmer, and he planted a vineyard. Then he drank of the wine and was drunk and became
uncovered in his tent. And Ham, the father of Canaan, saw
the nakedness of his father, and told his two brothers outside"
(Gen. 9:20-22). This is not love. People want to cover their
own faults but expose the sins of those around them. Prov.
16:27,28 says, "An ungodly man digs up evil, and it is on his
lips like a burning fire. A perverse man sows strife, and a whis-
perer separates the best of friends." Love doesn't want you to
look bad. Love leaves you better than when it found you.

Love covers a multitude of sins. Gen. 9:23 says, "But Shem
and Japheth took a garment, laid it on both their shoulders,
and went backward and covered the nakedness of their father.
Their faces were turned away, and they did not see their father's nakedness." Shem and Japheth did not look at their father in his current condition. They didn't see his nakedness,
and this reveals the nature of the Heavenly Father. He covers
our mistakes, failures, and sin with the blood of Jesus. God re-
members our sins no more (Heb. 10:17) and neither should you
remember the sins of others. We are called to forgive and release the sins of others just as God has graciously forgiven us.
Through Christ, God does not rehearse our failures but casts
our sins into the sea of forgetfulness, choosing mercy over

judgment. When we forgive and let go, we reflect His heart and walk in the freedom He intended for us.

Ezek. 18:21,22 states, "But if a wicked man turns from all his sins which he has committed, keeps all My statutes, and does what is lawful and right, he shall surely live; he shall not die. None of the transgressions which he has committed shall be remembered against him; because of the righteousness which he has done, he shall live" (see also Ezek. 33:16). If a person has genuinely repented, then do not ever bring up their past failures again. In heated arguments people keep bringing up things from the past. This is not right. This is devilish for the devil is the accuser of the brethren (Rev. 12:10). This is making a mockery of the shed blood of Jesus and is a blatant violation of the love command. People feel bad and hang their head in shame when you bring up their past sins. Don't gossip about other people and don't be a talebearer. Don't look at the speck in your neighbor's eye when you have a plank in your own (Matt. 7:3). You wouldn't want the skeletons from your past dug up from the grave so treat others as you want to be treated.

Love is gentle and kind, not harsh and abrasive. Paul wrote in 1 Thess. 2:7,8, "But we were gentle among you, just as a nursing mother cherishes her own children. So, affectionately longing for you, we were well pleased to impart to you not only the gospel of God, but also our own lives, because you had become dear to us." This is also what Jesus was willing to do and when you are dominated by this same love you will do the same thing. You are a love child of a love God and just as God is strong you also can be strong without being harsh. Those who are weak get harsh to make people think they're strong. This is deplorable and utter foolishness. Anybody can yield to their temper and be mean but it takes a strong man to be soft and gentle. Prov. 15:1 says, "A soft answer turns away wrath, but a harsh word stirs up anger." A strong man who obeys the love command will smile and speak softly and will not be moved by what's going on around them.

Prov. 16:24 tells us, "Pleasant words are like a honeycomb, sweetness to the soul and health to the bones." If you want people to accept what you say and do then don't walk around with a sour look on your face all the time. Sweeten up a little. Let people feel the warmth of love coming out of you and let them sense in their hearts that you honestly care about them. Let your words flow with pleasantness because it's not what you say that wins people over, it's how you say it. Never speak evil of somebody else. Never say things that will make people think less of another person. Your words have power and evil words can change the perspective people have toward others. Love does no harm to a neighbor so "let no corrupt communication proceed out of your mouth, but what is good for necessary edification, that it may impart grace to the hearers" (Eph. 4:29).

The Message Bible says, "Watch the way you talk. Let nothing foul or dirty come out of your mouth. Say only what helps, each word a gift. Don't grieve God. Don't break His heart. His Holy Spirit, moving and breathing in you, is the most intimate part of your life, making you fit for Himself. Don't take such a gift for granted. Make a clear break with all the cutting, backbiting, profane talk. Be gentle with one another, sensitive. Forgive one another as quickly and thoroughly as God in Christ forgave you" (vs. 29-32). Love builds up and edifies. Love recognizes and celebrates what's right about a person and does not focus on what is wrong. Just as a nursing mother tenderly cares for her own children so does love care for others and seeks to bring encouragement into their lives. David had the right idea when he cried out to God in Ps. 141:3, "Set a guard, O Lord, over my mouth; Keep watch over the door of my lips." He also said in Ps. 39:1, "I will guard my ways, lest I sin with my tongue; I will restrain my mouth with a muzzle."

Paul writes in Phil. 4:8, "Finally, brethren, whatever things are true, whatever things are noble, whatever things are just, whatever things are pure, whatever things are lovely, whatever things are of good report, if there is any virtue and if there is anything praiseworthy - meditate on these things." The Message Bible says, "Summing it all up, friends, I'd say you'll do best by filling your minds and meditating on things true, noble, reputable, authentic, compelling, gracious - the best, not the worst; the beautiful, not the ugly; things to praise, not things to curse." Love is the distinguishing mark of the believer and love always sees the best in other people. Love shows mercy and never judges another person. Jesus said in Luke 6:36,37, "Therefore be merciful, just as your Father also is merciful. Judge not, and you shall not be judged. Condemn not, and you shall not be condemned. Forgive, and you will be forgiven." How you treat others is how you'll be treated so judge not.

God didn't tell other people not to judge you; He told you not to judge them. This is a daily full-time job because you'll be tempted to judge and find something wrong with every person you meet. The word "judge' means 'to decide' and when you judge somebody you make a decision about them. You're deciding whether they're right or wrong, guilty or innocent, good or bad. To "judge not" means you don't have to make a decision concerning somebody else. There is only one Judge and you're not Him! Being a judge is not a pretty thing and reveals some serious flaws in a person's character. Too many people want to pass judgment on everything people do. They're always pointing a finger at somebody else saying, "You did this wrong and you did that wrong. I'd never do what you did." Judging reveals a spirit of superiority and if you're a judge, you're a hypocrite." Rom. 2:1 says, "Therefore you are inexcusable, O man, whoever you are who judge, for in whatever you judge another you condemn yourself; for you who judge practice the same things."

The Message Bible says, "Those people are on a dark spiral downward. But if you think that leaves you on the high ground where you can point your finger at others, think again. Every time you criticize someone, you condemn yourself. It takes one to know one. Judgmental criticism of others is a well known way of escaping detection in your crimes and misdemeanors. But God isn't so easily diverted. He sees right through all such smoke screens and holds you to what you've done. " You can't love and do what you want all the time. Don't get offended and make a list of what other people did wrong to you. Don't be a record keeper. The reality of life is that you will never have a relationship with a person who never does something to irritate you. Never! You won't have a perfect spouse, child, friend, pastor, co-worker, or boss. So let it go! Don't be so judgmental. Give people a break. Cut them some slack. Compliment them and keep records of all the good things people do and say, not the bad things. Remember, we all have faults and we probably irritate them as well.

God will put people into your life whom He wants you to love into wholeness. You need to lay your life down in order to help people feel good about themselves, to help them feel special and valuable. A lot of people feel worthless and how you treat them often determines how they feel about themselves. All people need to be encouraged so compliment them and magnify the good in them. Get people to talk about themselves for listening to people make them feel valuable. Lay yourself aside and don't bring your problems to other people. Selfishness always wants to talk about itself, and this won't make you any friends. People don't want to hear about all your problems every time you talk to them. When you walk in love you don't want people burdened with all your problems. Cast your care on Jesus (1 Peter 5:7) and don't tell people more than you need to tell them. They've got their own problems to deal with so don't bring your burdens to other people. Besides, if you're walking in faith other people won't know you've got problems.

Paul writes in Rom. 15:1,2, "We then who are strong ought to bear with the scruples (weaknesses) of the weak, and not to please ourselves. Let each of us please his neighbor for his good, leading to edification." The Message Bible says in vs. 1-3a, "Those of us who are strong and able in the faith need to step in and lend a hand to those who falter, and not just do what is most convenient for us. Strength is for service, not status. Each one of us needs to look after the good of the people around us, asking ourselves, 'How can I help?' That's exactly what Jesus did. He didn't make it easy for Himself by avoiding people's troubles but waded right in and helped out." John, the apostle of love, writes in 1 John 3:18, "My little children, let us not love in word or in tongue, but in deed and in truth." Love is patient and kind but it also honest. Insecure people are hard to have relationships with because you don't feel you have the freedom to be honest with them.

Paul rebuked the churches of Galatia for turning away from the gospel of faith and then wrote, "Have I therefore become your enemy because I tell you the truth?" (Gal. 4:16). You are not walking in love with people if you are dishonest with them. A selfish person will tell you what you "want" to hear but love will tell you what you "need" to hear. Eccl. 7:5 tells us, "It is better to hear the rebuke of the wise than for a man to hear the song of fools." In today's society lying is expected and accepted but still honesty is always the best policy. The Lord said in Zech. 8:16,17, "These are the things you shall do: Speak each man the truth to his neighbor; Give judgment in your gates for truth, justice, and peace; Let none of you think evil in your heart against your neighbor; And do not love a false oath. For all these things I hate." Don't have an attitude of superiority but in meekness speak the truth in love (Eph. 4:15). Use the truth to enlighten, edify, and enrich others. Yes, the truth may hurt but love helps ease the pain.

Biblical love is a commitment to seek the highest good of the one loved so be sensitive in how you talk to others. Truth without love can be brutal but love without truth is hypocrisy. There is a universal need for truth and honesty is a characteristic of the mature in Christ. Truth is the element in which we are to live, move, and have our being. Truth, however, must be married to love. They're inseparable twins. Good tidings spoken harshly are not good tidings. The charm of the message can be destroyed by the harshness of the messenger. Eph. 4:15,16 (AMP) says, "Rather, let our lives lovingly express truth [in all things, speaking truly, dealing truly, living truly]. Enfolded in love, let us grow up in every way and in all things into Him Who is the Head, [even] Christ (the Messiah, the Anointed One)." This is a verb that literally means "truthing in love" and has the idea of maintaining truth in both what you say and what you do. This is the recipe for which growth is maximized.

"Speaking the truth" pictures the right doctrine and "in love" pictures the right spirit and attitude. You cannot have a fiat truthfulness that speaks the truth with blunt rudeness. Love does no harm to a neighbor thus truth must be spoken with loving caution and kind allowance. Confronting people with the truth may not always be easy, but every sacrifice has its reward. The reward for speaking the truth in love is freedom. Jesus said in John 8:32, "And you shall know the truth, and the truth shall make you free." And whom the Lord makes free, is free indeed (vs. 36). Jesus said in Mark 8:34, "Whoever desires to come after Me, let him deny himself, and take up his cross, and follow Me." Love is always going to cost you something. It will cost you your time, money, effort and energy. It requires you to put aside selfishness and self-centeredness. The Amplified Bible says, "let him deny himself - forget, ignore, disown, and lose sight of himself and all his own interests."

You can't walk in love and be selfish. Love is an effort and you must do it on purpose. If you're not willing to pay the price you'll never love, and if you never love you'll never share God's glory. Paul writes in Rom. 8:16-18, "The Spirit Himself bears witness with our spirit that we are children of God, and if children, then heirs - heirs of God and joint heirs with Christ, if indeed we suffer with Him, that we may also be glorified together. For I consider that the sufferings of this present time are not worthy to be compared with the glory which shall be revealed in us." You were born to love so love on purpose! Love unconditionally even if people don't treat you right. You glorify God by living an excellent life and love is the most excellent way (1 Cor. 12:36). Love to glorify God! Sacrifice for Him! Love on purpose! Be willing to give up what you want so you can give to other people what they want. When you do this, God will step in and give you what you want. Bless others unconditionally and God will bless you.

| 12 |

"LOVE ON DISPLAY"

L ife is an adventure and those who walk in love will find that it is a glorious adventure. When the love of God has the first and last word in everything you do you'll see how greener the grass gets and the better the birds sing. It will be easier to get up in the morning and you'll be less concerned about what your hair looks like. As you abide and dwell in the manifested presence of His love you'll rise to a higher dimension of life for it gives you a different focus on what life is all about. Love is more than a sermon you hear on Sunday morning. It's a lifestyle that you live, a habit of life that you develop where you strive each and every day to make people feel better about themselves. People in the world don't want to hear about love, they want to see it in action. Paul wrote in 2 Cor. 8:24, "Therefore show to them, and before the churches, the proof of your love and of our boasting on your behalf." Love must be proven. Show people what Jesus is like.

God is love and people must see this love in how you walk, talk, and act. People want something real, something genuine, so make treating them with love the top priority of your life. Love not shown is not love at all. The world won't be won if you hide yourself in a closet all day and don't show them what the love of God is like. You owe them love. It's a debt that must be paid. You impress people by loving them because most people don't know what true love really is. The love of God is a love that sacrifices, that lays down its life for other people, that goes out of its way to bring a blessing into their life. People want to see by your actions what God is really like. They are not going to want Jesus until they first want what you have. People don't want sermons but when they see Christ in you they'll want your love, your peace, and your joy. Be aggressive with your love walk. Do it on purpose. Ask God to show you something you can do to be a blessing to somebody else.

Paul says in Phil. 1:9, "And this I pray, that your love may abound still more and more in knowledge and all discernment." Pray that your love will flourish and that you will not only love much but well. The Amplified Bible says, "And this I pray: that your love may abound yet more and more and extend to its' fullest development in knowledge and all keen insight [that your love may display itself in greater depth of acquaintance and more comprehensive discernment]." Love is the most excellent way to live so let your love abound and grow and display itself to greater measures every day of your life. No matter how good your love walk is it can grow to the point where you have abounding love, a love that chases people down and overtakes them, a love that displays itself openly. A crippling deception is in the church today where the majority of the people believe that the ministers and preachers are the only ones called upon to do the work of the ministry.

This type of thinking, if true, would cripple and limit the leaders of the church. They are all mortal and if they don't get the proper rest because they are overworked it will send them to an early grave. At the same time, it causes the people to not develop. You can't sit on a pew every Sunday and do nothing and expect to grow and mature in the things of God. You can't sit and watch and do nothing. Church is a place to work, a place of service. Paul says in Eph. 4:11,12 that it is the responsibility of the leaders in the church to teach the people how to serve one another with brotherly kindness and holy hospitality. Rom. 12:10-13 says, "Be kindly affectionate to one another with brotherly love, in honor giving preference to one another; not lagging in diligence, fervent in spirit, serving the Lord; rejoicing in hope, patient in tribulation, continuing steadfastly in prayer; distributing to the needs of the saints, given to hospitality." The Message Bible says, "Help needy Christians; be inventive in hospitality."

What good is being a Christian if you can't help somebody out during a time of need? If the need arises, don't hesitate to let people borrow your car or lend them some money. Don't be covetous or make an idol out of the things you have. People are more important than your material possessions so treat them like royalty and make them feel at home when they come knocking on your door. 1 Peter 4:8-10 tells us, "And above all things have fervent love for one another, for love covers a multitude of sins. Be hospitable to one another without grumbling.

As each one has received a gift, minister it to one another, as good stewards of the manifold grace of God." You can be a channel God uses to meet the needs of others when you open your heart, your hands, and your home with genuine love and humility. When hospitality is done properly, without grumbling or obligation, it becomes a joyful expression of service that blesses both the giver and the receiver.

God takes it personal when you bless one of His children. He took it personal when Saul persecuted the church. On the road to Damascus He said, "Saul, Saul, why are you persecuting Me?" (Acts 9:4). Likewise, He takes it personal when love is shown to them as well. Jesus said in Matt. 25:35-40, "'for I was hungry and you gave Me food; I was thirsty and you gave Me drink; I was a stranger and you took Me in; I was naked and you clothed Me; I was sick and you visited Me; I was in prison and you came to Me.' Then the righteous will answer Him, saying, 'Lord, when did we see You hungry and feed You, or thirsty and give You drink? When did we see You a stranger and take You in, or naked and clothe You? Or when did we see You sick, or in prison and come to You?' And the King will answer and say to them, 'Assuredly, I say to you, inasmuch as you did it to the least of these My brethren, you did it to Me.'"

Christianity is the life of the open hand, the open heart, and the open door. It is a great thing to have a door from which the stranger and the one in trouble know that they will never be turned away. The open door is the door of Christian welcome and Christian love for we are to identify ourselves with the needs of others and make them our own. Christianity is much more than a pat on the back and a handshake. It means sharing the burdens and the blessings with others so that all grow together and glorify the Lord. When God's children are in need be the one to help them out. Get into the habit of inviting guests home for dinner and, if need be, lodging for the night. Give freely to those in want and be eager for opportunities to show hospitality. Job 31:32 says, "But no sojourner had to lodge in the street, for I have opened my doors to the traveler." Job repels the very thought that he could let the sojourner be unprovided for.

Christ's direction to the apostles to "take nothing for the journey" (Mark 6:8) presupposes that they were sure of always finding hospitality. It was assumed that they would even be able to make their own choice of hosts (Matt. 10:11) and would be able to stay as long as they chose (Luke 10:7). In Biblical times travel was dangerous and inns were evil, scarce, filthy, and very expensive. They were targets for thieves and prostitutes. This being so, the early Christians would welcome traveling believers, especially those laboring in the gospel, into their homes even if they had never met them before (3 John 5-8). Hospitality was a highly valued Greek and Jewish virtue. It was absolutely necessary for the expansion of the gospel and for the maintenance of the fellowship within the church as well as the image of the church from without. The word "hospitality" means 'fond of guests' and the Greek word means literally 'a lover of strangers.' It means taking an interest in others and making them feel welcomed and at ease.

This is a quality that every Christian must strive for, and it should begin when people gather at church. If you're talking to someone you know and see a visitor all alone, don't keep talking to each other. Go to the visitor and make him feel welcome. 1 Peter 4:9 (AMP) says, "Practice hospitality to one another (those of the household of faith). [Be hospitable, be a lover of strangers, with brotherly affection for the unknown guests, the foreigners, the poor, and all others who come your way who are of Christ's body]. And [in each instance] do it ungrudgingly (cordially and graciously, without complaining but as representing Him)." Hospitality is a test for godliness because those who are selfish do not like strangers (especially needy ones) to intrude upon their private lives. They prefer their own friends who share their lifestyle. Only the humble have the necessary resources to give of themselves to those who could never give of themselves in return.

Heb. 13:1,2 states, "Let brotherly love continue. Do not to forget to entertain strangers, for by so doing some have unwittingly entertained angels." Do not neglect to show hospitality to strangers because you don't know who you're being kind to. The Message Bible says, "Stay on good terms with each other, held together by love. Be ready with a meal or a bed when it's needed. Why, some have extended hospitality to angels without ever knowing it!" Genesis 18 tells the story of three strangers who came to visit Abraham one day as he sat in the door of his tent in the heat of the day. "So he lifted his eyes and looked, and behold, three men were standing by him; and when he saw them, he ran from the tent door to meet them and bowed himself to the ground" (vs. 2). One must understand that Abraham was a very wealthy man who had hundreds of servants to do his bidding for him. Still, he personally took it upon himself to show holy hospitality to these three strangers who stood before him.

He then said, "Please let a little water be brought, and wash your feet, and rest yourself under the tree. And I will bring a morsel of bread, that you may refresh your hearts. After that you may pass by, inasmuch as you have come to your servant" (vs. 4,5). Abraham was called the friend of God because he would do anything God told him to do, go anywhere God told him to go, and give anything God told him to give. He was faithful and righteous and very wealthy but still he humbled himself to the point where he bowed down before these strangers and called himself their servant. Verses 6-8 continues the generous reception he gave his guests, "So Abraham hastened into the tent of Sarah and said, 'Quickly, make ready three measures of fine meal; knead it and make cakes.' And Abraham ran to the herd, took a tender and good calf, gave it to a young man, and he hastened to prepare it. So he took butter and milk and the calf which he had prepared, and set it before them; and he stood by them under the tree as they ate."

Abraham did not walk to the herd, he ran to it and this showed the fondness he had for his guests and his willingness to display his love by showing holy hospitality. Scriptures reveal that his guests were two angels and Jesus Christ in preincarnate form and it was shortly after this meal was prepared for them that they announced that Sarah his wife would have a son (vs. 10). Thus began God's plan to have a bloodline through which His Son would one day be born. All of this unfolded because Abraham was intentional and aggressive in his kindness toward the three guests who stood before him. He did not hesitate, delay, or offer the minimum - he ran, prepared the best he had, and served with honor. That bold hospitality became the doorway through which God released promise, revelation, and blessing. One can only imagine what would have happened had he not been hospitable to them.

In Genesis 19 a similar encounter happened to Abraham's nephew Lot. "Now the two angels came to Sodom in the evening, and Lot was sitting in the gate of Sodom. When Lot saw them, he rose to meet them, and he bowed himself with his face toward the ground. And he said, 'Here now, my lords, please turn in to your servant's house and spend the night, and wash your feet; then you may rise early and go your way.' And they said, 'No, but we will spend the night in the open square.' But he insisted strongly; so they turned in to him and entered his house. Then he made them a feast, and baked unleavened bread, and they ate" (vs. 1-3).

Lot demonstrated remarkable hospitality when he urgently welcomed the two strangers into his home, offering them protection and care without knowing they were sent to save his life. His kindness positioned him to receive divine warning and deliverance, showing that obedience and generosity often open the door to God's intervention. Had Lot refused hospitality, he might have missed the opportunity for rescue, reminding us that small acts of faithfulness can carry eternal consequences. Lot demonstrated remarkable hospitality when he urgently welcomed the two strangers into his home, offering them protection and care without knowing they were sent to save his life. His kindness positioned him to receive divine warning and deliverance, showing that obedience and generosity often open the door to God's intervention. Had Lot refused hospitality, he might have missed the opportunity for rescue, reminding us that small acts of faithfulness can carry eternal consequences.

Also, 1 Kings 17 tells the story of a widow woman who fed the prophet when she had almost nothing to give. Don't be prideful and turn people away because your couch has a hole in it. Love the stranger who comes knocking at your door, for compassion opens the way for God's purpose to unfold. When you choose mercy over fear, you create space for the Lord to work through your obedience. Trust Him to lead and guide your response, knowing that His wisdom will direct you in what you should do. This woman sustained the prophet during a time of famine and she put his needs above her own and those of her son. As a result of her kindness the bin of flour was not used up, nor did the jar of oil run dry, and she and the prophet and her household did eat for many days (vs. 15,16). What if she had not been hospitable to the stranger who came knocking at her door?

Some Christians have been known to build extra rooms onto their homes in order to provide for traveling evangelists and missionaries on furlough. This happened in 2 Kings 4 and we read in vs. 8, "Now it happened one day that Elisha went to Shunew, where there was a notable woman, and she constrained him to eat some food. So it was, as often as he passed by, that he turned in there to eat some food." This great woman constrained the man of God, and this means she literally grabbed onto him and physically forced him to eat food at her house. She and her husband were practicing holy hospitality. This is not passive kindness; it is an intentional pursuit of people with the same intensity, earnestness, and diligence used to chase a fleeing enemy. It means pressing hard after opportunities to welcome, serve, and love others, refusing to be casual or indifferent in our care.

In this way, hospitality becomes a disciplined, faith-driven pursuit to lay hold of hearts for Christ through deliberate, sacrificial action. Vs. 9,10 says, "And she said to her husband, 'Look now, I know that this is a holy man of God, who passes by us regularly. Please, let us make a small upper room on the wall; and let us put a bed for him there, and a table and a chair and a lampstand; so it will be, whenever he comes to us, he can turn in there.'" This took time and money, but they did it anyway. Like this couple Holy hospitality is not passive kindness; it is an intentional pursuit of people with the same intensity, earnestness, and diligence used to chase a fleeing enemy. It means pressing hard after opportunities to welcome, serve, and love others, refusing to be casual or indifferent in our care. In this way, hospitality becomes a disciplined, faith-driven pursuit to lay hold of hearts for Christ through deliberate, sacrificial action.

Like this couple you need to get into a position where you can bless other people. Take them out to eat, buy them things, let them stay with you for a while. Start now right where you're at. As a result of this couple's efforts, they were blessed with a son they were unable to have. What would have happened if hospitality had not been shown to the traveling man of God? Paul writes in Eph. 2:10, "For we are His workmanship, created in Christ Jesus for good works, which God prepared beforehand that we should walk in them." You were born again to do good works and the word "good" means 'pleasant; to do pleasant, beautiful works, appropriate, beneficial works.' The Message Bible says, "He creates each of us by Christ Jesus to join Him in the work He does, the good work He has gotten ready for us to do, work we had better be doing." Doing good works is to be the believer's supernatural and Spirit empowered lifestyle and habitual practice.

Continual earnestness and diligence must be displayed in order to show holy hospitality. Luke tells of the hospitality of Lydia when he writes in Acts 16:15, "And when she and her household were baptized, she begged us, saying, 'If you have judged me to be faithful to the Lord, come to my house and stay.' And she constrained us." In Acts 28 we read that on the island of Malta "there was an estate of the leading citizen of the island, whose name was Publius, who received us and entertained us courteously for three days" (vs. 7). Luke 10:38 tells where a certain woman named Martha welcomed Jesus and His followers into her home. To do this same thing will cost money and for sure people will get dirt on your carpet and leave water marks on your coffee table. Dirty dishes will be piled high in your sink but you can't look at this as an inconvenience. This is all part of your Christian testimony, your walk of love. Later

Martha's brother Lazarus died and got raised from the dead by Jesus. What if Martha had not been hospitable to her welcomed guests?

People are supposed to see your love. When they do, they see who God is and what He is like. Daily make a choice to do something on purpose that will bless another person. Treat people the way God told you to treat them whether you feel like it or not. Not feeling like it does not relieve you from the responsibility of doing it. Push your feelings aside and love on purpose. God said in Is. 55:8,9, "'For My thoughts are not your thoughts, nor are your ways My ways,' says the Lord. 'For as the heavens are higher than the earth, so are My ways higher than your ways, and My thoughts than your thoughts.'" God has a higher way of doing things, a better way, and the goal is for us to walk in His way. He'll direct you to where you should go and then He'll show you the way to get there. Prov. 16:25 says, "There is a way that seems right to a man, but it's end is the way of death." Every time you have an opinion it's right in your own eyes but if you see things His way you'll walk in the light.

David wrote in Ps. 138:23,24, "Search me, O God, and know my heart; Try me, and know my anxieties; And see if there is any wicked way in me, and lead me in the way everlasting." David asked God to look at his thoughts because at first he wanted to do things his way. He knew that God has a specific way of doing things and he asked God to show him where he was in the wrong and then to lead him in His way. God's way is the way of love. Love is not an emotion. It's a way, a spiritual force. It is God and love is the way of the Lord. When you "seek first the kingdom of God and His righteousness" (Matt. 6:33) you are seeking His way of doing things and of being right. You can't serve two masters. You can't serve God and still seek to do things your own way. Anything with two heads is a freak. There is one Lord, one Master, and His way is the way of love. Love is the highest way, the more excellent way. Get on fire for God and seek to love others on purpose.

Love will find a way to give when there seems to be no way. Luke 5 tells the story how some men brought on a bed a man who was paralyzed to Jesus so that he may be healed. Verse 19 says, "And when they could not find how they might bring him in, because of the crowd, they went up on the housetop and let him down with his bed through the tiling into the midst before Jesus." A heart motivated by love doesn't quit. When love sees a roadblock, it seeks a detour. Love can't be stopped. It's committed and when it saw no way into the house it literally took the high way and went up onto the roof. Jesus looked up and saw their work of faith motivated by love (vs. 20) and moments later the paralyzed man rose up healed and whole and began to glorify God. Your labor of love has possibilities of eternal value so never devalue that what you do in love. Faith and love working together always gets what it aims to achieve.

God is love and you can be also. Be love to somebody else. Choose to do acts of love and obey what Paul said to do in Col. 3:12-14, "Therefore, as the elect of God, holy and beloved, put on tender mercies, kindness, humbleness of mind, meekness, long-suffering; bearing with one another, and forgiving one another; even as Christ forgave you, so you also must do. But above all these things put on love, which is the bond of perfection." Love shown, love on display, can change the life of another person dramatically. It can change the direction of their life where in time they will become a completely different person than what they would have become had love not been shown to them. Love makes a difference, a big difference, so be determined day in and day out to display love wherever possible. Love will lead you and give you the opportunity to make people feel special and important. You help people change by letting them see Jesus in you. You do this by walking in the light of God's love.

| 13 |

"LOVING THY NEIGHBOR"

Y ou are here for a purpose. You didn't get saved so you
could have an easy life. No, you are here to be witnesses
for God. You were born to love and called to serve. You are
here to make a positive difference in the lives of other people.
That means you are here to help them have an easier life, a life
more blessed than had your path not crossed with theirs. People are watching you because the world is desperate for something real and genuine. They need help but they're tired of
phony believers who talk the talk but don't walk the walk.
More than anything, you need to upgrade your testimony by
the way you live your life. Don't just witness to people, be a
witness to them by displaying a tremendous outpouring of love
into their lives. Show people by your words and actions that
you truly care about them and their circumstances. Let them
know you'll be there for them if the need arises and even if it
don't. You'll be a friend who stands closer than a brother (Prov.
18:24) in good times and bad.

God wants to use you. You can be a light in a dark world if you'll get out of your comfort zone and do something good. Don't be content to just go to church, be the church. Too much emphasis is given to going to church on Sunday mornings. People think if they do this they've fulfilled their Christian obligation and then go off and live like the devil the rest of the week. These people are hypocrites and one day will hear Jesus say to them, "I never knew you; depart from Me" (Matt. 7:23). Know with certainty that God has a personal, individualized plan for your life. If you will follow that plan, you'll have a life that will amaze you and God will use you to bless people and to draw them out of the grasp of the evil one and into the kingdom of God. Quality workmanship is hard to find. Scarce are people who are truthful, honest, and keep their commitments. This is not pleasing to God. Do what you say you will do even if you have to suffer doing it.

God is not going to bless liars. Be led by the Spirit. Think before you sign on the dotted line. God will bless a person of integrity, a person who will do what they say they will do. The flesh is lazy and compromising and will only do what it absolutely has to. It thinks only about itself. A person controlled by their flesh will merge into the left lane of traffic when it sees a person pulled over on the right side of the road with a flat tire. It is impossible to be selfish and happy at the same time. You can't do it! Get your mind off yourself and be a blessing to somebody else. You are blessed to be a blessing, not to consume everything you get on yourself. Paul said, "I die daily" (1 Cor. 15:310). Every day he said "no" to his stinking flesh. Stop letting your flesh rule you and, once and for all, get your selfish self off your mind. You really haven't lived until you get free from "me"! Die to yourself daily and become an extreme, radical, over-the-top Christian. Go upstream when the rest of the world flows downstream.

The main theme of your life should be love, a love that gives and expects nothing in return. Don't complain about what you do for others, especially if they don't appreciate what you do. Zip your lip and do it unto God. Live to please Him. Good people always do more than enough. They go the extra mile. The rich young ruler didn't want to go the extra mile and he walked away from Jesus sad and grieved (see Mark 10:17-22). Jesus said in Matt. 26:41, "The spirit indeed is willing, but the flesh is weak." The Message Bible says, "There is a part of you that is eager, ready for anything in God. But there's another part that's as lazy as an old dog sleeping by the fire." Real life is hard and you must walk in the Spirit and be strong in the Lord to live a victorious life. If everything was easy you wouldn't get strong. Take notice of a selfish person and you will see how weak they are. It takes strength and spiritual energy to love thy neighbor because only a strong and mature believer will humble themselves under the mighty hand of God and not insist on their own way.

Paul didn't have to have his own way all the time. He was willing to adjust and adapt to the needs and personalities of the people he encountered. He wrote in 1 Cor. 9:19-22, "For though I am free from all men, I have made myself a servant of all, that I might win the more; and to the Jews I became as a Jew, that I might win Jews, to those who are under the law, as under the law, that I might win those who are under the law, to those who are without law, as without law that I might win those who are without law; to the weak I became as weak, that I might win the weak. I have become all things to all men, that I might by all means save some." The Message Bible says, "I didn't take on their way of life. I kept my bearings in Christ - but I entered their world and tried to experience things from their point of view. I've become just about every sort of servant there is in my attempts to lead those I meet into a God-saved life. I did all this because of the Message. I didn't just want to talk about it; I wanted to be in on it."

Jesus did the same thing. He was willing to adjust and adapt Himself to the needs of sinful man. Phil. 2:5-8 (MSG) says, "Think of yourselves the way Christ Jesus thought of Himself. He had equal status with God but didn't think so much of Himself that He had to cling to the advantage of that status no matter what. Not at all. When the time came, He set aside the privileges of deity and took on the status of a slave, became human! Having become human, He stayed human. It was an incredibly humbling process. He didn't claim special privileges. Instead, He lived a selfless, obedient life and then died a selfless, obedient death - and the worst kind of death at that: a crucifixion." Jesus ate with sinners. He related to them. He showed them that He cared. He discerned what the needs of the people were and He gave it to them. That's love to the highest degree. When you love people, the walls come down and they'll open up to you. God is knocking on doors and He'll use you to open up those doors.

Treating people right motivates them to open up the doors of their heart to God so He can change their lives. Daily follow the leading of the Holy Spirit and readily adjust yourself to other people and their needs. Learn the personalities of those you associate with and adapt the way you communicate with them. Paul said in Rom. 12:15,16, "Rejoice with those who rejoice, and weep with those who weep. Be of the same mind toward one another." Don't wait for other people to change, you change. You adjust! You adapt! You become all things to all men. If you're not careful, you'll give people what you need instead of what they need. You need to study people and listen to them in order to find out what they want and need. Very few people will be like you and like the same things you do. Adjust yourself to these people and adapt to them so that you'll be able to not give them what you need but rather what they need.

Married or not, your relationships with people are all over the place. Everywhere you go, you will encounter people who are different than you are. You need to realize that not everybody is like you and that they have different needs and desires, likes and dislikes. You must be educated on how to love thy neighbor and learn how to relate to and get along with other people. Paul wrote in Phil. 4:2 (MSG), "I urge Euodia and Syntyche to iron out their differences and make up. God doesn't want His children holding grudges." There is power in agreement and a house divided cannot stand (Luke 11:17). Strife destroys homes and churches and is a sign that love is lacking. You must humble yourself to stay out of strife since unity is the number one sign of maturity. Ps. 133:1 says, "Behold, how good and how pleasant it is for brethren to dwell together in unity." People need to network together and live in harmony because unity is the atmosphere through which the blessings of God flow.

Phil. 2:2 says, "Fulfill my joy by being like-minded, having the same love, being of one accord, of one mind." If you want peace, you're going to have to work at it. Eph. 4:2,3 says, "With all lowliness and gentleness, with longsuffering, bearing with one another in love, endeavoring to keep the unity of the Spirit in the bond of peace." The Message Bible says, "And mark that you do this with humility and discipline - not in fits and starts, but steadily, pouring yourselves out for each other in acts of love, alert at noticing differences and quick at mending fences." Prov. 20:3 says, "It is honorable for a man to stop striving, since any fool can start a quarrel." Where there is no peace, there is no power. Not treating people right quenches the Holy Spirit and strife will remove the anointing from off your life (1 Thess. 5:19). Love seeks not its own way so learn to adapt yourself to other people because more times than not they won't adapt to you.

Your success as a Christian is linked to your love walk so seek to do good and learn to "be at peace among yourselves" (1 Thess. 5:13). If you get mad because you don't get your own way all the time then not too many people will want to hang around with you. Don't be moody, touchy, and insecure where everybody has to always submit to what you want. People who complain all the time because they don't get their own way are takers and not givers and they don't obey the command to love. They are never happy and the more they get the more they want. Unhappy people want to make everybody else unhappy. Hurting people try to hurt other people. Let God supply all your needs and aggressively seek for ways to be a blessing to someone else. Love is not a feeling, it's something you do on purpose. Take time to plan ways to be a blessing to people. Don't wait for an angel to appear telling you what to do. Bless somebody for no reason at all, not just at Christmas or on their birthday.

If you follow Jesus you're going to have to be generous. You'll have to go the extra mile. Jesus said, "And whoever compels you to go one mile, go with him two. Give to him who asks you, and from him who wants to borrow from you do not turn away" (Matt. 5:41,42). This means that you go to work ten minutes early and stay ten minutes late. Go above and beyond what's asked or required of you. Be the type of person who on purpose does more than you have to. Kick it up to a higher level. God is El Shaddai, the God of more than enough. He goes the extra mile and so should you. God is able to do far more than you could ever think or imagine in your wildest dreams (Eph. 3:20 MSG) and you need to do the same. Your spirit wants to work and be fruitful and accomplish something good. Your flesh wants to eat donuts and play video games all day. The good news is that it is never too late to begin living a life led by the promptings of the Holy Spirit and not the flesh.

Go out into the world and begin to act like Jesus. Put a smile on your face. Too many people are frowning and act like they have nothing to live for. When people walk in the flesh there is agony and destruction and this is why the world needs Spirit-filled and Spirit-led individuals who will forget about themselves long enough to go the extra mile and be a blessing to someone else. As this becomes your lifestyle you also will be blessed because what you make happen for others God will make happen for you (Eph. 6:8). Be prepared to be a blessing. Don't wait until the last minute and then find out you don't have the time or resources to do it. Have a supply of finances and things with which to bless other people. Set up a blessing account at the bank so that when the need presents itself you'll be able to respond immediately. Make a sacrifice and give away something you value and that which cost you something. Don't give away broken down, second-hand things that you no longer want or need.

God gave you His best when He gave you Jesus so you also must be willing to give the best things you have. Give freely and abundantly with no strings attached. Expect nothing in return. Don't have the attitude, "I'll scratch your back if you'll scratch mine." If there are strings it's not a gift. It puts a burden on the receiver and it won't bless the giver. The value of the gift is diminished if people think you're trying to buy them and that they owe you something back. But gifts given with a pure heart has eternal value. Mark 12:41,42 tells of a poor widow who gave two mites and the value of her gift was determined by the heart giving it. People still talk today about the woman with the alabaster box of perfume that she gave to Jesus. David said in Ps. 57:7, "My heart is steadfast, O God, my heart is steadfast; I will sing and give praise." When a person has a heart that is steadfast and perfect toward God they'll give freely and willingly with no expectations except to see the person receiving the gift happy and blessed.

Follow the way of love (1 Cor. 14:1). Do what love does all the time. God is love and you also are to be love. The value of a gift is determined by the heart giving it. A gift without love attached to it has no eternal value and is not a gift at all. Go out of your way to make relationships special. Compliment people and bless them with your words. Edify, exhort, and encourage others. Accept people for who they are and don't put them on the potter's wheel and try to change them. Put them in God's hands and love them anyway. Love is knowing what somebody's weaknesses are and not making a big deal out of it. Don't be a fault finder and don't demand perfection out of other people. Love always believes the best of everyone and does not deliberately keep records of wrongs and past mistakes. This is not always easy to do because some people's behavior makes it hard to believe there's anything good in them. Still, love is God's command and loving the ungodly is what sets believers apart from the rest of the world.

A friend who walks in love will stay close in times of trouble, will hover over people to protect them during the storms of life rather than expose them and their flaws in the view of others. Love protects, shields, guards, seals, and safeguards people from exposure. Love strains forward with all its might refusing to give up and to always believe the very best in every situation. Love always expects and anticipates the best in others and the best for others. Love never disappoints, never fails, never falls, and never lets anyone down. Love is not blind. It sees the weaknesses and faults of people but it always endeavors to believe the best. If you will do this, if you will truly love people unconditionally in spite of their shortcomings, you will have more friends than you know what to do with. Love is something you see. Wounded people need to see unconditional love, and not just a little. They need a great abundance of love and patience and they need to know that somebody cares about them.

When you've been hurt by people, you don't respond well to other people. You put walls up and if you've been hurt you just automatically want to hurt someone else. What happens to you will flow through you. Love does not feel overjoyed when it sees an injustice done to someone else but when stretched to its fullest limit has a way of reaching into a person and pulling out the best in them. Love will seek to endeavor in some way to restore that person and is elated, thrilled, and overjoyed when that hurting person gets set free to become the person they truly desire to be. Hurting people need to be loved and feel that they are appreciated and understood. Love is seen in how you treat people so, if somebody is hurting, be nice to them, talk sweet and lower your voice tone. Don't have a rough tone to your voice for soft words turn away wrath (Prov. 15:1). Voice tone and body language is what hurting people notice first for words by themselves is a small part of communication.

Be straight forward with people and speak the truth in love (Eph. 4:15) and always remember, it's not what you say but how you say it. Don't try to correct somebody until you first tell them something you like about them. Show them you care and be willing to share your own faults with them. People won't respond to you well if you act like you're perfect and don't make any mistakes. All have sinned and fallen short of the glory of God but if people know you love them they'll receive your correction. 2 Sam. 19:7 says, "Now therefore, arise, go out and speak comfort to your servants. For I swear by the Lord, if you do not go out, not one will stay with you this night." Don't act "bossy" telling people what to do all the time, bossing them around in a cruel, harsh manner. Love edifies (1 Cor. 8:1) and makes allowances for other people so give them a break and don't be judgmental. Encourage people to grow to their full potential and speak kindly to those who are with you. If you don't, they'll all leave.

It's your job as an ambassador of the Lord to make people feel good about themselves. Use words to build up and not tear down. Paul said in Eph. 4:29, "Let no corrupt communication proceed out of your mouth, but what is good for necessary edification, that it may impart grace to the hearers." The Message Bible says, "Watch the way you talk. Let nothing foul or dirty come out of your mouth. Say only what helps, each word a gift." Don't be discouraged if you don't see any results right away. Some people have been beat down with negative words for so long that the concept of them being special is hard for them to grasp. A house is built one brick at a time and so it is with people's lives. They are edified and built up one kind word and one kind deed at a time. Don't grow weary telling people how special they are. Stay with it. Love never fails and if you'll stir it up and stay with it you will be a vessel of honor that God will use to bring a positive change into the lives of other people.

Take up the needs of the body of Christ as if they were your own. As you diligently seek the benefit of others, God will step in and meet your needs. This will give you the freedom to take your thoughts off yourself and onto other people, to put their needs above your own. When people see the love of God in you they see God because He put it there. Allow 1 Cor. 13:4-8 to be a description of who you are. You endure long and are patient and kind. You are never envious nor do you boil over with jealousy. You are not boastful and neither do you display yourself haughtily. You are not conceited, arrogant, or inflated with pride. You are not rude, unmannerly, and you do not act unbecomingly. You do not insist on your own rights or your own way because you are not self-seeking. Like a professionally cut diamond, love sparkles in many ways. Be the type of person other people will be thankful for. They are talking about you behind your back. The question is, "What are they saying?"

| 14 |

"BEAR MUCH FRUIT"

There are two super important things that you need to learn in life. You need to know what's important, and you need to learn what's not important. For example, some people think texting their friends is more important than staying in the proper lane on the highway. Or how about the pleasure seeking father who would rather play golf with his friends than attend his son's championship ball game? You need to learn what's important in life and what's valuable and what's worth spending your time and energy and your resources on. If you don't discern what's important you could spend your entire life on that which is not important. The truth be told, some things are not as important as people think they are. People are wasting days of their lives doing nothing important. They spend two hours fixing their hair and another two deciding what clothes to wear. Some people spend an entire day shopping and looking for things but leave the mall without buying anything.

Why do people spend three hours deciding which pair of shoes to buy and a couple days later spend more time taking them back to the store? If they were led by the Spirit they wouldn't have bought the wrong pair in the first place. Foolish people waste time doing whatever comes up, whatever their friends want them to do, and whatever strikes their mind and tickles their flesh. They do things that are not important and do it for days and weeks and months and years. The end result is a wasted life, a life that bears no fruit for the kingdom of God. When it comes to time, you can never get back that which you've wasted. Once it's gone, it's gone forever. The most valuable thing you have is your time. Not your job, your house, your car, or your money. You can't put a price on time for it is irreplaceable and precious beyond cost. Only a fool will take something that is priceless and trade it for that which is worth nothing, something that is common and useless. Still, people do this every day.

People think they have all the time in the world to do the things they're supposed to do when suddenly the curtain drops on their life and they pass on to the other side. Time is flying by quickly and there are only a few days left before it will all be over. Heb. 9:27 says, "It is appointed for men to die once, but after this the judgment." People act like life goes on forever and don't realize that their lifetime is a very brief amount of time. James 4:14 says, "For what is your life? It is even a vapor that appears for a little time and then vanishes away." The Message Bible says, "You're nothing but a wisp of fog, catching a brief bit of sun before disappearing." Job had a revelation of this when he wrote, "My days are swifter than a weaver's shuttle. Oh, remember that my life is a breath!" (Job 7:6,7). Time is precious so don't waste it. You get to live your life one time and one time only so spend it on eternal things and not on that which won't mean anything next week or next year. In just a few more days you're going to look up and your life is going to be over.

Time is precious but it is also short. Your life is like a mist. You're here one moment and gone the next. Years come and go quickly like telephone poles flying by on the highway. People live like this life is all there is and what they're doing now they'll be doing forever. They don't realize that nothing that's happening now is going to last very long. Not where they're living, not where they're working, and not with the people they associate with. Things are different today than it was yesterday and things will be different tomorrow. Change happens to everybody but soon and very soon it's all going to be over. When the time comes for your departure from this planet you don't want to look back at your life and find out that you've wasted a great portion of your time on things that have no eternal significance. Check up on yourself and take account of your life. Ask yourself, "What am I doing with the one life I've been given?" What am I doing and why am I doing it? What's it worth and what is it producing?

Don't live for self-gratification and don't make being rich and famous your primary goal in life. Reject the notion that "He who dies with the most toys wins" and "Let's eat, drink, and be merry for tomorrow we die." Both are a lie of the devil and he'll never reveal to you the severe consequences of living solely to satisfy your flesh. People who think this world is all there is live to satisfy their own lustful desires with no regard for anybody else nor do they consider or worry above the consequences. These are the people who need to take heed to the words of the apostle Paul written in Eph. 5:14, "Awake, you who sleep, arise from the dead, and Christ will give you light." Most of the world is either spiritually dead and not born-again or else they are born-again but are asleep. They're saved but are doing nothing with their lives to advance the kingdom of God. It is time for the church to wake up and get rid of all those mundane things that rob you of your time.

It has been estimated that people spend one year of their life looking for their socks and deciding what clothes to put on. Spend more time with God and He'll show you what's important and what's not important. He'll show you what to do and what not to do. He'll show you what to change and do more of and what to change and do less of. He'll show you how to do things in less time and how to get more results from your labor. Prov. 9:10,11 says, "The fear of the Lord is the beginning of wisdom, and the knowledge of the Holy One is understanding. For by me your days will be multiplied, and years of life will be added to you." With wisdom and God's direction you can produce more in one year than the previous ten years put together. God can make you fruitful beyond your wildest dreams. This is what your future and your life should look like. It doesn't matter what your background is. You may have been unfruitful for fifty years but you can be fruitful now. It's never too late to begin.

God is gracious and He loves you so much He'll help you make up for lost time. He'll restore the years the locust and the caterpillar have eaten up (Joel 2:25). You're here, you're breathing, and God is still on the throne. There's still time to be fruitful and do something good with your life. Don't go to heaven empty handed. God is expecting you to bear fruit and plenty of it. Jesus said in John 15:1,2, "I am the true vine, and My Father is the vinedresser. Every branch in Me that does not bear fruit He takes away; and every branch that bears fruit He prunes, that it may bear more fruit." You are not here just to get saved and then wait to die so you can go to heaven. Religious folks put a high emphasis on getting saved and going to church but say very little or nothing about bearing fruit. People are dazzled by church services with laser shows and bright lights and smoking mirrors and loud music. People get amazed and moon-eyed and follow these preachers down the path not knowing where it will lead.

People should not be so gullible and so easily swayed. The Bible says you will know them by their fruit, not by what they say or dream or by what type of brilliant show they put on. Some people all they do is talk, talk, talk but produce no fruit. You can put any type of label you want on an empty can but the bottom line is, "Where's the fruit?" Churches today are filled with much activity. There are plenty of meals to eat and much gossip to go around with all that food. Sunday services have turned the church into a social club with no thought of teaching on denying the selfish appetites of the flesh and rising up to advance the kingdom of God. These people have a form of godliness but deny its power (2 Tim. 3:5). Barrenness and doing nothing for God is a serious thing and has severe consequences. God expects a return on what He's poured into your life. He expects you to bear much fruit and to do what you're supposed to do.

Ezekiel 15 tells the "Parable of the Vine" that the Lord spoke to the prophet. It says in vs.2-4, "Son of man, how is the wood of the vine better than any other wood, the vine branch which is among the trees of the forest? Is wood taken from it to make any object? Or can men make a peg from it to hang any vessel on? Instead, it is thrown into the fire for fuel; the fire devours both ends of it, and its middle is burned. Is it useful for any work?" This passage of scripture says that branches are good for either bearing fruit or for burning. They are not good for building anything and they can not produce their own life. The branches actually display and bear the fruit of the vine. Jesus is the Vine and all born-again believers should be thinking about being fruitful every day of their lives. Going to church and warming a pew is not being fruitful. Most people don't even care if they're fruitful or not. For them the zeal languishes, the professed love is gone, prayer is neglected, the sanctuary is forsaken, and the soul becomes like a withered branch reserved for the fire on the last great day.

God will take from His church all professed Christians who give no evidence by their lives that they are truly united to the Vine, the Lord Jesus Christ. Heb. 10:30,31 warns, "For we know Him who said, 'Vengeance is Mine, I will repay, says the Lord.' And again, 'The Lord will judge His people.' It is a fearful thing to fall into the hands of the living God." The Message Bible says, "This is no light matter. God has warned us that He'll hold us to account and make us pay. He was quite explicit: 'Vengeance is mine, and I won't overlook a thing,' and 'God will judge His people,' Nobody's getting by with anything, believe me." Jesus said in Matt. 9:37,38, "The harvest truly is plentiful, but the laborers are few. Therefore pray the Lord of the harvest to send out laborers into His harvest." We are here for only a brief amount of time and you have got a job to do. You are here to produce and bear much fruit for the Master. If you are already bearing fruit you can produce a hundred times more than you have been.

God can make you fruitful beyond your wildest dreams. The question is, "What are you doing with your time?" If you are striving to serve God and please Him with it then that time becomes precious to Him. When you serve God with the time you now have and show Him what you would do if you had more, He'll give you the resources that will help free you up and give you more time with which to serve Him. He'll give you the finances so that you won't have to work all that overtime. He'll give you good health so you don't have to sit in the doctor's office for hours at a time. He'll give you a new car so you don't have to waste time waiting for the old one to get fixed. If you are faithful over a little time God will make you ruler over much time. Be a good steward with what you have now and God will give you more. He'll give you the things that will help you redeem the time (Eph. 5:16) and save more hours and days. He'll give you more money, more ability, more opportunity.

Let God lead you and make every day of your life count. He will lead you to greater fruitfulness when you abide in the Vine.

Withered up branches don't produce any fruit so let nothing hinder the full flow of His Spirit and His life that causes you to produce an abundance of fruit that pleases Him. What good is a branch that bears no fruit? Every branch that isn't bearing fruit needs to start doing so in a hurry before it becomes withered and cut off. This is serious business. Bearing fruit begins with the fear of the Lord. Abide in the Vine and get God involved in everything you do. The life is in the Vine and if that life is blocked the branch dries up and withers. When people don't stay connected to the Vine their creativity is cut off and their joy is dried up. They lead a dead, boring, fruitless life. To bear much fruit you need to stop wasting so much time and be led by God. Prov. 11:30 says, "The fruit of the righteous is a tree of life."

When you do what God tells you to do, it will be profitable for there will be life in it. It will be valuable and it will touch the lives of other people. It will quicken them and make them more alive. It will draw them deeper into the things of God. The Greater One inside you will lead you so that your life will be more sufficient and more profitable. Slow down and take time to hear from Him. You don't have to do a lot of the things you think you have to do. Check your heart and be more particular about the decisions you make. Prov. 3:5,6 says, "Trust in the Lord with all your heart, and lean not on your own understanding. In all your ways acknowledge Him, and He shall direct your paths." If you're more selective, you'll be more effective. People today are getting worn out doing things they shouldn't be doing. They're not being led by God and end up being at the wrong place at the wrong time. Things happen that wouldn't have happened had they taken the time to get before Him and be led by His direction. Ask God what you should do. Remember, pride assumes but humility asks.

You are a co-laborer with God (1 Cor. 3:9). You are not called to do things "for" God, you are called to do things "with" God. Do what He says. Don't add to it or take anything away. Don't change anything because you're not going to have a better idea than God. Jesus said, "Abide in Me and I in you. As the branch cannot bear fruit of itself, unless it abides in the vine, neither can you unless you abide in Me" (John 15:4). The word "abide" means 'stay' and Jesus is saying to stay in Him and He will stay in you. The enemy will tempt you to leave but stay hooked up to the Vine. Stay joined and stay connected. The nature of the flesh is impatience. It doesn't want to stay anywhere for very long. It's flighty. It's here, it's there. With the Lord you have to learn to be still and see and know that He is God. Wait on the Lord and He will renew your strength and He will make your heart strong. To be fruitful you must stay connected to the Vine and have continuous communion with Him.

You can be aware of God and commune with Him all day and all night. Stay in Him and His words will stay in your mind and in your heart and in your mouth. This is the way to make every second count and not waste your precious life here on the earth. You were called to the fellowship of Jesus Christ. The great deeds and miracles in the life of Jesus were a product of His fellowship with the Father. He did not waste His life on fleshly pursuits but did only what the Father told Him to do. He knew what to do and say every minute of every day. Look how much the Father did with Jesus in a little more than three years. What can He do with you in a year, or two, or three? Abide in the Vine and make your life count. There are many courses in the university of life. Some are painful but God uses these required lessons to drive people to a more intimate relationship with Him that in turn will produce spiritual fruit that remains for all eternity.

Jesus said that branches that produce fruit get purged and pruned so that they will bear much fruit that remains and glorifies God. Pruning involves the cutting away of dead branches, but also the cutting back of living branches to enhance the quality and quantity of the crop. The worst thing God could do would be to leave you alone and let you have your own way but, if you'll get before Him and listen to Him, He'll trim you up. He'll show you in the days to come those things that are a waste of your time and resources that need to be cut off. There is no such thing as a fruit tree that doesn't need trimming. Even the very best fruit trees and vines need some dead stuff cut off so it can put out new shoots and new branches and thus become more fruitful. Purging may not sound good but it's better than being cut off and burned. 1 Peter 5:10 states, "But may the God of all grace, who called us to His eternal glory by Christ Jesus, after you have suffered a while, perfect, establish, strengthen, and settle you."

The Message Bible says, "So keep a firm grip on the faith. The suffering won't last forever. It won't be long before this generous God who has great plans for us in Christ - eternal and glorious plans they are! - will have you put together and on your feet for good. He gets the last word; yes He does." Purging is not a pleasant experience, and most people wouldn't want to go through it again. Jesus said it was like plucking your eye out or cutting your hand off (Matt. 5:29,30). A useless life is an unproductive life, a life that bears no fruit. Start up that spiritual chainsaw and cut off those things that are hindering your walk with God and holding you back from bearing much fruit. Every believer needs some weed pulling and limb trimming and dead stuff removal. Discipline yourself and ask God to show you every hindering thing in your life that needs to be removed. Disdain the things that are wasting your time and your resources and your life.

If you live for only what's down here, you are throwing your life away. You only have a short window of opportunity to produce fruit that remains for all eternity. If all you do is live to please yourself and try to make your flesh comfortable then you have thrown away something that is precious and beyond price. There is a God, there is a heaven, there is a kingdom that lasts forever, and there is a judgment to come. The biggest fear in your life should be that you do not obey God. Don't be concerned about how much money you have or if you'll be comfortable in your retirement years. Seek first the kingdom of God and all these things will be added to you (Matt. 6:33). Now is the time to work. God wants you to enjoy your life but don't make having fun your top priority. The harvest is plentiful, but the laborers are few. You've got to double up on your work effort because there are millions of believers doing nothing and don't care about anything but their own ease and comfort. God says, "You fool! This night your soul will be required of you" (Luke 12:20).

As painful as pruning may be, those who go through the process wouldn't trade it for anything in the world for there is a benefit that comes through the pain that takes place. 2 Cor. 5:17 says, "Old things have passed away; behold, all things become new." Old branches that produce no fruit have become new branches that bear much fruit. What a glorious day that will be when it is revealed that you didn't waste your time, money, and opportunities on things that don't matter in the long run. Instead, you were fruitful and the Father was glorified by all you did for the kingdom. When you love God and people you just automatically want to do more. If you have a heart toward God, you'll want to do more this year than you did last year. Titus 3:14 (NIV) says, "Our people must learn to devote themselves to doing what is good, in order to provide for urgent needs and not live unproductive lives." Jesus said you will be known by the fruit you produce (Matt. 7:15).

There are wolves who wear sheep's clothing and people are swayed because they're not looking at the fruit. They're looking at the outward appearance and the brilliance of the show they put on. Jesus said you will know them not by their beliefs and opinions and their good intentions, but by what they produce. Ask, "Where's the fruit?" What have they produced with their lives and ministry? We don't want to know how they survived the hard times, we want to know what they produced for the kingdom of God. Where's the fruit? The fruit grows on the branch but the power to produce the fruit is in the Vine.

This is why every branch must abide in the Vine. You cannot bear fruit by yourself with your own effort and good intentions. You can only do it if you abide in the Vine. The more you are connected to Him, the fuller of life you are, the more vibrant you will be, and the more fruit you will produce. Your energy level and your patience will soar, and you'll be able to do those things that really matter and count.

You'll be led by the Spirit and you'll know what to do in every situation. One of the most tormenting things in life is being confused and not knowing what to do. That darkness is a result of withering, of not abiding in the Vine, of not being connected and trying to do your own thing. You don't hook up to God for a few moments, you've got to stay in His presence all day long, at work and at play. Is. 26:3 says, "You will keep him in perfect peace whose mind is stayed on You, because He trusts in You." If you don't know what to do, you won't have peace. But if you'll deny the flesh and say to Him, "Not my will but Your will be done," He'll show you what to do. As you contribute to His work and His plan and His kingdom you'll be spending your life wisely. The end will be here faster than you know and when it does you can hold your head up and say you ran your race, you finished your course. And when you are asked, "Where's the fruit?" you can say with all boldness and confidence, "Come, let me show you."

| 15 |

"SEEK YE FIRST"

It's a sign of the times. People everywhere are searching for something. We are all by nature a seeking people for there is just something about the act of seeking that captures our imagination. Shopping malls are crowded with people seeking the latest fashion design or the most updated version of the iPhone. We go to the movie theater where fascination grips our hearts as we watch the renegade pirate in search of buried treasure. We view on television a professional fisherman who travels the back waters of Africa searching for a river monster that is known to lurk there. We cheer on the gifted athlete as he seeks to win the gold medal at the Olympic games. We support them all and hope they find whatever it is they're searching for. The act of seeking is like a giant magnet that pulls us forward in life and barely a day goes by where we are not in search of something. A relentless pursuit goes forth as we seek fortune and fame, pleasure and power.

Some seek for a better education, a new job, and a new house to live in. Women seek husbands and men seek wives. That which is most important to you is what you will search for the most. People, possessions, power, prestige, and pleasure all compete for your attention and the addictiveness of these things will cause people to search for them at all costs.The great tragedy of life is that most people are only interested in themselves, their advancement in life, and their own personal concerns. They become selfish, are too busy to get involved with the needs of other people, and are too occupied with their own pursuits to care. There is more to life then having money in the bank, a new car in the garage, and a boat on the lake. Deep down inside themselves people know this but they've fallen into the trap of putting things first. They go to church and watch the clock more than they watch the preacher. It is a sad commentary that those who have received the grace of God don't extend it to others.

The apostle Paul spoke of this when he wrote Phil. 2:19-21, "But I trust in the Lord Jesus to send Timothy to you shortly, that I also may be encouraged when I know your state. For I have no one like-minded who will sincerely care for your state. For all seek their own, not the things which are of Christ Jesus." The city of Philippi was a Roman colony and the local church there was in need of nurturing and spiritual care. Evidently the church of Rome was wrapped up in their own affairs and their preoccupation with the things of this life caused them to forego the privilege of ministering to the saints of God at Philippi. There were burdens to be borne and shared and at one time the Roman church was interested in helping others. They had a reputation for sharing their faith (Rom. 1:8) but now they could care less. They appear to have lost their passion for other people but instead are now wasting their lives chasing after those things that in the end won't bring fulfillment to their innermost being.

The reason people keep searching for things is because what they originally sought after didn't satisfy them so they wake up each morning and begin the process all over again. The whole world around us is consumed with making a living and climbing the corporate ladder. They get ulcers and lose sleep worrying about these things. There should be more to life than spending all your time thinking about what to wear to work or what to eat when you get home or where to go on the next family vacation. As Christians we are in the world but not of the world and if one is not careful even the elect can get snared in the trap of seeking after worldly things, things that won't matter in the not-too-distant future. Paul wrote in Col. 3:1,2, "If then you were raised with Christ, seek those things which are above, where Christ is, sitting at the right hand of God. Set your mind on things above, not on things on the earth."

The Message Bible says, "So if you're serious about living this new resurrection life with Christ, act like it. Pursue the things over which Christ presides. Don't shuffle along, eyes to the ground, absorbed with the things right in front of you. Look up and be alert to what is going on around Christ - that's where the action is. See things from His perspective." Your life is shaped and ultimately defined by what you choose to pursue. When you seek after the right things - truth, purpose, integrity, and God's will - you position your life for peace, joy, and lasting blessing. What you chase will eventually claim your heart, your time, and your direction. Pursue the wrong things, and heartache and misery will follow you wherever you go, but pursue what is right, and fulfillment will meet you along the way. James 4:1 asks, "Where do wars and fights come from among you? Do they not come from your desires for pleasure that war in your members?"

The Message Bible in vs. 1-3 states, "Where do you think all these appalling wars and quarrels come from? Do you think they just happen? Think again. They come about because you want your own way, and fight for it deep inside yourselves. You lust for what you don't have and are willing to kill to get it. You want what isn't yours and will risk violence to get your hands on it. You wouldn't think of just asking God for it, would you? And why not? Because you know you'd be asking for what you have no right to. You're spoiled children, each wanting your own way." This is a description of the "me first" generation in which we now live. We are told in James 1:14, "But each one is tempted when he is drawn away by his own desires and enticed." James warns that such self-serving desires will cause divisions, wars, and fights (vs. 1,2) and will destroy your relationship with God.

James 4:4 says, "Adulterers and adulteresses! Do you not know that friendship with the world is enmity with God? Whoever therefore wants to be a friend of the world makes himself an enemy of God." The solution to all this is to seek after the right things. Jesus addressed this in Matt. 6:31-33 when He said, "Therefore do not worry, saying 'What shall we eat?' or 'What shall we drink?' or 'What shall we wear?' For after all these things the Gentiles seek. For your heavenly Father knows that you need all these things. But seek first the kingdom of God and His righteousness, and all these things will be added to you." Jesus did not say to seek "for" the kingdom of God which is what He would have said if He was addressing this command to unbelievers. This command was spoken to those who are kingdom citizens and Jesus was saying to make the interests of God's kingdom your top priority. Do not be anxious about what you will eat or wear.

God is faithful to provide for His own and we can have anything we can believe for. There is, however, something you should be anxious about, something good to seek after, something that creates enthusiasm and with great compulsion drives you forward. Paul tells us what that is in Phil. 2:2-4, "Fulfill my joy by being like-minded, having the same love, being of one accord of one mind. Let nothing be done through selfish ambition or conceit, but in lowliness of mind let each esteem others better than himself. Let each of you look out not only for his own interests, but also for the interests of others." This is how greatness is measured for when you forget about yourself you usually start doing something others will remember. The kingdom of God is an everlasting kingdom. History tells of many great kingdoms that have ruled the known world in times past. The Greek, Egyptian, and Babylonian kingdoms were all mighty and powerful at one time, as was the Roman Empire.

But these kingdoms are no more. Kingdoms rise and kingdoms fall but Luke 1:33 says, "Of His kingdom there will be no end."

As citizens of God's everlasting kingdom, we've been made in His image, and we are most like Him when our thoughts for ourselves are lost in our thoughts for others. This is what it means to "seek ye first" the kingdom of God. The word "kingdom" is a composite of the words 'king' and 'dominion' and is defined as the realm or territory where a king rules and his will is fulfilled. In the Lord's Prayer we read in Matt. 6:10, "Your kingdom come. Your will be done on earth as it is in heaven." God's will being done on earth is a description of the kingdom of God. When Jesus told us to seek first the kingdom of God, He was telling us to see to it that what God wants done, gets done! Stop making material things the center of your life but seek in earnest to be a blessing to other people.

Replace those desires for worldly treasures with a pursuit that has far greater significance in this life and the life to come. Be so eager for heavenly things that you leave altogether your earthly cares with Jesus. Seek God first and the rest will follow in due course. You've only got one life to live and if you will spend it on this one thing it will be a life well spent. The act of seeking demands an intensity, a perseverance that will not be denied, and a zeal to achieve the desired objective. Every nerve in your body should tingle and throb at the thought of being used by God to help somebody else. Make a conscious choice every day that your thoughts and actions will demonstrate that the kingdom of God is your top priority in a world that is quickly passing away. Prov. 3:27 says, "Withhold not good from them to whom it is due, when it is in the power of your hand to do it."

A noted evangelist once said, "Everything God has made is a solution to a problem. Your worth and significance are determined by the kinds of problems you are solving for someone." There is something in you and about you that someone else needs. Realize that you may be God's answer to somebody else's prayer. Daily be diligent and look for problems to solve. Think and look for extra ways to benefit others. Go the extra mile. Jesus said, "And whoever compels you to go one mile, go with him two" (Matt. 5:41). If you are sincere and willing God will cause you to cross paths with someone in need. It is only when we turn our eyes off of ourselves and focus on others that we will be able to experience the true, genuine God-given joy that being a blessing to others brings. As this becomes our lifestyle it will be proven over and over again that it is indeed better to give than receive.

God has a plan and purpose for each of our lives and one only has to read the first four words of the Bible to find out what His perfect will is, "In the beginning God..." (Gen. 1:1). In the beginning of the day, put God first. Every morning when you wake up begin your day by seeking with your whole heart and soul, first and foremost, the kingdom of God. Seeking for God will give you peace that passes human understanding and joy unspeakable. Happiness is not about having and getting, it consists in giving and serving. Jesus said to take no thought for tomorrow (Matt. 6:34) and the antidote to worrying is to make a daily choice to prioritize God's kingdom and His righteousness. Seeking is a heart issue so make it the habit of your life, your first and ever dominant concern. Seeking first the kingdom of God is a biblical concept that touches ones' motivations and priorities including how one spends their leisure time, the goals one sets in this life, and whether or not they experience spiritual growth.

The good news is that what you seek, you will find. We read in 1 Chron. 28:9, "As for you, my son Solomon, know the God of your father, and serve Him with a loyal heart and a willing mind; for the Lord searches all hearts and understands all the intent of the thoughts. If you seek Him, He will be found by you; but if you forsake Him, He will cast you off forever" (see also Deut. 4:29). Dan. 2:44 says, "And in the days of these kings the God of heaven will set up a kingdom which will never be destroyed; and the kingdom shall not be left to other people; it shall break in pieces and consume all these kingdoms, and it shall stand forever." God's kingdom will never end and this tells us that there will always be people doing nice things for other people. We are here on kingdom business, and the kingdom of the King requires haste. There's a lot to be done and not much time to do it. Darkness is ruling in too many places and we've been called to be a light in a dark and sinful world.

Col. 1:13 says God "has delivered us from the power of darkness and translated us into the kingdom of the Son of His love." God's kingdom is a kingdom of love and love always gives and serves. We're born to love and called to serve. 1 John 3:2 says, "Beloved, now we are children of God." Jesus is the Son of God and He came to serve. We also are sons and daughters of God and we also serve. Being kingdom-minded means you're always thinking about how you can be used by God to advance His kingdom. Of course, this can't be done if one is forever worried and concerned about the needs of this life. "Life is more than food, and the body more than clothing" (Luke 12:23). God feeds the birds of the air and clothes the lilies in the field and He'll more than take care of you. If you will take care of God's business by seeking first His kingdom, He will be faithful and just to take care of your business.

Jesus said in Luke 12:32, "Do not fear, little flock, for it is your Father's good pleasure to give you the kingdom." Think about that. God will give you the kingdom. This means He will provide you with opportunities to serve Him and others, to have His will fulfilled in your life. That's precisely what the kingdom of God is. We are living in the last days and laborers are needed like never before. Laboring is not a burden as some would think. It's a joy! Eccl. 5:20 assures us that "God keeps every man busy with the joy of his heart." God will use you in whatever area brings you the most joy. Take your natural gifts and talents and place them in the hands of God to be used according to His perfect will. Eccl. 9:1 says, "For I considered all this in my heart, so that I could declare it all that the righteous and the wise and their works are in the hand of God." When you go to work for God don't do it half-heartedly. Give it everything you've got and then some.

Paul says in Rom. 12:11 to be "not lagging in diligence, fervent in spirit, serving the Lord." To be "fervent in spirit" means to be aglow and burning with the Spirit of God in your heart. We are to maintain that spiritual glow in our work for the Lord and have the attitude that "whatever your hand finds to do, do it with all your might" (Eccl. 9:10). There are two ways to advance the kingdom of God. You can do something or you can help somebody else do something. God gave Moses instructions on how to build the tabernacle and in Ex. 31:2-6 (NIV) He speaks of two builders, "I have chosen Bezalel...and filled him with the Spirit of God, with skill, ability and knowledge in all kinds of crafts...Moreover, I have anointed Oholiab...to help him." God has made each of us unique and different from anybody else who has ever been born, and this means there are certain things you can do for the kingdom of God that nobody else can do.

Even in your mother's womb you were given special abilities and skills by God that only a person with your personality can develop and perform to the degree God wants them done. Paul encourages Timothy to "not neglect the gift that is in you" (1 Tim. 4:14). Develop those skills and turn yourself over to God to be used by Him to fulfill His purpose on planet earth. These skills may not be "religious" in a formal sense but there is a spiritual element to everything we do. Nehemiah was a wall builder, Daniel was a government man in Babylon, and Luke was a first century physician. When you use your job-related skills to advance the kingdom of God you are as called as any minister. When you know you're doing what God has called you to do, whether it's preaching before thousands of people or fixing a broken pipe in the church bathroom, you will experience a lasting pleasure that can't be found anywhere else.

Paul writes in 1 Cor. 15:58, "Therefore, my beloved brethren, be steadfast, immovable, always abounding in the work of the Lord, knowing that your labor is not in vain in the Lord." The

Message Bible says, "Throw yourselves into the work of the Master, confident that nothing you do for Him is a waste of time or effort." You can have fun in this life but our top priority is to seek first the kingdom of God and do the work of the ministry. Faithful laborers are needed and the work gets done when you combine the natural with the spiritual. Ps. 127:1 says, "Unless the Lord builds the house, they labor in vain who build it." A picture of how this works is painted for us in Ex. 17:8-13. After passing through the Red Sea the children of Israel were attacked by Amalek in Rephidim. Moses sent Joshua and his men onto the field of battle while he stood on the top of the hill with the rod of God in his hand.

"And so it was, when Moses held up his hand, that Israel prevailed, and when he let down his hand, Amalek prevailed" (vs. 11). You can have the best of the best in the natural but if you don't have the spiritual you will fail. The hands of Moses were in the air, and this was a sign of faith and a symbol of victory. Eventually Moses got tired and his arms got heavy, so Aaron and Hur stood beside Moses and held up his hands until the going down of the sun (vs. 12). All Aaron and Hur did was hold up an arm, but it was necessary and it shows that even the smallest of tasks can take on great significance. The warriors on the ground needed the spiritual element and the battle was won because of their efforts. We are in the kingdom, and the kingdom is in us. Jesus taught us to seek with utmost urgency the expansion and the full and total development of God's kingdom. This is why we're here, why we breath, why we're alive.

The longing of kingdom citizens is for the Lord to rule over their lives, for Godly character and behavior to be fully displayed in all that they do and say, and for the kingdom to extend into every life and corner of the globe. The highest form of happiness comes when one is in perfect submission to God's which must be obeyed perfectly, readily, and unceasingly. We cannot call Him "King" and not do His will. When you pray "Thy kingdom come. Thy will be done" you prove the sincerity of your prayer by laboring every day to make a positive difference in the lives of other people. There must be a willingness to forsake all to become a disciple of Jesus (see Luke 14:33) and it begins not outwardly but in the heart. Heart decisions determine the direction your life will take and direction determines destiny. When you make a quality decision to seek first the kingdom of God and His righteousness, it will set you on a course of action that will determine the outcome of your life.

| 16 |

"GOD'S BUSINESS"

One day an Ox said to a Mule, "Let's pretend to be sick." The Mule said, "No, we need to get this work done." The Ox feigned illness and the farmer brought him fresh hay. When the Mule came in from plowing the Ox asked how things went and the Mule said, "All right." The Ox asked, "What did the farmer say about me?" The Mule replied, "Nothing." The next day the Ox pretended to be ill again. When the Mule came home the Ox asked, "How did it go?" The Mule said, "All right." After a week of this the Ox asked, "Did the farmer say anything about me today?" The Mule replied, "Well, he said nothing to me personally, but he stopped and had a long talk with the butcher." The moral of this story is that you were born to fulfill a divine purpose and when you don't there will be consequences to pay, both in the here and now and in the age to come. The apostle Paul continually focused on his calling and shortly before he was executed he wrote, "I have finished the race..." (2 Tim. 4:7).

Notice that Paul didn't retire, he finished that which he was called to do. In the Parable of the Talents the man who buried his talent and did nothing with it paid a high price. He was thrown into outer darkness where there is weeping and gnashing of teeth. In God's eyes the greatest failure of all is the failure to invest the time, talent, and treasure He's given you to fulfill His purpose. One day your life will be audited. It's called "the judgment seat of Christ." Paul writes in 1 Cor. 3:13-15 that everyone's work will be put through the fire to see whether or not it keeps its value. If the work survives the fire, the builder will receive a great reward. But if the work is burned up, the builder will suffer great loss. God has something He wants to do in you, for you, and through you and it is imperative that you find out why you are here and what you can do to help advance His kingdom. If you're doing nothing then don't waste another day. Pray about it. Get still before God and ask Him what He would have you do.

Do it seriously until you find out what your part is. Your calling and assignment is not decided by you, it is discovered by you. Everything God creates is given a calling, purpose, and destiny and you need to quickly find out where you fit in. Don't bounce around and do nothing for the next twenty years. Your purpose for living is not to see how many vacations you can go on or how many fish you can catch or how many rounds of golf you can play. Your ultimate goal in life should not be to retire early so you can sit down and do nothing. Proverbs says that the prosperity of a fool will destroy him. With your life you need to be doing something for God. You were born to love and called to serve so find out where you fit and don't just sit. Do something and do it now! Work! Volunteer for every-thing! Don't rush home on Sunday to eat and watch a ballgame when the chairs at church need to be picked up and put away. He who is faithful over a little will be made ruler over much (Matt. 25:21).

Pretty soon it's all going to be over, and God is going to ask you what you did for Him. These are the days in which you need to be doing everything you can to keep yourself in the center of God's will and destiny for your life. Heb. 6:10 says, "For God is not unjust to forget your work and labor of love which you have shown toward His Name, in that you have ministered to the saints, and do minister." Work is God's idea and the work that pleases Him the most is your labor of love toward people, especially other believers. The Message Bible states, "God doesn't miss anything. He knows perfectly well all the love you've shown Him by helping needy Christians, and that you keep at it." God will not forget your labor of love but if you do no work for Him then He'll have nothing to remem-ber. The time to start working for God is now so lift up those idle hands and do more for the kingdom. Hang around people with a bigger vision than you and let their enthusiasm rub off on you.

Allow them to encourage you to do more and more for the kingdom and as you help them with their vision God will begin to show you specifically that which He would have you do. Work is not a bad thing. There is nothing glorious to sitting around and being lazy and getting nothing done and accom-plished. It doesn't make you feel good about yourself. Work is a spiritual thing, and the Bible commands you to work. Paul writes in 2 Thess. 3:6, "But we command you, brethren, in the name of our Lord Jesus Christ, that you withdraw from every brother who walks disorderly and not according to the tradition which he received from us." The tradition Paul is talking about is the tradition to work. The Message Bible puts it this way, "Our orders - backed up by the Master, Jesus - are to refuse to have anything to do with those among you who are lazy and refuse to work the way we taught you. Don't permit them to freeload on the rest."

Don't hang around people who refuse to work. Withdraw from those who have opportunities to work but won't take advantage of them. You know who these people are. They're your family and friends and coworkers but still you are commanded to stay away from them. "A little leaven leavens the whole lump" (Gal. 5:9) and if you associate with lazy people you will become just as disorderly and rebellious as they are. People who do not work "learn to be idle, wandering about from house to house, and not only idle but also gossips and busybodies, saying things which they ought not" (1 Tim. 5:13). Paul was a worker. He was a tent maker because he didn't want to be a burden to anybody. Faith people are workers and are not comfortable with other people taking care of them all the time. God is your source of supply, and you need not beg any man or government agency to help meet your needs. If the truth be told people are not victims of circumstance, they're lazy and slothful and victims of their own rebellion.

There are reasons people keep losing their jobs and floundering around year after year. They can work but don't want to and to these people Paul wrote, "For even when we were with you, we commanded you this: If anyone will not work, neither shall he eat" (2 Thess. 3:10). The Message Bible says, "Don't you remember the rule we had when we lived with you? 'If you don't work, you don't eat.' And now we're getting reports that a bunch of lazy good-for-nothings are taking advantage of you. This must not be tolerated. We command them to get to work immediately - no excuses, no arguments - and earn their own keep. Friends, don't slack off in doing your duty" (vs. 10-13). People who don't do anything don't want to do anything. The word "lazy" means 'to lean idly.' When the government pays your bills and provides your income people lose their incentive to work and as a result of that they get lazy. They are able to work and have opportunities to work but choose not to. They lean idly by and do nothing.

Believers, however, are supposed to work. Work is God's idea and even He works. He created the heavens and the earth and on the seventh day He rested. Jesus said in John 9:4, "I must work the works of Him Who sent Me while it is day; the night is coming when no one will work." You never retire from the work of God in your life. You should always be doing something fruitful and work that is profitable as long as you have breath. There is a Godly kingdom to be advanced and millions of people who need help. We need to work and keep busy and occupy until He comes. God will bless and prosper what you put your hand to. There is a work to be done so don't gripe and complain when you're asked to do something. Keep your mouth shut and do what you're supposed to do and do it diligently. Work can be fun! It can be satisfying, fulfilling, and greatly rewarding. If it's not, then you're doing the wrong thing or else you're not doing it right. You must do the right thing diligently.

Heb. 6:11,12 says, "And we desire that each one of you show the same diligence to the full assurance of hope until the end, that you do not become sluggish, but imitate those who through faith and patience inherit the promises." The Message Bible states, "And now I want each of you to extent that same intensity toward a full-bodied hope and keep at it till the finish. Don't drag your feet. Be like those who stay the course with committed faith and then get everything promised to them." People who are diligent do things vehemently, with intensity and passion. The word "vehement" is marked by forceful energy, it's powerful like a strong wind and intensely emotional. It's deeply felt and forcibly expressed. This describes the passion you should have for the things of God and the work He would have you do. Diligence sets a higher standard to your love walk and your service unto God and it's what separates the men from the boys. The word "diligence" also means 'wholly, completely, speedily.'

It means 'to dawn.' This is not early; this is a half hour before early. A consistent quality of diligent people is you don't have to wait on them. They're prompt and early, whereas lazy people are consistently late and tardy and are always making excuses. The father of our faith is Abraham, and he was not a lazy, slothful man. When God told him to offer up his son

Isaac, he got up early the next morning and set out on his journey. Paul says in Rom. 12:10,11, "Be kindly affectionate to one another with brotherly love, in honor giving preference to one another; not lagging in diligence, fervent in spirit, serving the Lord." The KJV says, "be not slothful in business." Everybody has a business. There is a family business, house business, work business, car business, garden business, pet business, ministry business, and God's business. At age twelve Jesus said, "Did you not know that I must be about My Father's business?" (Luke 2:49). Heb. 11:6 says that God "is a rewarder of those who diligently seek Him."

When you seek God, you seek His business. God is love and His business is the love business. You must be diligent and passionate about your love walk and the things you do for God. If God calls you to do something, get up early and do it promptly and speedily. Don't drag around and do it half heartedly. The Greek word for "diligence" means 'with earnestness, with speed, very promptly, energetic, to make effort.' Serve God with a wide-open throttle. Move fast and go forward with Jesus. Don't be lukewarm. People who are lukewarm are not idle but they're only doing a fraction of what they're capable of. In fact, most people do nothing. The body of Christ needs more workers and not just church goers. Some attend, fewer work. All of us have been put here for a purpose and we all have a job to do. The problem is too many people are too busy living life to have time for the things of God. They've got a time clock to punch and a round of golf to play. They don't realize that if you're too busy for God, you're too busy.

The first mention of diligence in the Bible is found in Gen. 2:15, "Then the Lord God took the man and put him in the garden of Eden to tend and keep it." The word for "keep" means 'diligence' and Adam was told to be fervent and passionate about watching over the garden and taking care of it. It was his responsibility to stay sharp, reject passivity, and don't fall asleep on the job. Unfortunately he failed to do any of these things and the world is in the mess it's in today because one man did not obey the Lord's command to be diligent. Don't be like Adam but instead take care of your business and don't wait for someone to do it for you. Being lazy will lower your standards and is a sign that your spirituality has slipped. The bad news is that what's on the inside of you will show up on the outside. If you're lazy on the inside you'll be lazy on the outside. You can't be diligent and walk in love if you look and smell like a slob. Jesus dealt with unclean spirits and the people who had them were filthy and nasty.

God is love and you are to imitate and represent Him. He is wonderful and He is glorious! He is light and there is no darkness in Him. Pay attention to how you dress and how you smell. Wash your car, vacuum your house, clean those dirty dishes and brush your teeth. We have a witness to keep for we're not just representing ourselves; we represent the King of kings and Lord of lords. There's a whole lot of business involved in living a spiritual life. Don't be too spiritual to clean your house and pay your bills. Don't let your home become a trash dump because you're too busy praying and reading your Bible. True believers who have it together are sharp, diligent, and are hard workers. They're not sloppy and slothful and they have their home and business in order. They're not too spiritual to let their lawn be overgrown or the paint to peel off their house. Their car is clean and vacuumed and in the garage their tools are in the proper place.

The sink is not full of dirty dishes and dirty clothes don't litter the laundry room floor and the garbage don't overflow and spill out onto the floor. Those who are diligent in taking care of worldly business will be diligent in taking care of God's business. These are the people who are willing to get up early and stay late. They are the ones who will put their flesh under and keep their mouths shut. People who walk in the spirit are not idle but are those who get things done. A car idles but goes nowhere. Believers who are diligent put the pedal to the metal and does the best they can do all the while believing God to help them do it better. Raise the standard in the business you perform. Put more effort into it and do it better. Gal. 6:9 tells us, "And let us not grow weary while doing good, for in due season we shall reap if we do not lose heart." Don't quit, don't give up, don't lose heart. Instead, be diligent week after week, month after month, year after year.

When you are given the freedom to do anything you want to do, what you choose to do reveals your heart. As a Christian you must choose to take care of God's business and be diligent to do your part to walk in love and advance the kingdom of God on the earth. Your love and obedience to God is shown in your life. People can see it and they can see the lack of it. If it's in you, it will come out of you. As you get stronger in your spirit the more diligent you will become. Instead of putting something off you'll get up and do it as early as you can. Taking care of God's business requires promptness and speed. Take it seriously when God tells you to do something. Put your hand to the plow and do it with fervor and diligence. Don't make faith confessions all day and do nothing. Add works to your faith for faith without works is dead. Nothing ventured, nothing gained. Eccl. 9:10 says, "Whatever your hand finds to do, do it with all your might." Do it! Do it now and do it well!

The Message Bible says, "Whatever turns up, grab it and do it heartily." The NL Bible says, "Whatever task comes your way, do it with all your strength." Whenever you find work to do, do the best you can and do it passionately and earnestly. Do it heartily and with all your might. Diligence is early and prompt and speedy so do it now and do it well! Be sharp, be ready, be prepared. This glorifies God and makes the gospel message look good to outsiders. Believers who are diligent are flexible and ready to work at a moment's notice. If you have to "get" ready, then you're not ready and if you're not ready, you're not going to be used by God. You will miss out on the rich blessings of God just like the five foolish virgins missed out because they weren't ready. We live in a lazy generation where people goof off, lay around, and are never ready. If something comes up, then they'll get ready but by then it will be too late.

The window of opportunity closed on them, and these are the people who will never be used by God. Don't "get" ready, "be" ready! Live ready and be ready when God calls on you. You're needed now, not three days from now. God used people who are ready so you must be ready at all times. Lighten your schedule and order your time and finances in a way so that you'll be ready to be used by God in a moment's notice. People who are diligent are ready not knowing the details or the time when they'll be called to work. These people walk in faith and they trust God and are forever ready to say, "Here I am, Lord. Send me." Never be without the time or the money to do what God tells you to do. If you don't have the resources to do what God tells you to do then you're wasting vast amounts of time, money, and energy. It is selfishness to make people wait on you all the time. This means you think your time is more valuable than their time.

The love of God is not selfish and is forever ready to give a helping hand no matter what time of day it is. This is diligence at the highest level. Procrastination is the manifestation of the lack of diligence. These are the people who are lazy and slothful and always puts things off until tomorrow. Solomon must have had these people in mind when he wrote Eccl. 5:4, "When you make a vow to God, do not delay paying it; For He has no pleasure in fools. Pay what you have vowed." When you know what to do, don't put it off until tomorrow. Do it now and do it well! The NIV says, "Do not delay in fulfilling it" and the NL Bible says, "Don't delay in following through." People who do little tend to do less. They waste time and get farther and farther behind on the things they should be doing. On the other hand, people who are diligent and do much tend to do even more. People who are laborers and one of the chosen few will take on another project and do it well.

It's as if they can't do enough for their Lord and Master. The Message Bible says, "If you tell God you'll do something, do it now. God takes no pleasure in foolish gabble. Vow it and then do it." Don't put it off! Do it now and do it well! Do it early and do it with speed! Ezra 7:23 says, "Whatever is commanded by the God of heaven, let it diligently be done for the house of the God of heaven." Diligence is a spiritual force just like faith and love is. Desire affects "how" you do something so do everything as unto the Lord with diligence, whether it be sweeping the floor, stocking a grocery shelf, or cleaning the toilet. Do everything as unto the Lord because people watch what you do and how you do it more than what you say. Get stirred up! Be enthusiastic and excited about what you do. Be eager and determined to "show the same diligence to the full assurance until the end" (Heb. 6:11b). Don't quit halfway through a project but see it through to the end.

Don't give up but instead keep after it until the work is done. Finish what you set out to do. A lot of people can start a project and keep at it for a few days but when the going gets tough they bale out and quit. They jump out of the will of God because of impatience, offenses, and anger and they leave the place where He put them. To get the job done you need persistence and perseverance, and it takes diligence to do this. Heb. 3:5,6 says, "And Moses indeed was faithful in all his house as a servant, for a testimony of those things which would be spoken afterward, but Christ as a Son over His own house, whose house we are if we hold fast the confidence and the rejoicing of the hope firm to the end." We are God's house if we persevere and hang in there until the end when the work is done. Heb. 3:14 says, "For we have become partakers of Christ if we hold the beginning of our confidence steadfast to the end." If you start a project, finish it.

Be like Abraham who patiently endured to the end and obtained the promise (Heb. 6:13-15). Don't try to do something. Do it! Do it well and persevere until the job is done. Even Jesus said, "No one, having put his hand to the plow and looking back, is fit for the kingdom of God" (Luke 9:62). In all things we are to be forever "looking unto Jesus, the author and finisher of our faith" (Heb. 12:2). Jesus is the example we follow and He is a finisher. He is the author and the finisher. He is the pacesetter and we follow in His footsteps. If you're falling behind, then pick up the pace. Lay aside those things that would hinder you and distract you. Turn off the TV and cancel that golf game. Lighten your load and stop doing those things that prevent you from serving God to the fullest and finishing those things you began to do. Follow after Jesus Who went all the way and finished the work He was sent to do. He said in John 4:34, "My food is to do the will of Him Who sent Me, and to finish His work."

Jesus didn't grow weary and quit. His faith was tried in the garden of Gethsemane, but He pressed forward and completed the work He was sent to do. The last words Jesus said on the cross was, "It is finished" (John 19:30). And if He did all this for us, we ought to do the same for Him. Don't give up! Don't quit! Persevere till the end. Finish the work God entrusted to you, because obedience is proven not at the start, but at the end. Many begin with enthusiasm, but only the diligent remain when the work becomes demanding. Diligence stays with the assignment, refusing distraction, discouragement, or delay. A faithful servant does not stop when it is convenient - he finishes when the work is done. You never retire from doing the work of God in your life and on the day you breathe your last breath you can agree with Solomon who wrote, "The end of a thing is better than its beginning" (Eccl. 7:8). Then and only then can you look into the heavenlies and say with bold confidence, "It is finished!"

| 17 |

"FERVENT IN SPIRIT"

You were born to be great. God wants you to be happy, but you were not born to be happy. You were born to be great. Greatness in the eyes of many means to have vast amounts of wealth and to occupy positions of power and authority where you are able to rule over many men. Having people do what you tell them to do is the accumulation of everything some people have ever worked for and many consider this the pinnacle of greatness. This is not so in God's eyes for He sees greatness in a different light. Jesus said, "You know that the rulers of the Gentiles lord it over them, and those who are great exercise authority over them. Yet it shall not be so among you; but whoever desires to become great among you, let him be your servant. And whoever desires to be first among you, let him be your slave - just as the Son of Man did not come to be served, but to serve, and to give His life a ransom for many" (Matt. 20:25-28).

Jesus came and set the example that we are all to follow. "He offered Himself as a sacrifice to free us from a dark, rebellious life into this good, pure life, making us a people He can be proud of, energetic in goodness" (Titus 2:14 MSG). You were born to love and called to serve, and this is greatness in the eyes of God. You are a masterpiece, created and formed by the Master Himself. "For we are His workmanship, created in Christ Jesus for good works, which God prepared beforehand that we should walk in them" (Eph. 2:10). When you become zealous for good works, you become great in the eyes of God. God won't leave you hanging. When you surrender your life to Him and answer the call to be great, He will show you in His Word how to achieve this ultimate way of life. He will lead you to the words of Rom. 12;10,11, "Be kindly affectionate to one another with brotherly love, in honor giving preference to one another; not lagging in diligence, fervent in spirit, serving the Lord."

To be great you must forever be serving the Lord with diligence and holy fervor. There is a certain intensity in the Christian life, and you must serve the Lord with a boiling spirit and keep yourself fueled and aflame. The Philips Bible says, "Let us not allow slackness to spoil our work, and let us keep the fires of our spirit burning as we do our work for the Lord." The NIV says, "never be lacking in zeal" and this is a rebuke to passivity, laziness, lethargy, apathy, and boredom. The Amplified Bible says, "Never lag in zeal, and in earnest endeavor be aglow and burning with the Spirit serving the Lord." The Greek word for "fervent" is 'zeo' which means "boil, to be hot, burn, and glow." This means you must be earnest, zealous, on fire, and enthusiastic in serving the Lord. Don't put a frown on your face if the pastor asks you to do something at church. Instead, smile from ear to ear, boil with heat, be white hot, and have a burning zeal to do the will of God.

God is calling you to invest your life in something great and with fervor and enthusiasm you must find ways to pour your life into the things of God. Col. 3:2 says, "Set your mind on things above, not on things on the earth." There are great things worth living for, such as the greatness of God and His glorious purposes in the world. We exist to spread a passion for the supremacy of God in all things. Rom. 12:11 is a verse about living life as unto the Lord and this is why you must boil in your spirit and stir up zeal for God and the cause of truth and life. Rom. 14:8 says, "For if we live, we live to the Lord; and if we die, we die to the Lord. Therefore, whether we live or die, we are the Lord's." All of life is a serving of the Lord and there is a work to be done. Work is spiritual. The Father works, the Son works, and you are to work also. Jesus said in John 5:17, "My Father has been working until now, and I have been working."

Paul said in 1 Cor. 15:58, "Therefore, my beloved brethren, be steadfast, immovable, always abounding in the work of the Lord, knowing that your labor is not in vain in the Lord." God has assigned us much to accomplish, and He will hold us accountable for the faithful performance of it. Every Christian has enough to do to occupy all his time until the Lord returns. He whose life is spent in ease and does nothing should doubt altogether his faith in God and whether or not he is truly saved. Jesus said in John 14:12, "Most assuredly, I say to you, he who believes in Me, the works that I do he will do also." He goes on to say in vs. 15, "If you love Me, keep My commandments. Being fervent in spirit is the capacity and ability of every Christian to be consumed and eaten up by the things of God. The call on your life is to do the will of God from the heart. Work with a smile on your face, always keeping in mind that no matter who happens to be giving the orders, you're really serving God.

There are different commitment levels to the Lord among all believers. Some people work fervently, others work a little, most work none at all. In Rom. 16:12 Paul told the brethren to greet two of his friends who labored in the Lord. He then said to greet "the beloved Persis, who labored much in the Lord." Two labored in the Lord but Persis labored much more than the others. Many people are deceived. They think they're more committed than they actually are. For some it's only talk but no action. We read in John 13:36-38, "Simon Peter said to Him, 'Lord, where are you going?' Jesus answered him, 'Where I am going you cannot follow Me now, but you shall follow Me afterward.' Peter said to Him, 'Lord, why can I not follow You now? I will lay down my life for Your sake.' Jesus answered him, 'Will you lay down your life for My sake? Most assuredly, I say to you, the rooster shall not crow till you have denied Me three times.'"

In the garden of Gethsemane Jesus asked His disciples to pray with Him but they fell asleep. It was after this that Peter denied Jesus. If you fail the little tests, it is foolish to believe you'll pass the big tests. Be diligently committed to seek first the kingdom of God for he who is faithful over a little will be made ruler over much (Matt. 25:21). The Lord said in Num. 14:24, "But My servant Caleb, because he has a different spirit in him and has followed Me fully, I will bring into the land where he went, and his descendants shall inherit it." Caleb went all the way with God and God took him all the way into the Promised Land. He went farther than Moses and all his elders. Jesus was committed and your commitment level should be the same as His. He said in John 14:31, "But that the world may know that I love the Father, and as the Father gave Me commandment, so I do." Jesus went all the way and gave everything He had. He offered His spirit for your spirit, His mind for your mind, His body for your body.

He gave all of His life's blood. He became sin when He knew no sin. He did all this willingly because He was committed to the Father and to you. He held nothing back. He gave it all. He went all the way. He went to hell for all mankind and you can't give any more than that. Even today He ever lives to make intercession for you. He is your Advocate. Every moment of every day and every night He pleads your case before the Father. His blood is speaking and proclaiming your innocence from off the mercy seat. His commitment level is without dispute and like Him you also should go all the way. Paul said, "In the last days perilous times will come for men will be lovers of themselves, lovers of money." (2 Tim. 3:1,2). Many people are only committed to themselves, lovers of pleasures more than lovers of God. Whatever you love the most, you will be committed to the most. There are folks highly committed to their pleasures and their lives are going nowhere.

They don't know that serving others is what gives meaning to life and brings complete satisfaction. Total fulfillment comes when God uses you to help another person's dream come true. This only happens when you love God more than you love yourself and when you desire what God wants more than what you want. Truly, it will be the most fulfilling life you could ever imagine. A Christian who is not fervent in spirit has become lukewarm through compromise. Compromise is like erosion; it happens slowly and before you know it, you're in a state of lukewarmness and you're only going through the motions. Those who have lost their fervency and passion for God become empty, slack, shallow, sluggish, and useless all because of compromise. God's people in the Old Testament were warned about being lazy and slothful. Amos 6:1 says, "Woe to you who are at ease in Zion" and Jer. 48:10 tells us, "Cursed is he who does the work of the Lord deceitfully, and cursed is he who keeps back his sword from blood."

Those who are not on fire on the inside will not do very much on the outside. Neglect and a do-nothing attitude will ruin your Christian life. Passivity is unacceptable to God and slothfulness should never be tolerated. The wet blanket of apathy, sloth, and laziness will put out your fire for God. Don't drag your feet spiritually but be full of zeal and enthusiasm, forever glowing in your spirit. The word "fervor" suggests heat and passion and only the fervency of the Spirit can overcome laziness and slothfulness. The heat of one's fervency will drive you forward and cause you to wake up each morning ready and willing to be used by God to serve Him and bless others. The only other place in scripture where "fervent in spirit" appears is Acts 18:25 where it describes the teaching ministry of Apollos, an eloquent man and mighty in his knowledge of the Word (vs. 24). His internal fervency produced an external fervency in his service for the Lord and "he greatly helped those who had believed through grace" (vs. 27).

Serving God is fun and the Christian attitude must be one of enthusiasm, a hot fervor which the Spirit promotes. Ps. 100:1,2 says, "Make a joyful shout to the Lord, all you lands! Serve the Lord with gladness; Come before His presence with singing." A joyful spirit is a fervent spirit in which the fire of your first love still burns. Despite all the hardships that you might encounter, be sure to complain less and not lose courage but rather display even more joy in the Lord and His work. You will succeed if the fire of faith, hope, and love burns brightly from within. Jesus said John the Baptist was "the burning and shining lamp" (John 5:35) and in Matt. 5:16 He said, "Let your light so shine before men, that they may see your good works and glorify your Father in heaven." This is a great motivator to be fervent in spirit because the brighter and hotter your light shines, the more glory the Lord receives. The word "Lord" is 'Kurios' and this describes someone who has undisputed possession of a person or thing.

It means 'Master' or 'owner,' Jesus is your Master and you are His servant. The word "servant" is 'doulos,' meaning you belong totally to the Lord. You have no rights of your own and your sole desire is to honor and serve Him with enthusiasm that comes from having a fervent heart. In the context of Christian service "fervent" means 'to be full of energy, to be on fire with zeal and enthusiasm.' It is a warning against settling into comfortable, shallow ruts in your spiritual life. The idea is that you are to be continually "hot" for the things of God. It is to be your habitual practice, your lifestyle before a critically watching world. The great in the eyes of God are those who serve. The Lord expects His children to be whole-hearted workers who are wildly willing and filled with an impassioned desire to please and serve Him faithfully. God wants on fire, red hot enthusiastic followers who love Him more than anything or anyone on earth, disciples who are determined to follow Jesus all the way.

You must always have a realization of what a great privilege it is to serve the Lord and that nothing can stop the man who is fired up with zeal and enthusiasm and is full of a fiery anointing that empowers him in everything he does. The person who is fervent in spirit will keep going no matter what the circumstances are that come against him. He will be driven by compelling compassion with an irresistible motivation that gives direction and meaning in everything he does, everything he says, and everywhere he goes. Paul said in 2 Cor. 5:14, "The love of Christ compels me." The Message Bible says, "Christ's love has moved me to such extremes. His love has the first and last word in everything we do." Don't waste time waiting for inspiration. When you address the task at hand, inspiration will come. Fervor and enthusiasm are the fundamental keys to success in the Lord's work. Fervency produces results (James 5:16) and gives boldness and power (Acts 18:25-28).

It brings rejoicing to God's people (2 Cor. 7:6-8) and makes up for other shortcomings (1 Peter 4:8; Jude 22). Most of all, fervency brings about a real and genuine love (1 Peter 1:22), a love that stays on fire and never burns out or grows cold (Matt. 24:120). A fervent spirit burns for God in such a way that you are consumed by Him. He is the reason you wake up in the morning. He is your One and only, your all in all. In Him you live and move and have your being (Acts 17:28). Your love and devotion have no ultimate value unless you are humbly and fervently serving the Lord. Work for Christ with feeling and live for Him with all your might. Intensity matters, zeal matters, wholeheartedness matters (see Jer. 29:13,14). Don't settle for anything less. Work for Christ passionately and be eager and earnest to accomplish what he has called you to do. Live your life in such a way that it shows openly your love and adoration for Him.

Become like the godly widow in 1 Tim. 5:10 who was "well reported for good works: if she has brought up children, if she has lodged strangers, if she has washed the saints' feet, if she has relieved the afflicted, if she has diligently followed every good work." Paul said in Titus 3:14, "And let our people also learn to maintain good works, to meet urgent needs, that they may not be unfruitful." The Message Bible says, "Our people have to learn to be diligent in their work so that all necessities are met (especially among the needy) and they don't end up with nothing to show for their lives." Serving God is not for the weak and timid. Paul said "according to my earnest expectations and hope that in nothing I shall be ashamed, but that with all boldness, as always, so now also Christ will be manifested in my body, whether by life or by death" (Phil. 1;20). It takes strength to be diligent so let the weak say "I am strong" (Joel 3:10).

Is. 40:29 says, "He gives power to the weak, and to those who have no might He increases strength." Stop talking about how tired you are because you're always busy. Say out loud, "I'm strong in the Lord and in the power of His might! I've got pep in my step! I've got all the strength I need! Greater is he that is in me than he that is in the world!" Those who are great have a strong desire to worship and serve and are always looking for opportunities to do so. At the last supper Jesus said, "With fervent desire I have desired to eat this Passover with you before I suffer" (Luke 22:15). Being fervent in spirit produces a diligence that is free from sloth. The slothful mind can be very creative and inventive in the excuses they make. Prov. 20:4 says, "The sluggard will not plow because of winter." In the winter it's too cold and in the summer it's too hot. Lazy people always have a reason for not working or an excuse for their laziness.

Prov.26:13,14 says, "The slothful man says, 'There is a lion in the road! A fierce lion is in the streets!' As a door turns on its hinges, so does the slothful turn on his bed." The door is moving but it's not going anywhere and so is the man who is slothful and forever making excuses. Solomon wrote in Eccl. 11:4, "He who observes the wind will not sow, and he who regards the clouds will not reap." The Message Bible says, "Don't sit there watching the wind. Do your own work. Don't stare at the clouds. Get on with your life." If you wait for the conditions to be perfect before you do anything, nothing will get done. As you wait for the perfect opportunities to do something the days will quickly pass you by. Months and years will go by and you'll still be waiting and doing nothing. Before you know it your life will be over and you'll have nothing to show for it. The Living Bible says, "If you wait for perfect conditions, you'll never get anything done." If you want an excuse not to work, you'll surely find one.

It is because of slothfulness that Jesus said in Matt. 9:37, "The harvest truly is plentiful, but the laborers are few." We live in a lazy generation. Gone are the days when a person had to walk across the room to change the channel on the television. Conveniences are everywhere. We now live in a world of drive-thru restaurants, microwaves, and remote controls. In Las Vegas there is even a place for drive-thru weddings. Well abled people are being programmed to eat potato chips and watch soap operas all day expecting the government to pay their bills and buy their food. Prov. 19:15 says, "Slothfulness casts one into a deep sleep, and an idle person will suffer hunger." We have returned to the days of Sodom. God said in Ezek. 16:49,50, "Look, this was the iniquity of your sister Sodom: She and her daughters had pride, fullness of food, and abundance of idleness; neither did she strengthen the hand of the poor and the needy. And they were haughty and committed abomination before Me; therefore I took them away as I saw fit."

Most people think it was sexual perversion that caused the destruction of this wicked city but here God says it was pride, gluttony, and the abundance of idleness. Slothfulness opens the door to the devil. Sin enters in and things go from bad to worse. Prov. 18:9 says, "He who is slothful in his work is a brother to him who is a great destroyer." Think about it. When you are diligent and fervent in spirit you are a child of God, but when you are lazy and slothful you are a brother to the devil. There are a lot of people doing nothing for God who think it's no big deal. All they want to do is eat, drink, and be merry and when they're all done, they go off and sleep their life away. They want God to supply their needs, but they don't think it's worthwhile getting involved in kingdom business. They are carnal and only think about what's in it for them. What they don't realize is that there's a lot in it for them if they would only adopt the lifestyle of being a blessing to somebody else.

Heb. 11:6 says, "But without faith it is impossible to please Him, for he who comes to God must believe that He is and that He is a rewarder of those who diligently seek Him." Believing God exists is easy but most people struggle to believe that God rewards people. He is a rewarder and you must believe this in order to please God. This is not optional! It is mandatory that you believe this! When you seek God and the expansion of His kingdom with passionate diligence good things will happen to you. You must believe this! People who say "you never know what God's going to do" don't believe that He is a rewarder of those who diligently seek Him and are fervent in spirit. A reward is a blessing; it is the goodness of God being poured into your life. It's increase, promotion, getting your needs met. God is a good God and He'll bless you! He'll protect you! He'll deliver you! He'll heal you! He'll prosper you! He'll fill you with the Holy Spirit! He'll fill your house with treasure!

He'll give you a good marriage and children you can be proud of! He'll make you rich and you'll never lack for anything as long as you live! Ps.122:1-3 says, "Praise the Lord! Blessed is the man who fears the Lord, who delights greatly in His commandments. His descendants will be mighty on earth; The generation of the upright will be blessed. Wealth and riches will be in his house, and his righteousness endures forever." Wealthy people have choices, poor people don't. People who are poor have no vision and no creativity, so they perish (Prov. 29:18). They cast off restraint and become a wandering vagabond like Cain in the Old Testament. They run wild and don't know if they're coming or going. They break loose without a guiding hand to direct them in the way they should go. These people need a vision of the goodness of God, that if you seek Him diligently, He will reward you. "Every good gift and every perfect gift is from above and comes down from the Father of lights" (James 1:17).

If it's good, it's from God and it's for you. Like Abraham you will be blessed and you will be a blessing (Gen. 12;2). You were born to love and called to serve and when you're rich you can bless people. You can feed them, clothe them, and help pay their bills. It is the will of God for you to be wealthy enough to bless other people, not so riches terminate with you, but so they flow through you. God desires you to be a living pipeline - receiving His provision and releasing it to meet needs, lift burdens, and advance His purposes. Wealth in God's hands is never about excess for self, but effectiveness for service. When God can trust you to give freely, He knows your heart is aligned with His purposes rather than possessions. Freely given hands become open channels through which God can pour His provision without restraint. What you release in faith, He multiplies in abundance because generosity proves you can be trusted with more.

As this happens your storehouse will be full, and all your needs will be met and all your desires fulfilled. God is not unjust and unfair. He remembers your labor of love, and He rewards it, now in this life and in the hereafter (Heb. 6:10). God is a rewarder and He talked about the reward part before He talked about the diligent part. "Therefore, do not cast away your confidence which has great reward. For you have need of endurance, so that after you have done the will of God, you may receive the promise: ' For yet a little while, and He who is coming will come and not tarry. Now the just shall live by faith; But if anyone draws back, My soul has no pleasure in him.' But we are not of those who draw back to perdition, but of those who believe to the saving of the soul" (Heb. 10:35-39). This describes the life of the diligent and the fervent in spirit. The Message Bible says, "But we're not quitters who lose out. Oh, no! We'll stay with it and survive, trusting all the way."

| 18 |

"A LIVING SACRIFICE"

Freedom is the prominent craving of every human heart. Wars have been fought and lives sacrificed all for the sake of freedom. Indeed, the taste of freedom is sweet and people will to anything and everything to bask in it's redemptive glory. We all love the heroics of William Wallace and Abraham Lincoln as they spent their lives for the sake of freedom. More important than all this, however, is the freedom that Christ came to give each of us. Freedom is what was taken from man in the Garden of Eden and four thousand years later God's gift of spiritual freedom was returned to man through the life and death of Jesus Christ. In John 8:34-36 (MSG) Jesus said, "I tell you most solemnly that anyone who chooses a life of sin is trapped in a dead-end life and is, in fact, a slave. a slave is transient, who can't come and go at will. The Son, though, has an established position, the run of the house. So, if the Son sets you free, you are free through and through."

Once freedom has been lived and experienced, never again will people let themselves be put under the yoke of whatever wants to control them. Surprisingly, there were a group of believers in the Bible who allowed themselves to be coerced into doing just that. Freedom from the law of sin and death was the message Paul was commissioned by God to teach the local church. he said in Rom. 8:2 (MSG), "The Spirit of life in Christ, like a strong wind, has magnificently cleared the air, freeing you from a fated lifetime of brutal tyranny at the hands of sin and death," Old time religious leaders, unfortunately, came into the churches in Galatia where Paul taught and tried to manipulate and coerce these freedom-loving believers back into the prison of religious rules and regulations. With strong-arm tactics these Jewish legalizers sought to control them and bring them back into a yoke of religious bondage to Old Testament law.

Paul was furious for these acts of intimidation but even more so at the Galatian believers who allowed themselves to be taken captive by these false doctrines. In Gal. 1:16 he said, "I marvel that you are turning away so soon from Him who called you in the grace of Christ to a different gospel." He comes on even stronger in Gal. 3:1 as he calls them "O foolish Galatians!" The Message Bible states, "You crazy Galatians! Did someone put a hex on you? Have you taken leave of your senses? Something crazy has happened, for it's obvious that you no longer have the crucified Jesus in clear focus in your lives. His sacrifice on the cross was certainly set before you clearly enough." Paul knew that freedom in Jesus was not an instrument to be used to control people and make them behave in prescribed ways. Jesus was a personal Savior whose love set us free from within in order that we might live a free life.

The book of Galatians was written to help these misguided believers regain back the freedom that only God can give. He boldly proclaimed in Gal. 5:1, "Stand fast therefore in the liberty by which Christ has made us free, and do not be entangled again with a yoke of bondage." The NIV says, "It is for freedom that Christ has set us free" and the Message Bible states, "Christ has set us free to live a free life. So take your stand! Never again let anyone put a harness of slavery on you." This precious freedom, priceless as it is, was bought and paid for by the shed blood of Jesus. This freedom is not free - it was purchased at a great price, secured through sacrifice, obedience, and unwavering love. It is neither offered nor given in vain but entrusted to us so we may walk in truth, live with purpose, and honor the One who paid the cost. There is a purpose for freedom and Paul's letter to the churches in Galatia sought to show them the true nature of Godly freedom and to give them clear direction on how to use it.

A preview of what Paul had to say is found in Is. 58:6,7, "Is this not the fast that I have chosen: To loose the bonds of wickedness, to undo the heavy burdens, to let the oppressed go free, and that you break every yoke? Is it not to share your bread with the hungry, and that you bring to your house the poor who are cast out; When you see the naked, that you cover him, and not hide yourself from your own flesh?" Paul mirrors these words in Gal. 5:13, "For you, brethren, have been called to liberty; only do not use liberty as an opportunity for the flesh, but through love serve one another." There is a call on your life. The Amplified Bible says, "For you, brethren, were [indeed] called to freedom; only [do not let your] freedom be an incentive to your flesh and an opportunity or excuse [for self-ishness], but through love you should serve one another." Paul is saying that you were called to freedom from servitude, now in love submit to servitude.

He said in 1 Cor. 9:19, "For though I am free from all men, I have made myself a servant of all, that I might win the more." Daily strive to promote each other's welfare and through love help each other mature in their spiritual salvation. When there is true, genuine love there is no sense of servitude. Duty is pleasant and acts of kindness agreeable. It gives you a reason to get up each morning. Love is the only behavior that we can do in freedom. The Message Bible translation of Gal. 5:13,14 states, "It is absolutely clear that God has called you to a free life. Just make sure that you don't use this freedom as an excuse to do whatever you want to do and destroy your freedom. Rather, use your freedom to serve one another in love; that's how freedom grows. For everything we know about God's Word is summed up in a single sentence: Love others as you love yourself. That's an act of true freedom." Love not shown is not love at all. It must be put into practice.

Paul continues in Gal. 6:2-4 (MSG), "Stoop down and reach out to those who are oppressed. Share their burdens, and so complete Christ's law. If you think you are too good for that, you are badly deceived. Make a careful exploration of who you are and the work you have been given and sink yourself into that." He goes on to say in vs. 9,10, "So let's not allow ourselves to get fatigued doing good. At the right time we will harvest a good crop if we don't give up or quit. Right now, therefore, every time we get the chance, let us work for the benefit of all, starting with the people closest to us in the community of faith." Paul is encouraging us to become like a cool mountain stream that services the valley with the water of love. The thought of freedom was heavy on Paul's mind when a year or two later he wrote to the church at Rome, "I beseech you therefore, brethren, by the mercies of God, that you present your bodies a living sacrifice, holy, acceptable to God, which is your reasonable service" (Rom. 12:1).

The NIV Bible says, "this is your spiritual act of worship" and the NLT states, "this is truly the way to worship Him." Worship is more than music and singing and lifting up holy hands. You can worship God with your service. In times past sacrifices were presented before the altar but now the altar is wherever you may be. A "living sacrifice" is an unselfish giving up of one's life for the sake of another. Jesus said in Matt. 16:25, "For whoever desires to save his life will lose it, and whoever loses his life for My sake will find it." The most miserable life you can live is the self-serving life. If all you do is serve yourself, you will be empty and unfulfilled. You will never be able to buy enough things to bring you complete satisfaction nor can you accomplish enough great deeds to make you happy. When Alexander the Great won his final battle, he wept because he had no more lands to conquer. You were saved to serve and until you make yourself useful there will always be a void in your life.

Being a living sacrifice is the walk of the mature Christian. In the world there is a struggle to always be on top where you call the shots and make all the decisions, where other people assist you and do what you say. Jesus spoke about this in Matt. 20:25, "You know that the rulers of the Gentiles lord it over them, and those who are great exercise authority over them." The Message Bible says in vs. 25-28, "You've observed how godless rulers throw their weight around, how quickly a little power goes to their heads. It's not going to be that way with you. Whoever wants to be great must become your servant. Whoever wants to be first among you must be your slave. That is what the Son of Man has done: He came to serve, not be served - and then to give away His life in exchange for the many who are held hostage." To be Christlike is to be service-minded and you must be spiritually mature to accept that cleaning toilets and changing dirty diapers is just as much spiritual worship as the one who stands in front of a crowd.

Spiritual babies only think of themselves and their own comfort and ease. They think they're too good to get on their hands and knees to scrub the floor but are always first in line to ask for favors and handouts from somebody else. But when you are spiritually mature you become more aware of what's going on around you and the needs of other people. Increased in you is the desire to have the Lord use you to help them and meet the need. Jesus set the example for all of us in John 13 when He laid aside His garments, took a towel and girded Himself, and began to wash the disciple's feet, and to wipe them with the towel with which He was girded (vs. 4,5). Jesus dressed like a bond slave, the lowest of the low, and proceeded to perform the lowest job around. This was not a high-profile job for there was dirt, grime, and donkey manure on those feet. It was the same as if he were cleaning toilets.

He then said in vs. 14, "If I then, your Lord and teacher, have washed your feet, you also ought to wash one another's feet." He then said in vs. 17, "Happy are you if you do them." Do you want to be happy? Then have a "foot washer" mentality. Be mindful of how God can use you to bless others. Wherever you go, whoever you see, ask God to reveal to you what you can do to be a blessing to them. Be a living sacrifice and shovel snow for your elderly neighbor and change the tire for the person stopped along the side of the road. Open the door for somebody and let them pass in front of you. Buy a coworker a cup of coffee at break time and carry the groceries out to the car for a mother with four children. This is how true happiness comes and will overflow in your life. On the other hand, if you want to be unhappy, then always look for people to do things for you.

The greatest joy a person can have is to know that their life counts for something, to know that they have made a positive difference in the life of another. There is no greater feeling in the world than usefulness, the feeling that your life matters, to know that you're doing something to help somebody else. Life has no meaning when all your energy, talents, finances, and desires are consumed only on yourself. To do that may seem nice for a season but quickly and most assuredly that lifestyle will grow old and stale. True peace and contentment comes by reaching out to others and making a positive difference in their lives. To know a person is better off because they have met you is what it means to take on the character of God. The lives of people everywhere are changed for the better when introduced to the loving kindness of our precious Heavenly Father.

As ambassadors of the kingdom, and because we are His children, it is our responsibility to be transformed into His image and express His nature by words and actions to whomever we come in contact with. Many believers, however, are bitter and unhappy because somebody didn't do something for them. Self-entitlement will destroy you and your relationships and the way to overcome a life that is downtrodden is to be service-minded. Daily look for ways to bless and benefit other people. It will put you on the mountain of joy and happiness from which no devil can knock you off. Let's face it, good help is hard to find. You know it, the boss at work knows it and, sad to say, God knows it as well. That is why faithfulness, diligence, and integrity stand out so powerfully in a world content with excuses and half-hearted effort. When God finds someone willing to show up, serve well, and remain trustworthy, He entrusts them with greater responsibility and lasting influence.

Matt. 9:35-38 records these words, "And Jesus went about all the cities and villages, teaching in their synagogues, preaching the gospel of the kingdom and healing every sickness and every disease among the people. But when he saw the multitudes, He was moved with compassion for them because they were weary and scattered like sheep having no shepherd. Then He said to His disciples, 'The harvest truly is plentiful, but the laborers are few. Therefore pray the Lord of the harvest to send out laborers into His harvest.'" Jesus said "the laborers are few." Since the beginning of time this has been a stark reality and an intense search has always had to be made to find "a worker who does not need to be ashamed" (2 Tim. 2:15). God said in Ezek. 22:30, "So I sought for a man among them who would make a wall and stand in the gap before Me on behalf of the land that I should not destroy it; but I found no one."

To be a servant of the Lord takes diligence, sacrifice, and a willingness to lay down one's own plans and desires in order to fulfill the will of the Master. In truth, the majority of believers don't have what it takes to be a servant of God and are content to step back and let others take on the responsibility of doing the work of the ministry. For these people the requirements of servanthood are too high for it comes with a price they are unwilling to pay. Jesus said to the rich young ruler, "If you want to be perfect, go, sell what you have and give to the poor, and you will have treasure in heaven; and come follow Me." When the young man heard that saying he went away sorrowful for he had great possessions (Matt. 19:21,22). Indeed, good help is hard to find. In the New Testament Paul gives a detailed, yet unlikely description of the person God takes delight in using to fulfill His will and purpose on earth.

We read in 1 Cor. 1:26-28 these words, "For you see your calling, brethren, that not many wise according to the flesh, not many mighty, not many noble are called. But God has chosen the foolish things of the world to put to shame the things that are mighty; and the base things of the world and the things which are despised God has chosen." The Message Bible puts it this way, "Take a good look, friends, at who you were when you got called into this life. I don't see many of 'the brightest and the best' among you, not many influential, not many from high society families. Isn't it obvious that God deliberately chose men and women that the culture overlooks and exploits and abuses, chose these 'nobodies' to expose the hollow pretensions of the 'somebodies'?" According to Paul, God delights in choosing people who are not highly educated or gifted with special insight and enlightenment according to worldly standards.

Rarely does He call those who are from the high class of society but instead chooses those from a normal, average background. Elisha was a farmer while Moses and David were both shepherds. Of the twelve disciples, one was a tax collector, another a thief, and several were smelly fishermen. God uses people the world will never recognize. Movie stars, big name athletes, stockbrokers, bankers, and those of high prestige and royalty are almost never called to be used by God. Instead, God calls those who are considered insignificant and despised by the world. Is. 53:3 tells us that even Jesus was "despised and rejected by men." The world is quick to discard those it deems weak, broken, or insignificant, but God never measures worth the way man does. Those whom society rejects are often the very ones God chooses to shape, strengthen, and position for His purposes. What the world throws away, God redeems and uses to display His power, grace, and glory.

A better and more detailed rendering of what Paul is saying to the Corinthian church is this, "For you see your calling, brothers, how not many of you were especially bright, educated, or enlightened according to the world's standards. Not many of you were impressive. Not many of you came from high-ranking families or from the upper crust of society. Instead, God selected people who are idiots in the world's view; yet God is using them to utterly confound those who seem smart in the world's eyes. God has picked out people who are laughable; yet through them, he is confounding those who think they are high and mighty. Low-class, second-rate, common, average. These are the ones God has chosen." The word "chosen" is a compound of two Greek words which literally means "Out! I say!" God says we are to separate ourselves and come "out" from the world choosing obedience and righteousness over compromise. When we do, we immediately become what Peter describes in 1 Peter 2:9,10.

"But you are a chosen generation, a royal priesthood, a holy nation. His own special people, that you may proclaim the praises of Him Who called you out of darkness into His marvelous light; who once were not a people but are now the people of God." Many people pull away from the privilege of serving God because in and of themselves they do not feel qualified to do so. For the most part, these people are correct in their thinking. They are not qualified and this is the exact reason God called them. Paul writes in 2 Cor. 3:5,6, "Not that we are sufficient of ourselves to think of anything as being from ourselves, but our sufficiency is from God Who also made us sufficient as ministers of the new covenant." Those who are highly qualified must remain vigilant, because it is easy to mistake God's work through them as personal achievement and quietly steal the glory that belongs to Him alone. When that happens, pride takes root and that is a spiritually dangerous place to stand.

Jesus said in John 15:5, "I am the vine, you are the branches. He who abides in Me, and I in him, bears much fruit for without Me you can do nothing." This being so, a servant of God must therefore be teachable and have a hunger to fulfill the will of God. Prov. 16:26 says that the laborer's appetite works for him and his hunger drives him on. In Matt. 5:6 we read, "Blessed are those who hunger and thirst for righteousness for they will be filled." A lazy and self-satisfied person will rarely be motivated to work but a person who is hungry for the things of God will be motivated to seek a course of action that will help fulfill and meet the need. David revealed that he had a servant's heart when he wrote in Ps. 25:4,5, "Show me Your ways, O Lord; Teach me Your paths. Lead me in Your truth and teach me for You are the God of my salvation; On You I wait all the day."

Solomon also testified that good help is hard to find when he wrote, "Most men will proclaim their own goodness, but who can find a faithful man?" (Prov. 20:6). To be a servant of God one must die to self and put aside their personal agendas and choose to live a life for a cause much more noble than their own self interests. Without much outside motivation a faithful person keeps moving forward each day driven by their mission and the Word of God in their heart. They do not grow weary in well doing as they perform the same righteous tasks day in and day out. A faithful person will never give up as they look for opportunities to serve and witness because of their love for Jesus and the Word of God. God is looking for those who are faithful and willing to do whatever it takes to get the job done. In Matt. 20:16 Jesus concluded the parable of the laborers by making what could be considered a shocking statement. He said, "For many are called but few chosen."

A careful study will reveal that, in truth, we are all called to be laborers for God (Rom. 8:28-30; 2 Peter 1:3). We are chosen only if and when we respond to the call. To do this we must first and foremost have a willing heart (Ex. 35:5) and mind (2 Cor.8:12) that is ready to obey (Is. 1:19) the voice of the Lord. A better example of a person willing to be used of God cannot be found than in the call on the life of the prophet Isaiah. In Is. 6:8 we read, "Also I heard the voice of the Lord saying; 'Whom shall I send, and who will go for Us?' Then I said, 'Here am I! Send me.'" David wrote in Ps. 110:3a, "Your people shall be volunteers in the day of Your power." God does not choose the idle or the hesitant; He calls those who are ready, willing, and prepared to labor faithfully in His kingdom. Those who submit to His call understand that obedience may demand sacrifice, but they count no price too high to fulfill the purpose God has placed on their lives. These are the ones who can rightfully be called "the chosen few."

| 19 |

"HOOKED ON MINISTRY"

A wonderful transformation took place the moment you were born-again. Once destined to a life of eternal destruction, Jesus snatched you from a fiery grave and placed you into His heavenly family. Gal. 4:7 says, "Therefore, you are no longer a slave but a son, and if a son, then an heir of God through Christ." God has elevated all believers to the high position of being His very own sons and daughters and in John 15:15 Jesus calls those who follow and obey Him "friends." Because of the great love poured out for the whole world on Calvary's tree it has become the privilege and honor of believers everywhere to give their lives back to Him in loyal and devout servitude. It will stir the fire of motivation inside if you to understand that servanthood is a promotion in the kingdom of God. You get born a child of God but get promoted to the high calling of being a servant of God. This promotion occurs when you choose to willfully surrender your will to the will of the Heavenly Father.

Joshua said, "Choose you this day whom you shall serve. As for me and my house, we will serve the Lord" (Joshua 24:15). For His service God is not going to use just anybody. He is only going to use those believers who are willing to make the necessary sacrifices required to become His servants. To do this you must count the cost by daily dying to your own self-will for a servant will always put the needs and desires of his Master above his own. In the New Testament Peter, Paul, James, Jude, and Jesus all classified themselves as servants. The willingness to serve is the mark of spiritual greatness. To be a servant Jesus said we must humble ourselves as a little child. To be humble means to be submissive. It means to take your authority, power, and independence and yield them to another. On a recent adventure a rock climber saw something that taught him a valuable lesson on the subject of humility.

Two mountain goats stood facing each other on a narrow ledge, one going up the mountain, the other coming down. There was not enough room for both of them to pass by at the same time so there they stood facing each other in a silent confrontational showdown. The climber watched in utter amazement as the goat going up the mountain lowered itself down onto its knees and then laid down further onto its stomach and became perfectly still as it allowed the other goat to walk over him on its way down the mountain. Once passed over the goat got to its feet and continued its journey up the mountain. The lesson here is that when you humble yourself in the sight of the Lord you may sometimes be walked over and downtrodden but ultimately the Lord will lift you up to success and victory. On the other hand, self-centered and prideful people who walk over others are all heading downhill on the path to defeat and destruction.

There is nobody in the body of Christ who's supposed to be doing nothing. You didn't get saved so you can play more golf or watch TV without pain. You got saved to serve. Paul told Titus, "This is a faithful saying, and these things I want you to affirm constantly, that those who have believed in God should be careful to maintain good works. These things are good and profitable to men" (Titus 3:8). The NIV says, "Those who have trusted in God may be careful to devote themselves to doing what is good." In vs. 14 Paul said, "And let our people also learn to maintain good works, to meet urgent needs, that they may not be unfruitful." You can be saved and filled with the Holy Spirit and still live an unproductive life. If all you do is live for yourself you will have an empty, useless life and, on the day you breathe your last breath, the words of Solomon will ring true, "Vanity of vanities, all is vanity. What profit has a man from all his labor in which he toils under the sun?" (Eccl. 1:2,3).

The reward for doing good works is that what you do for God will never be forgotten. "And whoever gives one of these little ones only a cup of cold water in the name of a disciple, assuredly, I say to you, he shall by no means lose his reward" (Mark 10:42). With God the smallest task can take on eternal significance. Ps. 84:10 says, "I'd rather be a doorkeeper in the house of God than dwell in the tents of wickedness." With utmost urgency make serving God the top priority of your life. Don't make it your second choice and don't put it off until tomorrow. Many people think it's highly spiritual to put their family first but, if they do that, then God is not first. There is only room at the top of your priority list for one person and it must be God. Some people are so busy with their families that they don't have time for God. There is grave danger in doing this because, if you put your family first, you are teaching them to put themselves first. You are teaching them that they are the center of the universe and not God.

Yes, love your spouse and your children with all that is within you and, together as a team, make God and your service to Him the top priority of your lives. There is no better example of a family who did this than the household of Stephanas. Paul said in 1 Cor. 16:14,15, "Let all that you do be done with love. I urge you, brethren - you know the household of Stephanas, that it is the firstfruts of Achaia, and that they have devoted themselves to the ministry of the saints." This family gave themselves wholly to the work of the ministry and did works of service with great heartiness, diligence, and zeal. The AKJB translation says, "They addicted themselves to the ministry of the saints." They were serving so consistently, so regularly, that it was like an addiction. They were hooked on ministry. There is something down on the inside of you driving you to get addicted to something. It's human nature to want to get "high" on some adrenaline rush that brings excitement.

Deep calls unto deep and people use worldly substances to fill that void. They drive fast cars, jump out of airplanes, take drugs, and go to casinos all for the purpose of feeling good. This "high" they feel is short lived and it never satisfies so they do it again and again until a lethal addiction occurs. This is all a substitute for serving God so don't be deceived by trying to satisfy your cravings with worldly things. Serving satisfies and, if you're not addicted to it, you'll be addicted to something else. Serving is one addiction that's good. It satisfies. It gives you what you're looking for. It fills the void that only God can fill and it makes you want to serve more and more. It will get you "high" on the Most High. Jesus said in John 15:10,11, "If you keep My commandments, you will abide in My love, just as I have kept My Father's commandments and abide in His love. These things I have spoken to you, that My joy may be in you, and that your joy may be full."

His joy becomes your joy when God's love flows through you to others. This gives you the "high" you so desperately need and crave. This is what happened in the churches of Macedonia. Paul writes in 2 Cor. 8:2-5, "That in a great trial of affliction the abundance of their joy and their deep poverty abounded in the riches of their liberality. For I bear witness that according to their ability, yes, and beyond their ability, they were freely willing, imploring us with much urgency that we would receive the gift and the fellowship of the ministering to the saints. And this they did, not as we had hoped, but first gave themselves to the Lord, and then to us by the will of God." The NLT says "they begged us again and again for the privilege of sharing in the gift for the believers in Jerusalem." Fierce troubles came down on these people but their trials only exposed how incredibly happy they were. They had given themselves without reservation to God and now they were earnestly pleading and begging with much urgency for the chance to help their brothers and sisters in the Lord.

The heart of these people wanted to serve and they, too, were addicted to ministry. They knew it's not a sacrifice to serve, it's a privilege, an honor! It's a privilege to push that broom, to clean that toilet, to change that diaper, to wash those smelly feet. This is all kingdom business and it never stops. It just keeps going and going and gets bigger and bigger. There is no task too small or insignificant if it does something to help somebody else. There is no such thing as a person who can't do anything. Even the useless can become useful. If you are paralyzed you can still pray and walk in faith. In Philemon 10, 11 Paul writes, "I appeal to you for my son Onesimus, whom I have begotten while in my chains, who once was unprofitable to you, but now is profitable to you and to me." Onesimus was in prison for being useless. If you're not occupied doing something good you'll be available for something bad. The NIV says about Onesimus, "Formerly he was useless to you, but now he has become useful both to you and me."

Paul told Timothy to be "useful to the Master and prepared to do any good work" (2 Tim. 2:21 NIV). He later told his young protege, "Get Mark and bring him with you for he is useful to me for ministry" (vs. 4:11). Mark had earlier abandoned Paul on a missionary journey but now the useless has become useful. Opportunities are there if you'll pursue them and make them your top priority. If you will take the first step God will enhance your ability to bring your service to people many times over. God will give you all things that pertain to life and godliness (2 Peter 1:3) so that you can serve Him and be a blessing to others. When you commit yourself to taking care of God's business, when you get addicted to ministry, He'll provide you with whatever you need to get the job done. Jesus told Peter to "Come" and Peter received the power to walk on the water. Jesus is also telling you to "Come, follow Me" and, when you embrace the call, He'll give whatever you need to fulfill that which you've been called to do.

Peter's mother-in-law was sick with a high fever and Jesus "stood over her and rebuked the fever, and it left her. And immediately she arose and served them" (Luke 4:39). This woman needed a healing in order to serve her guests and Jesus gave it to her. In Luke 8 certain women had been healed of evil spirits and various infirmities and they "provided for Him from their substance" (vs. 2,3). This is what Godly provision is for. You're healed to help others, set free to be a blessing to those around you. These women did not look back at their past problems but immediately set out to serve others. To serve is a privilege and, if you hesitate, you're not qualified. Too many people put too much time, energy, and effort into things that don't matter, things that don't have eternal significance. But when you addict yourself to the ministry of the saints, fullness of joy comes and true satisfaction will engulf your entire being. The more you help people the more happy you'll be and the higher you'll get.

John 15:13 says, "Greater love has no one than this, than to lay down his life for his friends." Paul said in 2 Cor. 12:15, "And I will very gladly spend and be spent for your souls." The Message Bible says, "I'd be most happy to empty my pockets, even mortgage my life, for your good." The NIV states, "So I will very gladly spend for you everything I have and expend myself as well." Everybody in the body of Christ has a ministry. 1 Cor. 12:28 lists the ministry of helps as a definite position in the church just like apostles, prophets, evangelists, teachers, and pastors. A small percentage of people have speaking gifts that allow them to stand behind a pulpit but all believers have been called to the ministry of helps. Don't think your position is unimportant because you're not on the platform in front of a large crowd of people. Most people have the need and desire to be noticed and acknowledged so they downplay the importance of the helps ministry. These people are carnally minded and of little value to others.

Those who are spiritually mature are always willing to be in the background where nobody sees them or knows who they are. The Lord knows everything and He sees all you do and He'll never forget your labor of love. Don't prompt people to sing your praises and don't boast about all you've done. Nobody says people have to notice and appreciate what you do. The Lord knows and, for the spiritually mature, that's all that matters. The ministry of helps is a big canopy that covers a wide area of things to do to help the body of Christ. 1 Samuel 10 tells the story of how Saul became king and shows how the ministry of helps is more important than most people think. After Samuel anointed Saul to be king, vs. 25,26 says, "Then Samuel explained to the people the behavior of royalty, and wrote it in a book and laid it up before the Lord. And Samuel sent all the people away, every man to his house. And Saul also went home to Gibeah; and valiant men went with him, whose hearts God had touched."

Saul needed help to be king and at the very beginning of his reign God touched the hearts of several brave men to help him. These men may have been naturally gifted in and of themselves but there is a spiritual aspect to being a good helper. God touched their hearts and they were able to go out and fulfill their mission. In like manner, there is also a spiritual aspect to cleaning carpets, changing diapers, and being a parking lot attendant. When God touches your heart, you'll do anything that needs to be done. Don't make restrictions on what you're willing to do and always be open minded. If you're pushing a broom to sweep the floor, just remember that it's God's broom and it's His floor. To be addicted to the ministry of the saints you must have the heart of a helper, a heart that God has touched. A true helper has an unselfish heart and these type of people are very rare. The nature of the flesh is selfishness and most people have themselves and what they want on their mind.

Many believers are afraid people will take advantage of them so they don't pray to God and ask Him to use them. There is a difference between being used and abused and, because they don't know the difference, they choose to do nothing at all. A good helper, however, has no such fears and doesn't have the need to make all the decisions. Faithful followers help leaders based on what's in the leader's heart and not what's in their own. 1 Samuel tells the story about the faith of Saul's son Jonathan and how he was willing to face the garrison of the enemy Philistine army on his own. Vs. 6,7 says, "Then Jonathan said to the young man who bore his armor, 'Come, let us go over to the garrison of these uncircumcised; it may be that the Lord will work for us. For nothing restrains the Lord from saving by many or by few.' So his armorbearer said to him, 'Do all that is in your heart. Go then, here I am with you, according to your heart.'"

This was an unselfish response and how encouraged Jonathan must have felt to have his servant respond this way. Jonathan had a plan on how to defeat the enemy and together these two men went out and won a major victory. There is a specific call on the life of every believer that goes above and beyond the ministry of helps. Before this call can be fulfilled, more times than not, God will use you to help fulfill the call on someone else's life. Jesus said in Luke 16:12, "And if you have not been faithful in what is another man's, who will give you what is your own?" Being a good helper brings maturity, growth, and proves faithfulness. Submit yourself to the leadership of those over you and do what needs to be done. Help them the way they want you to help them and not the way you feel they should be helped. Take yourself out of the equation and don't assume you know what's best. Ask for specific instructions on what they want you to do and then go out and do it with everything you've got.

1 Thess. 5:12,13 says, "And we urge you, brethren, to recognize those who labor among you, and are over you in the Lord and admonish you, and to esteem them very highly in love for their work's sake." Know those who are over you. Know what they like and don't like. Pride always has a better idea but humble yourself and help people the way they want to be helped. A faithful person is a dependable helper who can be counted on

to do what they say they'll do. They always show up on time, and they'll always be where they're supposed to be. Paul describes his helper Timothy in Phil. 2:20-22, "For I have no one like-minded, who will sincerely care for your state. For all seek their own, not the things which are of Christ Jesus. But you know his proven character, that as a son with his father he served with me in the gospel." Get to know the person you're helping and how they like things done. Like-mindedness is one aspect of an unselfish heart.

Know also that helping somebody doesn't mean you'll get close to them. A leader's privacy is precious to them and just because you're called to help them doesn't mean you're going to be their fishing buddy. You can help somebody without spending any personal time with them. If you get too close to a leader, whether it be the pastor at church or the boss at work, you'll have a hard time taking their correction or receiving direction from them. Some people want something in return for their help and if the leader doesn't give them the time they feel they deserve they walk away hurt and offended. This is not proper behavior for one who is addicted to ministry. A faithful helper is there when you need them and not there when you don't. Don't overstay your welcome. Don't hang around when it's not necessary. Do your job and leave. Don't stay unless you're asked to stay.

Helping is more than mechanical acts of labor. God looks at the heart, and a good helper is one whose heart has been touched by God. You must be unselfish, humble, and submissive. You are no longer your own. You were bought with a price and when Jesus is Lord you die to what you want. A faithful servant has no agenda of his own and each morning he wakes up and says, "Lord, not my will but Your will be done." There is amazing happiness and freedom in doing this. It's already been decided what you're supposed to do, and this means you don't have to figure everything out. The Master knows everything and all you have to do is hear from Him and discover what you're foreordained to do. God will not have compelled servants because love cannot exist where there is no choice. Life is short and opportunities to serve are precious. Become like the household of Stephanas. Get addicted to ministry and then go out and change your world.

| 20 |

"TOUR OF DUTY"

This world is like one big, giant airport. Every day there are thousands of arrivals and every day there are thousands of departures. Almost without fail those who are closing in on their departure date testify that the latter years of their life pass by much faster than the years of their youth. The Bible says your life is like a mist. You're here today, gone tomorrow. Ps. 39:4 (NL) says, "Lord, remind me how brief my time on earth will be. Remind me that my days are numbered - and that my life is fleeting away." Since our time here on earth is so brief we must all seriously consider that the day will soon be upon us when we will stand before God and be held accountable for what we did with the one life we've been given. Some people spend all their time and energy trying to get the corner office on the top floor of the highest skyscraper. They sacrifice their life, family, and any chance of having a relationship with God so they can one day retire, play golf, and go on Caribbean cruises one or twice a year.

They achieve their goals when suddenly and unexpectedly the doctor informs them that they've got six months to live. The result of all this is a wasted life with nothing of eternal value to show for it. Throughout the Bible we are warned to avoid the lifestyle that allows us to gain the whole world but lose our own soul. The rich young ruler refused to sell what he had and give to the poor so he could follow Jesus. Little did he know that no hearse ever had a U-Haul pulled behind it. In no way does God not want us to have nice things and live the good life. All He requires is that we put Him first and when you seek first the expansion of His kingdom then all these things will be added unto you (Matt. 6:33). Paul writes in 1 Tim. 6:17,18, "Command those who are rich in this present age not to be haughty, nor to trust in uncertain riches but in the living God, who gives us richly all things to enjoy. Let them do good, that they may be rich in good works, ready to give, willing to share."

The Message Bible tells us "to do good, to be rich in helping others, to be extravagantly generous." This is our purpose for living; the reason we arrived on this planet. Every person who is here is supposed to be in active service in God's kingdom, but too many people value their own life more than their service to God. They live for themselves and don't realize that God has something better for them, a life of greater influence in the world and usefulness in His kingdom. Sad to say, excuses abound as to why people don't step forward to serve God. They say they're too young or else they're too old, too poor, or too rich. They think they're too busy to serve God or else they're too important or live too far away. These people are too occupied with their own lives and don't realize this is the greatest enemy to serving God. They need to die to themselves and their own self-interests and put God first because time will come and go and before they know it their life will be over.

Jesus spoke about this in Luke 14 when He told the Parable of the Great Supper. He said in vs.16,17, "A certain man gave a great supper and invited many and sent his servant at supper time to say to those who were invited, 'Come, for all things are now ready.'" The Lord depicted a feast on a scale of great magnificence given for the purpose of bringing people together for a time of rejoicing and fellowship. In the East men of rank and affluence would send out two calls to a planned feast. The first was given so the people could make all the necessary preparations for accepting the invitation. The second call came later and told the people the feast was now ready and that the invited should stop what they were engaged in and go to the feast. This same invitation has gone out to every person who's ever been born, and it is a great privilege to be invited by the Lord to be a part of what is His. Unfortunately, not every person feels this way.

Jesus said in vs 18, "But they all with one accord began to make excuses." Animated by one spirit and moved by the same impulse all those who received the first invitation to the supper begged to be excused. In their refusal to go is the implication of hostility toward the host so they began to make up excuses for refusing his generous offer. "The first one said to him, 'I have bought a piece of ground, and I must go and see it. I ask you to have me excused'" (vs. 18). This is a lame excuse for one can hardly conceive of anybody buying anything before seeing it first. He would need to know if the land was flat or if rolling hills covered the landscape. Was the soil rich for planting or was the acreage covered with stony ground? How would the land respond to a heavy rainfall? Could it retain moisture and sustain itself during a dry season? All these facts needed to be considered before a purchase was made.

Also, this grand feast took place at supper time which was in the evening so even if he had foolishly bought the land without seeing it first, he could have easily seen it earlier in the day or else wait until the following morning. "And another said, 'I have bought five yokes of oxen, and I am going to test them. I ask you to have me excused'" (vs. 19). A small farm would only need one or two oxen but five yoke of oxen would be for a large plantation which means that like the landowner this was a wealthy man. Nobody ever bought oxen without testing them first to see how strong they were, so this was another lame excuse. "Still another said, 'I have married a wife, and therefore I cannot come.'" (vs. 20). This was the rudest response and had this man not been so selfish he could have gone to the feast with his new bride and given her a pleasant night out. All three excuses may differ in terms but all three express an immersion in worldly affairs that left them with no time for God.

Multitudes today are invited to the same gospel feast and respond in the same way as described by Jesus so long ago. It was for this reason that Paul wrote in 2 Tim. 2:3,4, "You therefore must endure hardship as a good soldier of Jesus Christ. No one engaged in warfare entangles himself with the affairs of this life, that he may please him who enlists him as a soldier." The word "entangle" means 'braid, twist, to weave like a crown of thorns.' It means to become involved in an activity to the point of interference with other activities of objectives. There is a difference between involvement and entanglement. Like a ram whose horns are caught in the brush one is entangled when he is not free to get loose. When worldly pleasures and the business affairs of this life hem us in so tightly that we can't get loose to fulfill the Lord's commands then we have become entangled in the thorns of non-eternal pursuits.

Entanglement is the act of getting so involved in something that one becomes restricted and controlled and is no longer free to do what should be done. Samson got entangled with Delilah and Lot got entangled with Sodom. Deut. 20:5-8 warns a man not to go to war if there are unsettled affairs in his life. The battle is serious and a soldier cannot be distracted by entanglements of business and worldly affairs. We are all called to be soldiers in the army of the Lord, and our tour of duty begins when we arrive on this planet and ends when we leave. We've got a job to do and we're not here to wile away the hours just to see how much fun we can have or how many toys we can buy. Paul describes the Christian soldier as one who is wholly focused, refusing to be distracted by the entanglements of this world, with a heart undivided in its devotion to Christ. His life is marked by singleness of purpose where loyalty, discipline, and commitment outweigh every competing interest.

Detachment from extraneous cares is essential for successful service and we must not entangle ourselves with worldly affairs to the point that we are diverted and drawn away from our tour of duty and the great concerns of our Christianity. No one when engaged in military service allows himself to become involved in civilian pursuits nor does he waste his time doing the things that most people do. A soldier in the fight needs to concentrate on the task of doing the Lord's work and must avoid all preoccupation with the daily affairs of life in order to be free to obey without hesitation or hindrance the orders of the commander-in-chief. He must not let anything distract him or stop him and he must put all of his effort and energy into the fight for his aim is to please the one for whom he is fighting. Like soldiers, Christians should work hard to do what the Lord wants and not get involved with things that would prevent them from doing this. Their main purpose is to please the Lord whom they serve.

We are called to be in the world but not to be entangled by it. 1 John 2:15 says, "Do not love the world or the things in the world. If anyone loves the world, the love of the Father is not in him." If you want to get serious about serving God, then there are going to be times when you can't do some of the things that other people do. Moses refused to be called the son of Pharoah's daughter choosing rather to suffer affliction with the people of God than to enjoy the passing pleasures of sin (Heb. 11:24,25). Soldiers in the field must avoid anything that hampers their effectiveness in battle. They are to be so consumed with their duties that they are oblivious to the enticements of this world and the non-essentials of life. In the Parable of the Sower Jesus said, "Now he who received seed among the thorns is he who hears the word, and the cares of this world and the deceitfulness of riches choke the word, and he becomes unfruitful" (Matt. 13:22).

Many concerns and activities in this life are innocent in and of themselves, but people have allowed them to crowd out the primary purpose of serving God in the advancement of His kingdom (see Luke 9:57-62). Instead, the active service for Christ must always occupy the prominent place in our hearts while the things of this life are kept in the background. The active soldier must forever be on guard against becoming so involved in such matters that he no longer feels free to give himself fully to the call of Christian service. We cannot have the mentality of a civilian who sits on the sidelines and does nothing. Some believers think they can be Christians but not have to fight as a soldier but they are deceiving themselves. All believers are called, delivered, and set free so they can be in active service to the Lord and will always be on the front lines of battle whether they realize it or not.

Serving God is hazardous duty and one must be able to endure hardship and be strong in the grace that is in Christ Jesus (2 Tim. 2:1-3). Soldiers find out early on that they're not called to a life of ease and comfort. They are tough warriors and there is no room for whining crybabies in the army of the Lord. A soldier fights in all conditions whether it be in the rain, snow, or 110-degree heat. They'll crawl in the mud, run in a storm, eat out of a can, sleep under the stars, carry heavy equipment, and go long hours without rest or sleep. They train hard and will do whatever it takes to win and overcome. They will go anywhere, at any time, at any cost. Active service calls for rigorous self-discipline and unquestioning obedience for a soldier is always on duty and needs to be alert around the clock. Total commitment is necessary to be a good soldier, and his training is designed to make him obey the word of command.

A soldier is conditioned for obedience and with much vigilance puts priority on his calling and the task at hand. Wholehearted devotion, marked by hard work and careful attention to God's Word, brings the greatest glory to the Lord. Time is going by fast and what you do for yourself won't matter a short time from now. Life is more than having fun all the time and only those who are doers of the Word get fully developed and receive eternal rewards and benefits. You will never be satisfied and fulfilled on the inside until you do something for somebody else. People of honor are always ready and willing to serve anytime, anywhere. The greatest expression of love is giving (John 3:16) and your service is the keeping of the love command. This doesn't mean you can't have a family, job, or hobbies. You just need a revelation that this is not what life is all about. It is foolish to live just for this life. People live like they'll be here forever, but the truth is that your life on this planet is the shortest thing you'll ever do.

The longer you live the faster you realize this life is passing you by quickly. You were not made for this life; you were made for eternity. A good soldier must not allow the ordinary affairs of life to become the main object of his existence. Paul was a tent maker, but this was only a means to further his passion of preaching Christ crucified. You will have no regrets if you sacrifice things in this life in order to complete your mission. This world is not your home, so live with the awareness that life here is brief and every moment carries eternal significance. Fix your heart on the world to come, where God's promises are fulfilled and true, lasting life awaits. All Christians have been delivered from the fear of death and if you're not afraid to die you can become a courageous soldier in the army of the Lord. We've all been invited to the great feast of the Master and when the call comes the only acceptable response is "Here I am."

Gen. 22:11 says, "But the Angel of the Lord called to him from heaven and said, 'Abraham, Abraham!' And he said, 'Here I am.'" In Gen. 46:2 we read, "Then God spoke to Israel in the vision of the night, and said, 'Jacob, Jacob!' And he said, 'Here I am.'" Moses said the same thing in Ex. 3:4 as did Samuel in 1 Sam. 3:4. Is. 6:8 tells how the Lord needed somebody to go on a mission for Him and Isaiah said, "Here am I! Send me." Jesus called the fishermen Peter and Andrew to follow Him and "they immediately left their nets and followed Him" (Matt. 4:20). To go on with the Lord and fulfill the call He has for you requires great levels of commitment and dedication. Daniel continued in his service to the Lord and through decades he did not swerve from his loyalty to God and his devotion to the high interests that were committed to his charge (see Dan. 1:21). The world does not want the flash of a meteor but the constant radiance of a fixed star.

When you put your hand to the plow never look back to the fleeting pleasures that this life has to offer. God will call you out of your comfort zone and if you're willing to turn loose of some things you'll quickly find out how better off you'll be when you obey the Lord in every way. If God calls you to another state of country, then you must go where He tells you to go and stay where He tells you to stay. Good soldiers go where they're sent and stay where they're stationed. Soldiers come and go on command, and you must follow Him and go where He is at for you. If you are called to the wastelands of Siberia, then that is where God is at for you. It takes faith to turn loose of what seems like security to you and go to a place you are not familiar with. Abraham left his home not knowing where he was going but he knew God's commands were His enablings. He didn't know the details, but he knew the direction and he promptly obeyed.

Like Abraham follow the orders of the Commander-In-Chief and His Word will give you the faith and ability to overcome any fear and to fulfill that which you've been called to do. There is a place for you and a service you are to perform. When you turn loose of your self-will and submit to the will of God then fullness of joy will overwhelm you. If you don't step out and obey, you'll never know what you've missed. The children of Israel didn't cross over the Jordan River and died in the wilderness. Do whatever it takes to fulfill your role as a soldier of the Lord. If you don't, you'll be unhappy all the time and you'll never be satisfied or fulfilled. Rarely will things go right for you, and it was all brought about by selfish disobedience. The selfish life is a miserable life, and the giving life is the fulfilled life. There are sacrifices to be made and much effort is needed but it will make you feel good and want to wake up each morning.

Spend your time doing something useful and worthwhile. Be not unfruitful but be productive and excel in good works and hospitality. The word "excel" means 'to super abound' and means you will do way more than what is adequate, to go above and beyond what is needed. Soldiers in the army of the Lord are eager and enthusiastic about doing good works, advancing the kingdom of God, and pushing the devil out of the way. When on duty soldiers are always busy doing something. They're never idle or lazy and they never lay around and do nothing. James 2:20 says, "faith without works is dead." A better rendering would be to say, "Faith without working is dead." Faith that does nothing is a dead faith and is worth nothing. The woman with the issue of blood was weak from her ailment but she pressed through the crowd anyway. She worked to get to Jesus, and this is what secured her healing. You, also, cannot be idle. You must get up and do something.

There are too many non-working people in the church today and Paul says we are to keep away from such people. 2 Thess. 3:6 (NIV) states, "In the name of the Lord Jesus Christ, we command you, brothers and sisters, to keep away from every believer who is idle and disruptive and does not live according to the teaching you received from us." If the non-working man is included in everything you're doing, then he'll think everything is all right. Paul continues in vs. 7, "For you yourselves know how you ought to follow our example. We were not idle when we were with you." Vs. 10, "For even when we were with you, we gave you this rule: 'The one who is unwilling to work shall not eat.'" Vs. 11, "We hear that some among you are idle and disruptive. They are not busy; they are busybodies." Vs.

12,13, "Such people we command and urge in the Lord Jesus Christ to settle down and earn the food they eat. And as for you, brothers and sisters, never tire of doing what is good."

1 Cor. 3:9 says, "We are God's fellow workers." We are laborers in the kingdom of God and work is what we've been called to do. What are you doing in your service to the Lord? At church most people come, they sit, they listen, and then they leave. You will not see them or hear from them again until the following Sunday morning. These are the very people Paul says we are to avoid. The Message Bible translation says, "Our orders - backed up by the Master, Jesus - are to refuse to have anything to do with those among you who are lazy and refuse to work the way we taught you." This may seem like a harsh command but if you fellowship with the wrong people long enough there is the chance that you will become as they are. Bad company corrupts good habits. In the Parable of the Talents the man who buried his was idle and got thrown into everlasting darkness where there will be weeping and gnashing of teeth (Matt. 25:30).

We are warned several times in scripture not to be idle, lazy, and slothful. Rom. 12:10,11 tells us, "Be kindly affectionate to one another with brotherly love, in honor giving preference to one another; not lagging in diligence, fervent in spirit, serving the Lord." The Living Bible says, "never be lazy in your work but serve the Lord enthusiastically." An enemy to your service to the Lord is slothfulness so never put off until tomorrow what you can be doing today. Your window of opportunity to serve is short and if you put things off long enough you won't do it. There is a limited time window on your life and if you're not careful, you'll miss the chance to serve and then you'll depart this planet without having done anything at all. Jesus wept and wailed over Jerusalem because they failed to recognize the moment of God's visitation and rejected the Messiah sent to bring them peace (Luke 19:41-44).

The book of Proverbs has a lot to say about slothfulness. Prov. 6:9 says, "How long will you slumber, O sluggard? When will you rise from your sleep?" Laziness loves to sleep. It goes to bed early, sleeps late, gets up to eat, and then takes a nap. Prov. 26:14 says, "As a door turns on its' hinges, so does the slothful turn on his bed." A door moves but doesn't go anywhere and so it is with the slothful. It's all about being comfortable but the more you yield to slothfulness the worse you'll feel. Prov. 20:4 tells us, "The sluggard will not plow because of winter; Therefore, he will beg during the harvest and have nothing." The slothful person yields to the flesh and is always making excuses. The sluggard will not plow his fields for it's either too cold or else it's too hot. There is a specific season to plant and pretty soon it will be too late to plow and prepare the soil. Poverty comes on the slothful man, and he'll beg in harvest but will have nothing. If you don't work, neither shall you eat.

Prov. 24:30,31 states, "I went by the field of the slothful, and by the field of the man devoid of understanding; and there it was all overgrown with thorns; Its' surface was covered with nettles; Its' stone wall was broken down." Prov. 22:13 says, "The slothful man says, 'There is a lion outside! I shall be slain in the streets!'" The slothful man is safety conscious and always has a reason not to work. He looks out his window and says, "Lions, and tigers, and bears! Oh my!!" These savage predators dwell in the wilderness and never roam on city streets. This is all an excuse not to work, and the slothful man returns to his bed where he will sleep his life away. In this life you are going to serve something or someone and there is nobody better to serve than the Lord. Because of His great mercies upon us it is just reasonable that we serve Him. He created us, He sustains us, and He purchased us with His own blood. God set you free from the chains of bondage in order that you may serve Him.

God sent Moses to Egypt with these instructions, "Then you shall say to Pharoah, 'Thus says the Lord: "Israel is My son, My firstborn. So I say to you, let my Son go that he may serve Me"'" (Ex. 4:22,23). The same thing was said in Ex. 7:16; 8:1,20;9:1,13;10:3. The people were already serving the Egyptians, but God set them free so they could serve Him and so it is with us today. After the people crossed the Red Sea and were delivered from bondage God gave them the Ten Commandments and the first one said, "You shall have no other gods before Me" (Ex. 20:3). Our God is a jealous God, and we are not to make a god out of material things. Worship is intimate and worshipping a false god is spiritual adultery and unfaithfulness. You will serve something and if you don't serve God, you will serve something else. God said in Deut. 28:47,48, "Because you did not serve the Lord your God with joy and gladness of heart, for the abundance of all things, therefore you shall serve your enemies."

Paul wrote in Rom. 6:16, "Do you not know that to whom you present yourselves slaves to obey, you are that one's slaves whom you obey, whether of sin to death, or of obedience to righteousness?" You are a servant to whom you obey. Some people serve their own belly and lustful appetites. They serve alcohol, drugs, money, and power. The devil wants to be served like God (Matt. 4:9) and he uses these fleshly cravings to draw you into a web of deceit where these entanglements will destroy your life. Serving God, however, is a joy, a privilege, and we are to serve Him with gladness. We are not here merely to enjoy the moment or drift through life seeking comfort and ease. We are here on a mission, called to serve with purpose, discipline, and resolve. A good soldier understands that this life is a tour of duty meant to be completed faithfully, not abandoned for temporary pleasures.

We're in the trenches with the devils and the diseases. We're here to rub elbows with those who are hurting and need a friend to lean on. We are here to make a positive difference in the world by living out the love God has poured into our lives. Our devotion to Him is not proven by words alone, but by the way we serve, uplift, and care for others. When we love people well, we reflect God's heart and become instruments of His grace in a hurting world. Nothing is too little or trivial if done with the right attitude and a heart of love. The older you get the faster the years go by so do something that matters today. Don't waste precious opportunities to serve God. Wake up every morning and say, "Lord, here I am. What would you have me do today? How can I be of service to You? Where can I help? What can I do to advance Your kingdom? How can I be

of service to Your children and the church today? Here am I!
Send me."

| 21 |

"A WILLING HEART"

Christianity is more than just you and God. It's more than getting saved and being healed and becoming prosperous. It's more than sitting back in a comfortable chair waiting to see what God is going to do for you next. If all you do is think about yourself and how your faith can get you a new house and a new car then you have missed the heartbeat of God. True Christianity is about giving something back once you've tasted the goodness of the Lord. Matt. 10:8b says, "Freely you have received, freely give." The only people in the body of Christ who are blessed are the doers. Many go to church and take notes and read books and listen to CD's and that's all they do. They're so heavenly minded they're no earthly good. They don't understand that you won't grow up and develop into a mature Christian if you don't step out and become a doer of the Word and not a hearer only (James 1:22). Christianity is fulfilling the call on your life; the plan and purpose God has for you and that includes serving other people.

You were born to love and called to serve and 1 John 4:11 says, "Beloved, if God so loved us, we also ought to love one another." Mature Christians understand service for the love of God stirs them up and motivates them to meet the needs of other people. It's their call, their destiny, it's what they were predestined to do. Paul writes in Eph. 2:10, "For we are His workmanship, created in Christ Jesus for good works, which God prepared beforehand that we should walk in them." The Message Bible says, "He creates each of us by Christ Jesus to join Him in the work He does, the good work He has gotten ready for us to do, work we had better be doing." Those who truly love God with all their heart, soul, and mind do not see service as a burden but as a joyful expression of their devotion. Their love for Him overflows into a genuine excitement to serve others, knowing that in serving people they are honoring God Himself. They do good and ask for nothing in return.

Heb. 10:24,25 says, "And let us consider one another in order to stir up love and good works, not forsaking the assembling of ourselves together, as is the manner of some, but exhorting one another, and so much the more as you see the Day approaching." The Message Bible says, "Let's see how inventive we can be in encouraging love and helping out..." Indeed, the great day of the Lords' return is upon us. In fact, it could happen in the next minute or two. Since this a reality those in the body of Christ should be busy doing more for the kingdom of God instead of storing up non-perishable food hoping to survive the great apocalypse that is to come. Jesus spoke about this in the Parable of the Ten Minas when He said, "A certain nobleman went into a far country to receive for himself a king-dom and to return. So he called ten of his servants, delivered to them ten minas, and said to them, 'Do business till I come'" (Luke 19:12,13).

Other translations say, "Occupy till I come" and this means to keep busy while the Master is away. These words are the marching orders of the end-time church that is on the earth to-day. Believers should take the Lord's command to "occupy" se-riously for it is spoken to all who profess and call themselves Christian. Believers should stop letting themselves be brain-washed by this selfish culture and begin to occupy as one who looks for Christs' return. This does not mean to sit in a pew once a week and passively listen to a sermon. It's much more aggressive than that. It means to be bold and courageous, to stand up for what you believe in. To occupy means to take and hold territory, to take back what the enemy has stolen, to strive, to mold and shape the land into the image of God. Peo-ple who occupy are on the streets, day after day, clamoring for change. They are forceful, determined, and committed.

Jesus said in Matt. 5:14-16, "You are the light of the world. A city that is set on a hill cannot be hidden. Nor do they light a lamp and put it under a basket, but on a lampstand, and it gives light to all who are in the house. Let your light so shine be-fore men, that they may see your good works and glorify your Father in heaven." Rather than being swept along with the trends of society people who occupy follow and obey the teach-ings and lifestyle of Jesus. They turn their world upside down because they have the same kind of passion and persistence and willingness to sacrifice for what they believe in. This is what Jesus meant when He told His followers to take up their cross and follow Him. Make no mistake about it, there is a price to pay to serve God. It's not all fun and games and Paul tells us, "For to you it has been granted on behalf of Christ, not only to believe in Him, but also to suffer for His sake, having the same conflict which you saw in me and now hear is in me" (Phil. 1:29,30).

Paul was saying the church would suffer as he had suffered and this is why we are told to count the cost of becoming a disciple of Jesus. He writes in 2 Tim. 3:12, "Yes, and all who desire to live godly in Christ Jesus will suffer persecution." Many are the afflictions of the righteous (Ps. 34:19a) and you must be willing to pay the price to get the job done. God got angry with Moses because he didn't want to suffer and pay the price to serve Him (see Ex. 4:14). Like the rich young ruler, millions of believers are unwilling to give up anything for the privilege of being used by God. All they do is make excuses and if they do that too much it will make God angry at them as well. Paul, on the other hand, was willing and he writes in 2 Cor. 12-15a, "And I will very gladly spend and be spent for your souls..." Rev. 17:14b says about Jesus, "for He is Lord of lords and King of kings; and those who are with Him are called, chosen, and faithful." God will not beg you to do anything for Him. He calls you and then you respond.

Many are called but few are chosen (Matt. 20:16) because only a handful of believers value the call and are willing to count the cost and pay the price. God is looking for a heart that is right toward Him. 2 Chron. 16:9 says, "For the eyes of the Lord run to and fro throughout the whole earth, to show Himself strong on behalf of those whose heart is loyal to Him." A person with a royal heart is a person who is willing to do whatever God wants done without giving it a second thought. This person will obey God with no reluctance or hesitation and will do so without murmuring or complaining about the task he's been asked to do. Is. 1:19,20 says, "If you are willing and obedient, you will eat the good of the land; But if you refuse and rebel, you shall be devoured by the sword; For the mouth of the Lord has spoken." God does not look at the outward appearance of a person but He does look at the condition of the heart (1 Sam. 16:7b). You can be obedient all you want but if you're not willing it won't do you any good.

You must be willing and obedient. The willingness of your heart, followed by the obedience of your actions, determine the acceptability and the reward for all that you do in your service unto the Lord. When Paul was struck down and blinded on the road to Damascus "he, trembling and astonished, said, 'Lord, what do You want me to do?'" (Acts 9:6). Paul's willingness to obey God was the secret to his amazing success and he verbalized what the believers' view of suffering should be when he wrote Rom. 8:18, "For I consider that the sufferings of this present time are not worthy to be compared with the glory which shall be revealed in us." Having a heart that is willing and obedient will amazingly alter the way you look at things. Paul wrote in 2 Cor. 4:17, "For our light affliction, which is but for a moment, is working for us a far more exceeding and eternal weight of glory."

This man overcame shipwrecks, being lost at sea, assassination attempts, riots, beatings, stonings, imprisonment, and more (2 Cor. 11:23-33) yet he calls all this a "light affliction." From a damp and dirty prison cell that smelled of raw sewage he wrote, "Rejoice in the Lord always. Again I will say, rejoice!" (Phil. 4:4). Paul was in a dungeon but the dungeon was not in him. God never promised you an easy life but if your heart is willing and obedient toward Him you can have a victorious life. Jesus said in John 16:33, "These things I have spoken to you, that in Me you may have peace. In the world you will have tribulation; but be of good cheer, I have overcome the world." Another time He said, "Come to Me, all you who labor and are heavy laden, and I will give you rest. Take My yoke upon you and learn from Me, for I am gentle and lowly in heart, and you will find rest for your souls. For My yoke is easy and My burden is light" (Matt. 11:28-30).

The Wuest translation says, "for My yoke is mild and pleasant, and My load is light in weight." The Amplified Bible says, "For My yoke is wholesome (useful, good - not harsh, hard, sharp, or pressing, but comfortable, gracious, and pleasant), and My burden is light and easy to be borne." This yoke that we are to carry is not laid upon us by another but is one which we are to place upon ourselves. It is an act of conscious surrender to His authority and a willingness to be ruled only by Him. Paul took this yoke upon him when he said, "Lord, what do You want me to do?" Christs' yoke is the obligation to live a spiritual life, a life of thanksgiving and gratitude unto God. It is the obligation to receive Him as the Messiah, to believe His doctrine, and to be in all things conformed to His Word and to His Spirit. In coming to Jesus there is a peace that passes all understanding. Subjection to the love of God, when cheerfully complied with, will bring with it an abundance of spiritual pleasure and true delight.

His yoke is easy and His burden is light because He helps you to bear it. The commandments of God are not grievous and the services He requires of you are not burdensome but are easily rendered. His gospel imposes nothing that is difficult. On the contrary, it provides for the complete removal of all that which oppresses and renders man miserable. The love of God is a love in which the soul rests supremely satisfied and is infinitely happy even during times of trial and persecution. His yoke is easy to bear. His yoke is pleasant. His yoke is sweet, gracious, and delightful and His burden is one of ease, liberty, and honor. All who come to Jesus receive rest as His gift to them and obtain peace and comfort in their hearts. But in coming to Him you must take up your cross and follow Him. You must take His yoke and surrender to His Lordship, submit to His rule, and let His will become your will. Here you will find rest for your soul, and here only.

His yoke is easy, but it requires self-denial and a willingness to follow Him at any cost. Forced obedience is a heavy burden to bear and is far from being light and easy. On the other hand, those who die to themselves and take up their cross find that the yoke of heaven is lined with love and pleasantness. The way of duty is the way of rest and brings with it inward peace and joy. Love is as rich and vast as God Himself for God is love. Whatever God is, love is and true love is the mark of a genuine Christian. You need a firm grasp and footing on the love of God and apply it to everything you do. Your whole life is to manifest the love of God so let your words and actions be interwoven with love. You can show the world what God is like by the way you treat them so have a willing heart to gladly spend and be spent for someone else. The key to living a happy, fulfilled, and satisfied life is really very simple. Just be the person God made you to be and have the courage to do what God called you to do.

God has a unique and individual plan for your life and the way to become a champion for God is to discover that plan and follow it wherever it may lead. God doesn't just want you to do something, He wants you to want to. Paul writes in 2 Cor. 8:12, "For if there is first a willing mind, it is accepted according to what one has, and not according to what he does not have." David writes in Ps. 110:3, "Your people shall be willing in the day of Your power." Other translations say, "Your people will offer themselves willingly..." and "Your people will volunteer freely..." There is a connection between God's manifested power and your willingness to take up your cross and follow Him. At the Pool of Bethesda Jesus asked the crippled man, "Will thou be made whole?" In other words, "Are you willing?" When the man affirmed that he was the healing power of Jesus touched his life and he picked up his bed and walked away. If you're not experiencing God's best, then get more willing and obedient.

The mistake many people make is they focus too much on the "doing" and not enough on the "willing." It's not enough to just obey God. God wants you to want to. He wants you to be willing. Elevate your willingness and obedience to match God's Word. Press toward the mark to become just like Jesus. Live like Him, pray like Him, love like Him, receive like Him, obey like Him. How did Jesus obey? He did it willingly. Jesus told the Father, "Not My will but Your will be done." 1 John 2:6 says, "He who says he abides in Him ought himself also to walk just as He walked." The condition of your heart is what matters to God. In fact, it's a matter of life and death because it's the heart that determines if you are willing or unwilling to obey Him. Consider 2 Chron. 25:1,2, "Amaziah was twenty-five years old when he became king, and he reigned twenty-nine years in Jerusalem. His mother's name was Jehoadda of Jerusalem. And he did what was right in the sight of the Lord, but not with a loyal heart."

Amaziah did the right thing but his heart wasn't right. We are commanded not to judge people because we don't know their heart and motives even if they do the right thing. Only God can judge righteously because He looks at the condition of the heart. Another example of obeying God with the wrong motive is found in Matt. 6. Jesus said in vs. 2, "Therefore, when you do a charitable deed, do not sound a trumpet before you as the hypocrites do in the synagogues and in the streets, that they may have glory from men." He also said in vs. 5, "And when you pray, you shall not be like the hypocrites. For they love to pray standing in the synagogues and on the corners of the street, that they may be seen by men." The religious leaders in the days of Jesus were doing what God commands all of us to do. Doing charitable deeds and praying is all part of a Godly lifestyle but these leaders had an evil heart and all they wanted was the praise of their fellow man.

On the other hand, it's possible to make mistakes and still have a perfect heart toward God. This is good news because God doesn't look at our mistakes, He looks at the heart. In 2 Chron. 15 Asa rose up to lead Israel at a time when the nation was "without the true God, without a teaching priest, and without law" (vs. 3). The people worshipped false idols and "great turmoil was on all the inhabitants of the land" (vs. 5). Asa rose up and removed all the idols (vs. 8) and all the people "entered into a covenant to seek the Lord God of their fathers with all their heart and all their soul." Asa led these people to God but look what happened next. Vs. 16,17 says, "Also he removed Maachah, the mother of Asa the king, from being queen mother, because she had made an obscene image of Asherah; and Asa cut down her obscene image, crushed it, and burned it by the Brook Kidion. But the high places were not removed from Israel. Nevertheless, the heart of Asa was loyal all his days."

In the midst of all the good that Asa did a mistake was made. The "high places" where pagan worship took place were not removed and thus was a constant reminder of the abomination that had taken place. Asa made mistakes but his heart was perfect and complete toward God all the days of his life. People who take up their cross and walk in love will never suffer "burn out" because His yoke is easy and their light affliction is but for a moment. This is good news because being fully willing and fully obedient will keep you busy all day long. Remember, if you want what you do to be accepted and blessed then you must do it willingly. God sees the heart. He doesn't just want you to pray, He wants you to want to! He doesn't just want you to witness to somebody, He wants you to want to! Don't obey God out of a sense of religious duty or obligation. Do it because you want to. Paul writes in 2 Cor. 9:7, "So let each one give as he purposes in his heart, not grudgingly or of necessity; for God loves a cheerful giver."

This same attitude about giving should apply to all we do for the Lord. We must be cheerful and prompt to obey God. We must be willing! If not, stop what you're doing, get willing first, and then obey God. The Lord told Moses in Ex. 35:5, "Take from among you an offering to the Lord. Whoever is of a willing heart, let him bring it as an offering to the Lord, gold, silver, and bronze." Notice the people's response in vs. 21, 22, "Then everyone came whose heart was stirred, and everyone whose spirit was willing, and they brought the Lords' offering for the work of the tabernacle of meeting for all its service and for the holy garments. They came, both men and women, as many as had a willing heart." Chapter 36 records that these people were so willing to give they had to be restrained from giving more. One thing a lot of people don't realize is that in God's eyes having it in your heart is the same thing as doing it.

When Abraham laid his son Isaac on the altar to offer him up to the Lord, he did not know the angel was going to stop him. Heb. 11:17 says Abraham offered up Isaac but what really happened is that he was willing to offer up his son. His willingness made the sacrifice acceptable. If you do it in your heart, you do it. If you do it but your heart is not in it, then in God's eyes you didn't do it. In heaven people will receive rewards for what was in their heart even if they didn't get the chance to do it in the natural. God rewards you not for what you were able or unable to do but according to your heart. With a true heart you want to obey God always and further your efforts to please Him. If you make a mistake or come up short it wasn't because you weren't trying. You wanted to and this is what God sees. That alone should make you want to "want to." God wants you blessed so get willing. Don't be spiritually lazy. Submit to God and yield to His will.

Unwillingness prevents God from speaking to you. It keeps you in a foggy state and darkens your understanding. It will cloud your judgment, and you won't know if you're coming or going. But with a willing heart comes spiritual discernment. Jesus said in John 7:17, "If anyone wants to do His will, he shall know concerning the doctrine, whether it is from God or whether I speak on My own authority." When you get willing it is amazing how quickly and powerfully things can change. When you are unwilling, you hinder the plan of God for your life. The good news is that the moment you get willing God will give you revelation and direction for your life and ministry. In John 6 Jesus was walking on the water and when the disciples saw Him they were afraid. Vs. 20,21 says, "But He said to them, 'It is I; do not be afraid.' Then they willingly received Him into the boat, and immediately the boat was at the land where they were going."

A few moments before this happened the disciples were not willing, and they thought Jesus was a ghost. But after they got willing the boat was miraculously transported to their destination. Connected to this miracle was their willingness. When you get willing you immediately start to move toward where you're supposed to go. The disciples did a whole lot of rowing but got nowhere until they got willing. The quicker you get willing, the quicker you get there and the easier it is on you. The wisest thing you can ever do is get willing. Jonah learned this the hard way. God called him to preach repentance to the wicked Ninevites, but the prophet was unwilling to obey the call on his life. He ran away from his assignment and began a journey to Tarshish instead, a journey where he learned that unwillingness can get you in a whole lot of trouble. Today millions of people all over the world are doing the same thing. They are running from the presence of God and the call He placed on their lives.

Jonah 1:4 says, "But the Lord sent out a great wind on the sea, and there was a mighty tempest on the sea, so that the ship was about to be broken up." The Lord does have a way of getting your attention. Vs. 13, "Nevertheless the men rowed hard to bring the ship to land, but they could not, for the sea continued to grow more tempestuous against them." Like the disciples in John 6 they did a whole lot of rowing but got nowhere. This is what unwillingness does to you. Jonah knew this storm was because of his disobedience, so he told the men to throw him overboard. "So they picked up Jonah and threw him into the sea, and the sea ceased from its' raging" (vs. 15). They got rid of Jonahs' unwillingness and the sea grew calm. If peace is missing from your life, check and see if there is any unwillingness in your life. Jonah did but look where he did it from.

"Then Jonah prayed to the Lord his God from the fish's belly. And he said: 'I cried out to the Lord because of my affliction, and He answered me. Out of the belly of Sheol I cried, and You heard my voice'" (Jonah 2:1,2). People don't realize this but Jonah died in the belly of the whale and went to hell. This is where unwillingness will take you. If not literally then for sure all the hosts of darkness will be unleashed in your life. It can't be emphasized enough, if you're not willing, get willing! Eventually Jonah did and a great revival took place in the city of Ninevah. It is a privilege and an honor to be used by God. It's not always easy, but it is an honor. Paul was glad God counted him worthy to be put into the ministry. King Agrippa was almost persuaded (Acts 26:27,28) but almost is not good enough. If you are almost willing, then you are not willing. That's just like saying, "I almost went to church." God calls us to be fully committed because lukewarm faith reflects a heart that has not truly chosen Him.

He is calling for total and complete commitment to Him and His will, and He requires that you lay down your life to Him. Nothing less will do. You can't be a casual "Sunday only" Christian and fulfill the will of God for your life. He asks for and requires more than people realize. Jesus said to count the cost and daily take up your cross and follow Him. Some people get close enough to God to get their prayers answered and then afterward pull away and draw back. To follow God fully you must die to yourself. Yes, you will lose your life but then you'll find true life. You'll find the good life. Do you want all God has for you? If so, God wants all of you. Raise your commitment level to God and be willing to do anything for Him. You can love God more today than you did yesterday and as your love grows so will your desire to please Him. Paul was willing. Jonah was not willing. King Agrippa was almost willing. Which are you? Decide quickly for it truly is a matter of life and death.

| 22 |

"ANOINTED BOUNDARIES"

In a conversation with God about Job, the made this statement, "Have You not made a hedge around him, around his household, and all that he has on every side? You have blessed the work of his hands, and his possessions have increased in the land" (Job 1:10). What the devil was referring to is also described in the 23rd psalm. After proclaiming that the Lord was his shepherd David wrote in vs. 5, "You prepare a table before me in the presence of my enemies; You anoint my head with oil; My cup runs over." In Biblical times a shepherd would lead his flock to a field of grass. He would then pour a special oil around the feeding place, and this would prevent the serpents from coming in to attack the sheep. The sheep would be led inside this boundary and eat to their hearts' content. That oil, which is symbolic of the anointing, had become the hedge of protection that circled the herd of sheep. The master shepherd prepared a table for his flock in the presence of their enemies.

The good life is when you also have a hedge of protection round about you. The good shepherd provided his sheep with a luscious feeding ground, and they ate the good of the land as the hungry serpents were on the outside looking in. The sheep were willing to follow the voice of their master and were obedient to stay within the hedge of protection that was set for them. If one of those sheep wandered outside the hedge of protection, if they went off and did their own thing, they would be exposed and subject to the lethal appetites of those hungry serpents. Likewise, we must follow the leading of the Good Shepherd and go where He tells us to go and stay where He tells us to stay. This is serious business. Consider Ps. 80:12,13, "Why have You broken down her hedges so that all who pass by pluck her fruit? The boar out of the woods uproots it, and the wild beast of the field devours it."

Also, we read in Ps. 89:40,41, "You have broken down all the hedges; You have brought his strongholds to ruin. All who pass by the way plunders him; He is a reproach to his neighbors." In the parable of the vineyard Isaiah wrote in Is. 5:4b,5, "Why then, when I expected it to bring forth good grapes, did it bring forth wild grapes? And now, please let me tell you what I will do to My vineyard: I will take away its hedge, and it shall be burned; and break down its wall, and it shall be trampled down." God has predetermined a plan for your life. 1 Cor. 12:18 says, "But now God has set the members, each one of them, in the body just as He pleased." Don't go off and start doing your own thing. You'll step into darkness if you do. You'll trip and fall in the darkness that will consume your life. You'll be confused and if you can't see where you're going, you'll have no direction for your life. Life will be hard and frustrating, and you'll have no satisfaction or fruitfulness.

Prov. 4:18,19 says, "But the path of the just is like the shining sun, that shines ever brighter unto the perfect day. The way of the wicked is like darkness; they do not know what makes them stumble." God cannot and will not put His full measure of blessings and protection on your plan if it's different from His. Millions of people are doing their own thing and as a result of this disobedience they are unhappy and unfulfilled. People need to understand that the good life only comes when you step into that specific plan that God prepared beforehand for your life. The Amplified translation of Eph. 2:10 says, "God predestined, planned beforehand for us, taking the paths that He prepared ahead of time, that we should walk in them, living the good life which He prearranged and made ready for us to live." Parents should never tell their children, "You can be anything you want to be." They mean well when they say this but if Jesus is your Lord, then it's not up to you to decide what you will be and what you will do.

It's already been decided for you and it's up to you to discover by His grace what you've been foreordained and predestined to become and do. That's the good life. Included in God's plan for your life is a God-ordained place where you are supposed to be. Paul says this about God in Acts 17:26, "And He has made from one blood every nation of men to dwell on all the face of the earth, and has determined their pre-appointed times and the boundaries of their dwellings." Consider also 2 Sam. 7:10 where God said, "Moreover I will appoint a place for My people Israel, and will plant them, that they may dwell in a place of their own and move no more; nor shall the sons of wickedness oppress them anymore as previously." Just like those shepherd-led sheep, if the people of Israel stayed within their anointed boundaries the hungry serpents, the sons of wickedness, could not come in and destroy their lives. There is a place for everyone and to live the good life everyone must be in their place.

Provision and protection come to you when you are in your proper, predesigned place. If God tells you to go minister in some mosquito-infested swampland then don't go to some nice tropical island and try to serve God there. No, go where God tells you to go and stay where He tells you to stay. If you get out of your place judgment and destruction will come. Jude 6 says, "And the angels who did not keep their proper place, but left their own abode, He has reserved in everlasting chains under darkness for the judgment of the great day." These angels left the place God gave them and paid a heavy price for doing so. Yes, getting out of your place has serious consequences. Jesus once told His followers to "look at the birds in the air" and to "consider the lilies of the field" (Matt. 6:26,28). There is a place where those birds and flowers are supposed to be and, in order to flourish, they must be in their proper place. Orange trees don't grow in cold temperatures, and a whale can't live on dry ground.

A cactus flourishes in desert conditions and an elephant don't swim in the ocean. Nobody ever saw a kangaroo romping alongside a polar bear in the Arctic cold or penguins galloping with the wild horses in Montana. Do camels swim with Alaskan trout or do zebras soar with the eagles? No, there are boundaries where each of them belong and so it is with us. Even the planet earth is in it's proper place. If it was one mile closer to the sun it would burn up and if it was one mile further away it would freeze over. The whole universe testifies that it is important to be in your proper place. If you run away from the place you are supposed to be like Jonah did you will be vulnerable to destruction. It is dangerous and sometimes deadly to be out of your place. Like a roaring lion Satan is forever roaming the earth seeking whom he may devour (1 Peter 5:8). An easy target for that hungry serpent are those who have drifted out beyond their anointed boundaries, people who are in the wrong place at the wrong time.

The Bible is filled with stories of many such people, those who were not where they were supposed to be. When Lot left the side of Abraham and moved to Sodom he was in the wrong place. Sodom was an evil city and eventually Lot lost everything he owned, his wife died, and he just barely escaped with his own life. When the children of Israel refused to enter into the promised land but instead wandered around in the wilderness for forty years they, too, were not in their proper place. When the prodigal son was eating food fed to the pigs he was most definitely in the wrong place. All these people were not in the place they were supposed to be and all of them paid a heavy price for being in the wrong place at the wrong time. There is no better example of this than the time when one evening David walked out onto his balcony and saw Bathsheba taking a bath. It was a time of war and he should have been out on the battlefield with his men.

Instead, he wandered outside his anointed boundary, he stayed home, and eventually the serpents of lust and murder filled his life with their deadly venom. This one act of disobedience has forever tarnished the legacy of this great king who the Bible describes as "a man after God's own heart." Months later when the baby born through his union with Bathsheba died David learned all too well that the safest place on earth was within the anointed boundaries that surround the place where you are supposed to be. David learned the hard way that the biggest enemy to God's plan is your plan. Job was a man who went through a series of harsh trials but look what he said in Job 13:15, "Though He slay me, yet will I trust Him. Even so, I will defend (maintain) my own ways before Him." Job was a righteous man who trusted God but when the trials came he began to complain and grow self-righteous. Job 3:25 says, "For the thing I greatly feared has come upon me, and what I dreaded has happened to me."

This verse tells us that Job was in fear and dread before the trials came. So how did the fear get in? If you go off and do your own thing, if you hold on to your plan and maintain your own ways, you can't keep the fear out because your heart knows you've chosen your own way instead of God's. You know on the inside that you're out of your place. We read in Prov. 1: 30-32, "They would have none of my counsel and despised all my reproof, therefore they shall eat the fruit of their own way and be filled to the full with their own fancies. For the turning away of the simple will slay them, and the complacency of fools will destroy them." The safest place on the planet is the place of God's perfect will for your life. Prov. 1:33 says, "But whoever listens to me will dwell safely, and will be secure, without fear of evil." Even Jesus said in John 10:27,28, "My sheep hear My voice, and I know them, and they follow Me. And I will give them eternal life, and they shall never perish; neither shall anyone snatch them out of My hand."

Obedience has many benefits and God's protection is one of them. When you go where God tells you to go and stay where God tells you to stay you will be in the cocoon of divine protection. The good life is to obey God at all costs and that includes being in your proper place. There is a location where you will develop and increase and be a blessing like you can in no other place. It's the place that God has predetermined for you before you were even born so stay where you're planted and reap the benefits. Don't be like the prodigal son and go off and do your own thing. God can not and will not bless rebellion, defiance, and disobedience. Luke 17:33a says, "Whoever seeks to save his life (to do his own thing) will lose it." In order to eat the good of the land you must be willing and obedient to do the will of God. You must go where He tells you to go and stay where He tells you to stay. The plan of God is exciting and there is a place where the enemy touches you not.

To live the good life, you must seek for and find that place where you are supposed to be. Ps. 66:12 says, "You have caused men to ride over our heads; We went through fire and water; But You brought us out to a wealthy place." God has a wealthy place for you, a place of rich fulfillment, and it is found within the anointed boundaries that surround your life. Sad to say, many believers are not in this place. Instead, they're in a place of lack and defeat, a place of inability, a place where there is no victory in their lives. Everybody has a place to serve but most people aren't doing it. It hurts the whole church when people are not in their proper place. Millions of born again believers are off doing their own thing and are doing nothing at all for the kingdom of God. They don't even go to church let alone serve. God, however, wants you in a specific place so that His grace will allow your full potential to shine forth brighter and brighter.

With God's grace you can become more than you ever thought you could become and do more than you ever thought you could do. All people have potential for greatness. Just having potential, however, is not enough unless you are willing to take a risk, to step out of your comfort zone, and let God do a work in your life. Having potential does not mean that what you set out to do is positively going to happen. It means that it can happen if you are in your proper place. Encourage yourself knowing that the place God has for you is a well-watered, well-filled place and you should seek for this place with all that is within you. Ps. 37:23 says, "The steps of a good man are ordered of the Lord" and those steps will lead you to your wealthy place. That place is calling out to you, trying to draw you in. Every fall geese fly hundreds of miles southward to warmer climates. How do they know where to fly? The place is calling out to them.

Salmon swim upstream and go against the flow, even to the point of jumping over waterfalls, to get to the place they are supposed to be. They don't think, plan, or reason. They just go. They don't stop and hesitate to try to figure it all out. They just follow the call and go. You must do likewise. Heb. 11:8 tells us,

"By faith Abraham obeyed when he was called to go out to the place that he would afterward receive as an inheritance. And he went out, not knowing where he was going." Abraham was convinced that God would direct his steps. In 1 Kings 17 Elijah prophecied that a drought would come upon the land and we read in vs. 2-4, "Then the word of the Lord came to him, saying, 'Get away from here and turn eastward, and hide by the Brook Cherith, which flows into the Jordan. And it will be that you shall drink from the brook, and I have commanded the ravens to feed you there."

You can count on God to lead you to your rightful place and, if by chance you miss Him, He'll find you in you will remain forever faithful and don't lose faith. Elijah received divine direction again in vs. 7-9, "And it happened after a while that the brook dried up, because there had been no rain in the land. Then the word of the Lord came to him, saying, 'Arise, go to Zarephath, which belongs to Sidon, and dwell there. See, I have commanded a widow there to provide for you.'" Once again he was told by God precisely where he was supposed to go. Had he gone anywhere else he would have not received the provision that God had graciously prepared for him beforehand. Likewise, God is calling out to His people (1 Thess. 5:12) and they need to obey His voice and respond to that call. In John 11:28 we read where Martha told her sister Mary, "The Teacher has come and is calling for you."

He Who calls you is faithful (1 Thess. 5:24) and you can trust Him to lead you and guide you to your predetermined place. The wise men were led to the infant Jesus and shortly thereafter Joseph was led to take the Child and mother to Egypt to escape those who would try to take His life. Consider also that God once called a ram to be in a specific place so Abraham could offer it up as a sacrifice to the Lord in place of his son Isaac. If a ram can respond to the calling of God, can you not much more do so? There is a place where you will excel and prosper like no other, but this is no guarantee that your circumstances will always be nice and comfortable. Consider Gen. 26: 1-3, "There was a famine in the land, besides the first famine that was in the days of Abraham. And Isaac went to Abimelech king of the Philistines, in Gerar. Then the Lord appeared to him and said: 'Do not go down to Egypt; dwell in the land of which I will be with you and bless you.'"

There was a famine in the land, life was definitely not comfortable, but Gerar was the predetermined place where Isaac was supposed to be. He sowed in that place and reaped in the same year a hundredfold and became very prosperous (vs. 12-14). God will bless and comfort you if you will go where He tells you to go and stay where He tells you to stay. 2 Cor. 1:3,4a says, "Blessed be the God and Father of our Lord Jesus Christ, the Father of mercies and God of all comfort, who comforts us in all our tribulation…" Elisha was called to stand beside Elijah the prophet and this was not an easy task because his mentor was not always an easy man to get along with. Elisha, however, walked in the fear of the Lord and in the comfort of the Holy Spirit (Acts 9:31) and faithfully remained in the place he was supposed to be. His reward for doing so is that he received double the spirit that was on Elijah when he witnessed the fiery chariot come and take Elijah to heaven.

The first thing a lot of people want to do if they are not happy or comfortable in their place is run away and go someplace else. Gen. 16 tells how Sarah gave her maidservant Hagar to her husband Abraham for the purpose of bearing him a son and "when she saw that she had conceived, her mistress became despised in her eyes" (vs.4). When Sarah dealt harshly with her Hagar fled from her presence (vs. 6). Later, the Angel of the Lord found her by a spring of water in the wilderness and said to her, "Return to your mistress, and submit yourself under her hand" (vs. 9). Hagar had left her rightful place and God was directing her back to it. We are in the army of the Lord, and we don't write up our own orders. We are supposed to go where we're sent and stay where we're stationed. Those who run away from hardship are spiritual babies who refuse to grow up.

Hagar did obey and we read in vs. 10, "Then the Angel of the Lord said to her, 'I will multiply your descendants exceedingly, so that they shall not be counted for multitude.'" For going where God told her to go and staying where God told her to stay Hagar received the exact same blessing as the father of our faith, the great Abraham (Gen. 13:16). You would not exist if there was not a plan for your life and a place where you are supposed to be. You are saved to serve, and the most miserable life is to live for yourself. Heb. 13:21 says the great Shepherd will "make you complete in every good work to do His will, working in you what is pleasing in His sight." God is working in you to desire and pursue His perfect will, and His will is for you to be in your proper place. He'll get you there if you will listen to His voice and obey His leading. God's direction is connected to spiritual desire so take heed to the desire down in your spirit.

Ps. 42:7 says, "Deep calls unto deep" and that desire down inside will guide you to the place you are supposed to be. God put that craving inside of you and He is working in you through that desire. Phil. 2:13 says, "For it is God Who works in you both to will and to do His good pleasure." Once you know what God's plan is for your life you must exercise free will and step into that plan. It is a serious thing and very dangerous to be out of your place. God will not bless disobedience and if you stay out of your place long enough it will cost you. It will cut years off of your life and you'll never reach your full potential. Jesus said in Luke 9:23, "If anyone desires to come after Me, let him deny himself, and take up his cross daily, and follow Me." To live the good life, you must die to your own plans and dreams and submit to God's plan for your life. John 5:11 says, "They forsook all and followed Him."

Matt. 20:16 says, "Many are called but few are chosen." You are chosen when you step away from your own personal plan and separate yourself unto the plan of God. It is a privilege to be chosen so stop making excuses and go forward and never look back. Blessings, satisfaction, fulfillment, and development are in your predetermined place so go where you are supposed to go and stay where you are supposed to stay. And, by all means, stop comparing yourself with other people and their call and their place. If God is calling you to the frigid wastelands of Siberia, then don't murmur and complain that you're not sent to the sandy beaches of the Dominican Republic. Stop thinking the grass is greener on the other side. It is an honor to serve God, wherever that may be, so never act like you are doing Him a favor. You are special in God's eyes, and the body of Christ needs you so never consider yourself to be of little significance and value.

God has already designed a plan for your life, and it is neither accidental nor uncertain - it is intentional and purposeful. He has prepared a specific place for you to walk in, a calling and assignment that fits you exactly as He formed you. When you put on your marching shoes in faith and obedience, you declare your readiness to move when He says move. You may not see every turn ahead, but the Lord promises to order your steps and guide your path with wisdom and clarity. Trust Him fully, because as you walk forward, He will lead you faithfully every step of the way. The good life God promised is already set before you, but it must be entered, claimed, and possessed through obedient faith (Deut. 1:8, 21, 25). You cannot experience what lies ahead by standing still - forward movement is the gateway to promise, purpose, and blessing. Start today, because choosing to move toward what God has prepared for you may be the wisest decision you ever make.

| 23 |

"RULER OVER MUCH"

Jesus is coming soon. We know it today and those who walked with Jesus knew it also. Jesus said openly that He would one day die and leave this planet and at an appointed time known only by the Father would one day return for those who were faithfully His. Two days before His death Jesus sat on the Mount of Olives and the disciples came to Him privately, saying, "Tell us, when will these things be? And what will be the sign of Your coming, and of the end of the age?" (Matt. 24:3). He then proceeded to tell them seven parables, each one building truth upon truth on the one previous to it. Verse 17 says, "For as the lightning comes from the east and flashes to the west, so also will the coming of the Son of Man be." Lightning is self-evident and seen by all. It is sudden and unexpected and awesome in appearance. This describes His second coming when He returns to the earth to consummate the age.

The rapture takes place seven years prior to this and like the second coming will be sudden but will not be discerned by everyone. He taught in these parables that He will appear only for those who are looking for His coming and who love such an appearing (2 Tim. 4:8). Three of these teachings can be called "rapture parables" because they speak of the same time period and talks about an absent Lord who returns to deal aright with those who were left with certain responsibilities during His absence. Each parable gives specific directions that were to be followed while the Master was away, and these same instructions should govern our behavior as well. They teach us that the lives of faithful servants are forever marked by sincere fellowship, holiness of life, and continual service that brings honor to the Master. The first of these three teachings is "The Parable of the Faithful and Wise Servant" and is found in Matt. 24:45-51.

We read in vs. 45-47, "Who then is a faithful and wise servant, whom his master made ruler over his household, to give them food in due season? Blessed is that servant whom his master, when he comes, will find so doing. Assuredly, I say to you that he will make him ruler over all his goods." Right now, Jesus is in heaven keeping busy as He prepares a place for us to dwell once we get there. In like manner, we should be busy doing things for Him as we await His glorious return. The first thing He tells us to do deals with communal responsibility as we faithfully labor with and among our fellow believers in the Masters' absence. In the days of Jesus the Pharisees had failed as servants because they were not faithful and only did things in the open to win the approval and praise of others. They didn't do behind closed doors what they did in front of an audience. A faithful servant, on the other hand, knows you can't live any way you like if one truly believes the Master could return at any moment.

They know that they must be diligent to live their lives in the Masters' absence the same way as if He were there among them. A faithful servant must be wise and skillful in dealing with other people. They must be able to laugh with those who laugh and weep with those who weep (Rom. 12:15). They know how to lift up and encourage the meek and timid and are able to confront and reprove the forward. They speak the truth in love because a key element of faithfulness is honesty. Jesus is faithful and true and He showed us that you can't be faithful and dishonest at the same time. The Lord said in Zech. 8:16,17, "These are the things you shall do: Speak each man the truth to his neighbor; Give judgment in your gates for truth, justice, and peace; Let none of you think evil in your heart against your neighbor; and do not love a false oath." To be faithful means to be trustworthy, reliable, true, and dependable.

A faithful employee is one who always shows up for work on time. He's there before anybody else arrives and is always the last person to leave. Likewise, a faithful servant is a person who is always there. Ps. 46:1 states, "God is our refuge and strength, a very present help in trouble." Ruth proved her faithfulness by always being there for Naomi, as did Elisha with Elijah. You can't trust everybody. Trust is earned and there is no better way for this to happen than to be where you are supposed to be. People notice such things and are forever looking for a ruler who will lead them by example. Just as a faithful and wise servant is obedient to their heavenly Master, so also do they lead others to be subject to Him as well. They are able to unite and inspire others to take the same straight and narrow path they themselves are taking. The reward for such behavior is that upon His return the Master will make him ruler over all His goods. He was faithful over a little, now he'll be made ruler over much.

In the second parable Jesus continues to declare the uncertainty of the time of His return and of the importance of being ready when He does. Interestingly, the Parable of the Ten Virgins is only found in the gospel of Matthew and speaks about the necessity of inward character and the responsibility we have for our individual lives. As with all parables there is much symbolism associated with this tale but it's central theme is summed up in the first two words of Matt. 25:13, "Watch therefore..." The bridegroom had gone away and upon his expected return the ten virgins went out to meet him. Night time had fallen and the five wise virgins brought oil for their lamps and the other five did not. An unexpected event occurred when the bridegroom was delayed and all ten virgins slumbered and slept (vs. 5). When he did arrive the five wise virgins trimmed their lamps and went out to meet him.

The unwise virgins had no oil and when they went away to buy some the bridegroom came and "those who were ready went in with him to the wedding; and the door was shut" (vs. 10). This is a parable about preparation, especially in the event of a long and unexpected delay. Most people think the rapture should have already happened and that Jesus has delayed His return. The result of such thinking is that these people have become careless and unwise in how they conduct their daily lives. Everything would be so much easier if the bridegroom came quickly but most people lose heart in the face of uncertainty and as a result to not prepare and persevere to the end. This is what happened to the five unwise virgins and their fate is recorded in Matt. 25:11-13, "Afterward the other virgins came also, saying 'Lord, Lord, open to us! But he answered and said, 'Assuredly, I say to you, I do not know you.' Watch therefore, for you know neither the day nor the hour in which the Son of Man is coming" (see also Luke 12:40).

Being ready means preparing for whatever contingency or disruption arises in our lives and keeping our eyes fixed on Jesus at all times. There is no excuse for not being ready and the five unwise virgins learned the hard way that once the Lord returns there is neither the time nor the opportunity to change their behavior and course of unbelief. Since no second chance will be given we must continue to persist in the things which lead to spiritual preparedness. Obedience is an outward form of preparation (Rom. 6:17,18) and further instructions are given in Titus 2:11-14, "For the grace of God that brings salvation has appeared to all men, teaching us that, denying ungodliness and worldly lusts, we should live soberly, righteously, and godly in the present age, looking for the blessed hope and glorious appearing of our great God and Savior Jesus Christ, who gave Himself for us, that He might redeem us from every lawless deed and purify for Himself His own special people, zealous for good works."

When one is truly prepared, they will keep alert and be watchful at all times. And although the coming of the Bridegroom is delayed, still the faithful continue to desire, believe, and remain committed with every breath they take. Jesus was well-rounded in everything He taught and when He finished this parable about watchfulness, He immediately began to reveal the necessity of outward exertion in the things we do for God. Back in His time many people believed Jesus was going to set up His earthly kingdom right away so they reasoned they should stop working and depend on the charity of others to supply their daily food and other needs. Jesus foresaw the peril this would bring and with a strong enforcement of words exhorted His followers to not only watch for His return but to work in earnestness until that day arrived. The same combination of vigilance and activity was seen in Nehemiah's workers as they rebuilt the wall around Jerusalem while under the threat of attack from the opposition.

It was no accident that Jesus taught the Parable of the Ten Virgins first because it's the condition of the heart that prepares a person to be a good and faithful servant of the Master. The apostle Paul wrote in 1 Cor. 4:2, "Moreover it is required in stewards that one be found faithful." Here in the Parable of the Talents Jesus uses bold words to reveal that we are living epistles and there is a proving time in our walk with the Lord and our service unto Him. The Master knows what we are capable of and He expects each of us to do something with the abilities, resources, and opportunities He gives us. Matt. 25:14-30 tells how a man traveling to a far country called his servants to him. To one he gave five talents, to another two, and to another one, to each according to his own ability. The man who had five talents went and doubled his investment as did the man who had two talents. The man with one talent buried his and did nothing for his master.

A promise was given to these servants that when the master returned he would deal with them individually according to what they did with the talents entrusted to them. It would be revealed by their actions what was in the heart of each one. The Lord tests the hearts of people (Prov. 17:3) and we are told in Jer. 17:10, "I, the Lord, search the heart, I test the mind, even to give every man according to his ways, and according to the fruit of his doings." Abraham was asked to offer up his son Isaac and when he quickly obeyed the Lord stopped him and said, "Do not lay your hand on the lad, or do anything to him, for now I know that you fear God..." (Gen. 22:12a). God is looking for faithfulness and Abraham went through a time of observation because big responsibilities are not given to a novice, Faithfulness is not a one-time act but is an attitude that should characterize the entire life of those who say they have faith in God.

President Theodore Roosevelt once said, "It is better to be faithful than famous." God says the same thing. In todays' world many esteem wealth, notoriety, and fame as valued character traits. Everybody strives to be rich and famous. However, ask anyone what they desire most in a relationship and you'll find faithfulness high on the list. Faithfulness inspires confidence and assurance and throughout the Bible faithfulness eclipses fame and fortune as the mark of greatness. Joseph stayed faithful in the midst of much adversity and eventually became the second highest ruler in all of Egypt. God said about Moses, "He is faithful in all My house" (Num. 12:7). Daniel "purposed in his heart" (Dan. 1:8) that he would serve God even at the risk of his own life. Dan. 6:4 tells us, "So the governors and satraps sought to find some charge against Daniel concerning the kingdom; but they could find no charge or fault, because he was faithful; nor was there any error or fault found in him."

David was proven faithful as he tended his fathers' sheep in spite of much opposition. He killed the lion and the bear that attacked his flock and heard ridicule from his older brothers who thought his task was of minimal value. What his brothers didn't realize is that with God little things matter. Jesus said in Luke 16:10, "He who is faithful in what is least is faithful also in much; and he who is unjust in what is least is unjust also in much." Faithfulness is proven in how we deal with little things. Are you on time for a scheduled appointment or are you consistently late? Do you pick up that piece of scrap paper on the floor or do you sweep it under the rug? Do you return the grocery cart to its' proper place or leave it in the parking lot? Know with certainty that God is watching those very things that seem trivial to us because how we deal with them shows integrity and reveals character.

A faithful person is a humble person who accepts his assigned task and fulfills his calling with devotion and integrity. The reason so many are unfaithful in little things is because they place no importance on them and never stop to consider that others do. What they don't understand is that it is the little things that determine how we deal with the bigger things and is the very thing the Lord uses to determine our faithfulness. Prov. 25:19 says, "Confidence in an unfaithful man in time of trouble is like a bad tooth and a foot out of joint." We must pass the test of faithfulness before we can move forward and increase in the blessings of God. It shows Him that we can be trusted with more responsibility, revelations, finances, or anything else He wants to give us. God is trustworthy and dependable, and He is always looking to bring favor and increase to the faithful person He can trust to be a yielded vessel to Him.

This was the very message Jesus sought to convey to His disciples as He taught them the Parable of the Talents. Notice the first thing the two faithful servants did with the talents entrusted to them. Immediately they went out and traded them with the intention of making an increase for their master. There was no hesitation or delay in their actions. They knew not how long their master would be away so as soon as he left they started to trade. Ps. 119:59,60 says, "I thought about my ways, and turned my feet to Your testimonies. I made haste and did not delay to keep Your commandments." Our deeds reveal our true convictions and the motivation for service and producing good fruit should be our love for the Master. A faithful person abounds in doing good and is constant in faith regardless of whatever situation they may be in. Through their actions they demonstrate that they won't allow negative circumstances to move them from their efforts to please their master.

Eccl. 9:10 says, "Whatever your hand finds to do, do it with your might." There must be consistency in your life. You can't be up one minute and down the next. Some people want the reward and not the work but don't realize that the Lord expects a return on what He gives them. Jesus said in Luke 12:48b, "For everyone to whom much is given, from him much will be required; and to whom much has been committed, of him they will ask the more." The Message Bible says, "Great gifts mean great responsibilities; greater gifts, greater responsibilities." A talent is not something we possess but are spiritual gifts possessed by the Master and dispensed to all born-again believers. They are like matches in a box. Matches unlit are useless but God wants us fired up, to burn and glow for Him. The trading of the wise servants indicates the faithful use the Lords' people should make of spiritual gifts and opportunities for service.

Decisions determine your direction, and direction determines your destiny. Decide today to be a faithful person who follows through on your commitments even if it means personal sacrifice. Committed and persistent work pays off and diligence is always rewarded. God will not reward you for the worldly success you attain but He will reward your faithfulness to do what He has called you to do. Prov. 28:20a says, "A faithful man will abound in blessings." Faithfulness to God is the key to prosperity and it will bring you to that place where God can cause the blessings to overflow in your life. God keeps an account of all your good deeds and surely you'll be blessed in the city and blessed in the field. You'll be blessed coming in and you'll be blessed going out. The best way to be truly happy and blessed of the Lord is to serve Him faithfully and to be honest in your dealings with your fellow man.

As Jesus continued His tale of the Parable of the Talents, He said in Matt. 25:19, "After a long time the lord of these servants came and settled accounts with them." Both the servants with the five and two talents brought everything they had to the master and kept nothing for themselves. You can hear the excitement in their voices as they told the master how they doubled their investment. Faithfulness will energize you to be diligent and bold even if you've never been that way in the natural. They had nothing to fear and 1 John 4:17 tells us that we can have boldness in the day of judgement. The master was well pleased and to both of them he said, "Well done, good and faithful servant; you were faithful over a few things, I will make you ruler over many things. Enter into the joy of your lord" (vs. 21,23). Usefulness shall be the reward of faithfulness, and it is a good reward. In fact, it is the greatest reward there is, more meaningful and valuable then fortune and fame.

Prov. 20:6 asks, "Most men will proclaim each his own goodness, but who can find a faithful man?" The wicked are not faithful, nor the lost, and certainly not those who don't know the Lord. It is His children that are expected to be faithful. Notice that the masters' praise was given for their faithfulness and not for the results they achieved. The first assignment God gives you may be a small task but if you'll be faithful with it the next assignment will be bigger and better. Faithfulness is the path to success and promotion so be faithful where you're at now. Faithful service leads to increased responsibilities in God's kingdom and eternal joy in the presence of the Master. The servants didn't keep the money for themselves, and their true reward was to share in the masters' happiness.

As you serve to create increase for others you will have the reward of happiness that no person can take from you. Happiness is a quality you inject into your work, not something you derive from it. It is something you exhale, not something you inhale. A faithful person does not quit in the face of adversity and has cheerful boldness in times of danger and opposition. Faithfulness to God means having the courage to be creative and to take bold steps to do whatever needs to be done to complete the task at hand. The faithful in Christ Jesus truly believes in Him, stands by His truths, and abides by His ordinances. They are faithful to one another and charitable and beneficial to all. Be faithful in all you do for your labor is not in vain. God is faithful to us so why can't we be faithful and do good works for Him? Who can find a faithful man? Hopefully you'll find one the next time you look at yourself in the mirror.

| 24 |

"TAKE UP YOUR CROSS"

A good life is when you've always got something good to look forward to. The thrill of anticipation is the fuel that drives us forward through good times and bad. Knowing that something good and wonderful and exciting awaits you will put a bounce in your step and will cause you to climb onto your roof and shout for all the world to hear, "This is the day the Lord has made; I will rejoice and be glad in it" (Ps. 118:24). Throughout the Bible we are commanded to make a joyful shout unto the Lord. Ps. 98:4-6 says, "Shout joyfully to the Lord, all the earth; Break forth in song, rejoice, and sing praises. Sing to the Lord with the harp, with the harp and the sound of a psalm. With trumpets and the sound of the horn; Shout joyfully before the Lord, the King." We also read in Ps. 100:1,2, "Make a joyful shout to the Lord, all you lands! Serve the Lord with gladness; Come before His presence with singing."

No matter what it is you are going through, whether you are on the mountaintop of victory or you are walking through the valley of the shadow of death, you can shout and rejoice because you know God is with you and something good is about to happen. David writes, "I will fear no evil; For You are with me; Your rod and Your staff, they comfort me. You prepare a table before me in the presence of my enemies; You anoint my head with oil; My cup runs over. Surely goodness and mercy shall follow me all the days of my life; And I will dwell in the house of the Lord forever" (Ps. 23:4b-6). Jesus stepped into a lost and dying world to bring hope where despair had taken root and light where darkness seemed to reign. He came not only to rescue humanity from sin, but to restore hearts weighed down by pain, shame, and brokenness. In Him, the hurting are given something sure and eternal to look forward to - new life, lasting peace, and an unshakable hope.

When told that His friend Lazarus was sick He said, "This sickness is not unto death" (John 11:4). When Lazarus did die, Jesus told his sister Martha, "Your brother will rise again. I am the resurrection and the life. He who believes in Me, though he may die, he shall live. And whoever lives and believes in Me shall never die. Do you believe this?" (vs. 23,25,26). These were words of hope and inspiration and Jesus wept (vs. 35) when they refused to grasp the good life and believe that Lazarus would soon be alive. Because of their unbelief Jesus could have easily walked away but He is forever merciful and moments later "cried with a loud voice, 'Lazarus, come forth!' And he who had died came out bound hand and foot with graveclothes, and his face was wrapped with a cloth. Jesus said to them, 'Loose him, and let him go'" (John 11:43,44). When times are bleak and situations hopeless, when you're at the end of your rope, Jesus is the light that shines in the darkness.

He is not the light at the end of the tunnel; He's the light in the tunnel. Just prior to the darkest moment of His life, when He would be beaten, scourged, and hung on a cross between two thieves, Jesus gave hope to His disciples and to those who would afterward believe in Him, "Let not your heart be troubled; you believe in God, believe also in Me. In My Fathers' house are many mansions; if it were not so, I would have told you. I go to prepare a place for you" (John 14:1,2). Contrary to popular belief, not everybody who goes to heaven will live in a mansion. No place in scripture does it say they will and, in fact, this is the only place in the Bible where heavenly mansions are mentioned. Jesus said in Rev. 22:12, "And behold, I am coming quickly, and My reward is with Me, to give to everyone according to his work." A heavenly mansion is but one of many rewards that will be given out in heaven for services rendered unto Him during our lifetime.

The key to having a mansion in heaven is to become a mansion for God here on planet Earth. Paul writes in 1 Cor. 3:9, "For we are God's fellow workers, you are God's field, you are God's building." You are God's house, the place where He dwells (see 1 Tim. 3:16). Paul continues in vs. 16, "Do you not know that you are the temple of God and that the Spirit of God dwells in you?" The type of house you are for God will be the same type of house you'll live in once you get to heaven. Does God live in a broken down cardboard shack or does He live in a gloriously constructed mansion? The way you live your life determines the answer. We read in 1 Peter 2:4,5, "Coming to Him as to a living stone, rejected indeed by men, but chosen by God and precious, you also, as living stones, are being built a spiritual house, a holy priesthood, to offer up spiritual sacrifices acceptable to God through Jesus Christ."

The Message Bible says, "Welcome to the living Stone, the source of life. The workmen took one look and threw it out; God set it in the place of honor. Present yourselves as building stones for the construction of a sanctuary vibrant with life, in which you'll serve as holy priests offering Christ-approved lives up to God." God is building a spiritual house out of living stones of which you are one. You've been made a king and priest unto God (Rev. 1:6) and we serve Him in this house by offering up spiritual sacrifices that He would accept in Jesus Christ. In Phil 4:18 Paul talks about "a sweet-smelling aroma, an acceptable sacrifice, well pleasing to God." Making sacrifices is not an Old Testament concept only but we are to offer up sacrifices in the new covenant as well. We are priests and the bulk of the work done by Old Testament priests was to offer up sacrifices which were mostly slain animals.

Today as New Testament priests we present our bodies as a "living sacrifice, holy, acceptable to God" (Rom. 12:1). God smells offerings when they're done right and given cheerfully with a willing and pure heart. God loves a cheerful giver (2 Cor. 9:7) and if you don't enjoy giving it, God don't enjoy receiving it. The heart of the giver determines the value and acceptability of the gift. A sacrifice will cost you something and our love is shown in what we're willing to pay. God asked

Abraham to offer up his son Isaac and Jesus asked the rich young ruler to sell all that he had. In 2 Sam. 24 David went to the home of Araunah the Jebusite to build an altar and make a sacrifice unto the Lord. All that was needed was offered to him freely, but David said, "No, but I will surely buy it from you for a price; nor will I offer burnt offerings to the Lord my God with that which costs me nothing" (vs. 24).

Jesus said in Luke 14:33, "whoever of you does not forsake all that he has cannot be My disciple." What does the Master ask of you? Everything! Great glory is attached to great sacrifice and you won't know how much you love God until it costs you something. Every person God has used in a substantial was has sacrificed heavily. Faith people don't tell you about their sacrifices because they do it cheerfully and with a glad heart and would do it again without hesitation. Most believers are only interested in what God can do for them and not what they can do for Him. They'll go to all the seminars that teach them how to prosper and be healed and set free from all their burdens. But when they're called upon to do something for God they're no where to be found because it will cost them something to do it. If God is going to use you more than somebody else He has to have a fair and just reason for doing so. It's because you were willing to sacrifice and obey when others would not.

In vs. 27-30 Jesus said, "And whoever does not bear his cross and come after Me cannot be My disciple. For which of you, intending to build a tower, does not sit down first and count the cost, whether he has enough to finish it - lest, after he has laid the foundation, and is not able to finish it, all who see it begin to mock him, saying, 'This man began to build and was not able to finish.'" It will cost you everything to follow Christ like you're supposed to. If you would count the cost before He asks you, you won't struggle so much when He does. As the bearing of His own cross was rapidly approaching, the Lord's appeal to all who desired to follow Him to bear their own cross took on a deeper significance. He said in Matt. 10:37-39, "He who loves father or mother more than Me is not worthy of Me. And he who loves son or daughter more than Me is not worthy of Me. And he who does not take his cross and follow after Me is not worthy of Me. He who finds his life will lose it and he who loses his life for My sake will find it."

Christ's demand is far reaching. Loyalty to our Lord must be above the highest and most noble affections we have for our loved ones. All earthly, natural loves and the love of life and the love of self must all be subordinate in our love for Him. The life to which Christ calls us is a life in which His words must have the preeminence. If He is not Lord of all, He is not Lord at all. The cross that we are to bear is the pain of self-denial. The cross is the symbol of doing our duty even at the cost of denying ourselves of the things that we want. James 4:3 (MSG) says, "if all you want is your own way, flirting with the world every chance you get, you end up enemies of God and His way." In bearing the cross of self-denial we become the companions of Christ. To follow the Master believers must bear this cross in order to conform to His example and to follow in His footsteps like faithful disciples.

Paul writes in Gal. 5:24, "And those who are Christ's have cru-cified the flesh with its' passions and desires." The Message Bible states, "Among those who belong to Christ, everything connected with getting our own way and mindlessly respond-ing to what everyone else calls necessities is killed off for good - crucified." The biggest way you'll ever suffer is to not get your own way. This is a battle many struggle with and a victory few ever win. Too many are like the tower builder who failed to count the cost before he started to lay the foundation and was ridiculed for his shameful failure. The demand for your whole heart is strong and those who would follow Jesus all the way must grasp the Lord's teaching of self-renunciation as the one indispensable condition of discipleship. All who taste of His supper (Luke 14:24) must count the cost of full fellowship with Him. The life to which Christ calls us is not one of perpetual ease. The good fight of faith must be fought against principali-ties and powers.

Hardness must be endured as valiant soldiers of Jesus Christ. All that true discipleship entails must be accepted for "no one, having put his hand to the plow, and looking back, is fit for the kingdom of God" (Luke 9:62). Paul had to rebuke those in the Galatian church who began in the Spirit but ended up in the flesh. Like the tower builder, failure to adequately count the cost of following Christ results in an unfinished life. When Jesus said "take up your cross and follow Me" a whole legion of Christians sat down or walked away. The rich young ruler turned his back on Jesus because he had great riches and didn't want to sell all that he had and give to the poor. Too many peo-ple think "suffering" is a bad word. They think we shouldn't have any hardships or inconvenience in life. All they want to do is have fun. They think being a Christian is to walk in faith all the time and getting everything you want. No, that's some of the benefits but if that's all you do you'll be unhappy, unfulfilled, and live a dissatisfied life.

The mark of the true, genuine Christian is that they have love for one another. Very few have embraced this lifestyle because it will cost them something to do so. They may have to give away their last dollar or stay up all night in order to do what needs to be done. All they ever think about is their own comfort where the only reason they got faith was so they could get a new car and a new house. The time is upon us when the sheep and the goats are being separated and made known publicly. The deciding factor is whether or not you will take up your cross and live a life of radical obedience that entails self-denial and a dying to self. If you are to emulate Jesus' sacrificial ministry you must embrace a perspective wherein life for His sake is perceived as of greater value than your own physical life. When it comes time to sacrifice, you'll see what you love the most.

If you follow Jesus and are going to love your neighbor it's going to cost you, and not just a little. God will ask you for your Isaac, the one thing closest to your heart, the thing you've desired and prayed for most of your life. Do not cry or hesitate when He asks. To get what's in God's hand, you have to turn loose of what's in your hand. "Again, the kingdom of heaven is like treasure hidden in a field, which a man found and hid; and for joy over it goes and sells all that he has and buys the field"

(Matt. 13:44). This man was not down or depressed. He considered walking with Jesus, knowing His plan, and doing His will more valuable than all his riches and for joy sold all that he had. Paul wrote in Phil. 3:7-9a, "But what things were gain to me, these I have counted loss for Christ. But indeed, I also count all thing loss for the excellence of the knowledge of Christ Jesus my Lord, for whom I have suffered the loss of all things, and count them as rubbish, that I may gain Christ and be found in Him."

The Message Bible states, "Yes, all the things I once thought were so important are gone from my life. Compared to the high privilege of knowing Christ Jesus as my Master, firsthand, everything I once thought I had going for me is insignificant - dog dung. I've dumped it all in the trash so that I could embrace Christ and be embraced by Him. I didn't want some petty, inferior brand of righteousness that comes from keeping a lot of rules when I could get the robust kind that comes from trusting Christ - God's righteousness. I gave up all that inferior stuff so I could know Christ personally, experience His resurrection power, be a partner in His suffering, and go all the way with Him to death itself. If there was any way to get in on the resurrection from the dead, I wanted to do it." 1 Peter 3:17 tells us, "For it is better, if it is the will of God, to suffer for doing good than for doing evil." It is going to cost you something to be a real Christian and to follow Jesus fully.

We are called upon to make spiritual sacrifices and there is suffering according to the will of God, suffering that is an honor. It's a suffering for the cause of Christ, for the benefit of the kingdom. It's a willingness to take up your cross and lay down your life for the sake of another. People are the most important thing on this planet, and we need to walk in love toward them and do what's best for them. True followers of Christ are prepared to go forth no matter what the cost and have a willingness to cheerfully suffer for the sake of blessing somebody else. Paul said, "I now rejoice in my sufferings for you." (Col. 1:24). The Message Bible says, "I welcome the chance to take my share in the church's' part of that suffering. When I became a servant in this church, I experienced this suffering as a sheer gift, God's way of helping me serve you." Love is always accompanied by true joy so suffer with a smile on your face. You should be happy and joyful that the Lord would use you to bear one another's burdens.

The true love of God is all about being used to meet somebody else's needs and this should bring you joy and a deep sense of satisfaction (see John 15:10,11). Sad Christians are not walking in love, but when this love is true and genuine you will take pleasure in being inconvenienced and sacrificing for other people. Heb. 10:34 tells of a people who joyfully accepted the plundering of their goods because they knew they had a richer inheritance waiting for them. Only the true love of God allowed them to do this. Just as there is a suffering according to the will of God, there is also a suffering not according to the will of God. If your suffering does not benefit somebody else then you are deceived if you think this is Christian suffering. Jesus suffered nothing unless it benefited somebody else. Perverted suffering is when you think you suffer for your own benefit.

Many believe they're poor and sick because God is trying to teach them something. They think their suffering will cause some mystical, spiritual development to take place in their lives. This is all an attempt to cover up their lack of growth and spiritual maturity. You never suffer for that which you've been redeemed from and to do so is to make a mockery of Christ and His death on the cross. Sadly, this type of suffering is taught in many churches, and it is a deception. You may also suffer for your own faults, failures, and mistakes. There is no glory in this type of suffering, no reward for it, and you don't get better for going through it. These people try to justify this type of suffering by saying it's all for the glory of God. It's not! The only time God gets glory for your suffering is when it benefits somebody else. If another person is not blessed by your sacrifice, then your suffering is in vain and for nothing.

A Godly sacrifice is when you stay home from your dream vacation in order to help a family whose house has just burned down. It's when you miss a meal or two during the week so you can give more in the offering. You never suffer for your spiritual growth and well-being, but you do suffer so somebody else can be helped, set free, and blessed. This type of suffering is a sweet aroma, well pleasing to God. Paul said in 2 Cor. 4:17,18, "For our light affliction, which is but for a moment, is working for us a far more exceeding and eternal weight of glory, while we do not look at the things which are seen, but at the things which are not seen." Do not look at your suffering which is seen but look instead at people getting helped and saved as a result of your sacrifice. The joy of the Lord is your strength (Neh. 8:10) so count it all joy when you are called upon to sacrifice in order to help another person. If you don't enjoy giving and serving, then you're not doing it right.

David said, "I delight to do Your will, O my God, and Your law is written in my heart" (Ps. 40:8). The man who bought the field with the hidden treasure sold all that he had and was full of joy. Nobody is making you do anything. You love God and you want to do it even if it costs you everything you've got. If it's God it doesn't matter how much it costs or how long it takes. You would be disappointed if you weren't called upon to help, to share in the "sufferings for the gospel according to the power of God" (2 Tim. 1:8). You love God with all your heart and the person who loves much, gives much. From a dark prison cell Paul wrote, "Yes, and if I am being poured out as a drink offering on the sacrifice and service of your faith, I am glad and rejoice with you all" (Phil. 2:17). The Message Bible says, "I'll rejoice in being an element in the offering of your faith that you make on Christ's altar, a part of your rejoicing." This is the same Paul who said in Phil. 4:4, "Rejoice in the Lord always. Again I will say, rejoice!"

Paul knew the price you pay cannot be compared to the glory that is going to be revealed. You have been redeemed from the curse of the law (Gal. 3:13) but you have not been redeemed from all suffering. Believers will suffer persecution for their faith but still we are to follow Jesus fully and be like Peter who said, "See, we have left all and followed You" (Luke 9:28). It's going to cost you something to follow Jesus and serve Him. It's going to cost you everything you've got. It will interfere with your schedule and the plans you've made for your life. You will need to lay aside your own plans and get God's plan. Your dream is whatever His will is and you must be willing to pay the price to be successful in whatever it is you do. People who are successful are envied. People want what they have but are unwilling to count the cost and pay the price to get it. Some things are well worth any price or sacrifice you'll have to make.

It is time to sacrifice and give up some things in order to do what needs to be done. Those who don't will eventually become unhappy and unfulfilled. Millions of people start to build their tower but never finish because of a lack of sacrifice and commitment. Faith is needed along with patience and perseverance. Hardships will come but those who count the cost will be prepared for it and will overcome any obstacle. That which costs nothing is worth nothing. Rich folks spoil their children by giving them things that don't cost them anything. This is what was happening to Moses, but we read in Heb. 11:24,25, "By faith Moses when he became of age, refused to be called the son of Pharaohs' daughter, choosing rather to suffer affliction with the people of God than to enjoy the passing pleasures of sin." Moses made the right choice. He chose suffering! He knew there is no price too high to pay. When you love God more than anything this world has to offer you also will make the right choice and will be glad to do it.

Jesus charges those who would follow Him to actively and cheerfully take up and patiently bear their cross and follow Him in a voluntary act of self-denial and obedience. We live in a selfish generation because people have left God out of their lives. This same God who they ignore gives each of us a free will. We can live our own life and make our own plans, or we can submit to His will and His plan. As kings and priests we are here to make spiritual sacrifices unto Him and we need to take pleasure in doing so. Helping other people will give you a sense of purpose and satisfaction along with joy unspeakable. True Christianity is to be like the Master, to love like Him and to give like Him. Jesus was not sad. He was anointed with the oil of gladness and He gave willingly. He had joy, He had strength, and He had victory. Paul wrote in 2 Cor. 12:15, "And I will very gladly spend and be spent for your souls." Don't take up your cross reluctantly. Do it willingly and cheerfully. Do it with a smile on your face.

SUMMARY

Every journey must come to an end, but the journey of love never truly does. It only deepens, matures, and expands. As you close these pages, you are not reaching a conclusion - you are stepping into a calling. For love is not merely the theme of this book; it is the purpose of your life.

Love remains the final frontier because it demands more of us than any other pursuit. It challenges our motives, confronts our wounds, and exposes our pride. Strength can be learned. Knowledge can be acquired. Discipline can be practiced. But love - true, Christlike love - must be received before it can be released. It begins not with what we do for God, but with what God has already done for us.

Throughout "Born To Love Called To Serve," you have seen that love is the ultimate expression of who God is. He does not merely instruct us to love; He demonstrates it. Through the life, sacrifice, and resurrection of Jesus Christ, God revealed a love that is unconditional, sacrificial, and transformational. This love does not stop at forgiveness - it restores identity, awakens purpose, and calls us into action.

When you truly understand how deeply God loves you, everything changes. Fear loses its grip. Shame loses its voice. Selfishness loosens its hold. In its place rises a new capacity - to love your neighbor as you love yourself. Not from obligation, but from overflow. Not from effort alone, but from grace at work within you.

This book has shown that love and service are inseparable. Love that is genuine will always move toward others. It serves, sacrifices, and seeks the good of those around it. To love as Christ loved is to take up your cross daily - to lay down self-interest and follow His example. Yet this surrender is not loss; it is gain. For in giving ourselves away in love, we discover who we were always meant to be.

The world does not need more religious activity - it needs lives marked by love. Lives that forgive when it is difficult, serve when it is inconvenient, and remain faithful when it is costly. This is the life Jesus modeled. This is the life He calls us to live. And this is the life you were born for.

As you go forward, remember this truth: you were born to love, and you are called to serve. Let love be the measure of your faith, the motive of your actions, and the legacy of your life. The final frontier now lies before you - not as a mystery to be explored, but as a life to be lived.